Addiction Pain Management®

Recovery Guide: Managing Pain and Medication in Recovery

Second Edition

Addiction-Free Pain Management®

Recovery Guide: Managing Pain and Medication in Recovery

Second Edition

**Developed by
Dr. Stephen F. Grinstead**

*Foreword
by Terence T. Gorski*

 Based on the Addiction-Free Pain Management® System and the Gorski-CENAPS® Model

Notice of Proprietary Information: This document contains copyrighted and proprietary information of Dr. Stephen F. Grinstead and The CENAPS® Corporation. Its receipt or possession does not convey any right to reproduce it; disclose its contents; or manufacture, use, or sell anything it may describe. Reproduction, disclosure, and use without the specific written authorization of Dr. Stephen F. Grinstead and The CENAPS® Corporation are strictly forbidden.

Additional copies are available from the publisher:
    Herald House/Independence Press
    1001 West Walnut
    P.O. Box 390
    Independence, MO 64051-0390
    Phone: 1-800-767-8181 or (816) 521-3015
    Fax: (816) 521-3066
    Web site: *www.relapse.org*

For training contact:
    The CENAPS® Corporation
    6147 Deltona Blvd.
    Spring Hill, FL 34606
    Phone: (352) 596-8000
    Fax: (352) 596-8002
    E-mail: *info@cenaps.com*

© 2008, 1996
Stephen F. Grinstead

13 12 11 10 09 08   5 4 3 2 1

Library of Congress Cataloging-in-Publication Data

ISBN 978-0-8309-1376-3

Printed in the United States of America

Contents

Foreword by Terence T. Gorski 8
Preface 10
   The Recovery Guide Road Map 10
   Your Call to Action 10
Acknowledgments 12
Chapter One: The Road to Empowerment 14
   Exploring the Problem 14
   Discovering the Solution 24
   Call to Action for the First Chapter 29
Chapter Two: The Addiction Pain Syndrome® 30
   Exploring Addiction and Pain 30
   Understanding Addictive Disorders 30
   Defining Misunderstood Terms 36
   Learning More about Pain Disorders 38
   The Pain System 49
   The Pain Spiral 54
   The Addiction Pain Syndrome® Defined 56
   Call to Action for the Second Chapter 60
Chapter Three: The Addiction-Free Pain Management® System 61
   The Developmental Model of Recovery 61
   Addiction-Free Pain Management® Defined 63
   The Development of Addiction-Free Pain Management® 64
   APM® Core Clinical Exercises 71
   APM® Medication Management Components 75
   APM® Nonpharmacological Treatment Processes 89
   Call to Action for the Third Chapter 94
Chapter Four: Learning to Live Again 95
   Understanding Your Chronic Pain 95
   Learning to Connect 99
   Making an Important Decision 100
   Detoxification Issues 101
   Developing Support Systems 106

A Guide for Managing Chronic Pain in Recovery 109
Getting Started: Transition and Stabilization Tasks 110
Call to Action for the Fourth Chapter 112

Chapter Five: Beginning the APM® Treatment Process 113
APM Core Clinical Exercise One: Understanding
    Your Pain 113
Exercise One, Part 1: Acute Pain versus Chronic Pain 113
Exercise One, Part 2-A: Identifying and Rating the
    Severity of Your Pain Symptoms 117
Exercise One, Part 2-B: Exploring Biological versus
    Psychological Pain Symptoms 120
Exercise One, Part 3: Exploring Your TFUARs on a
    Bad Pain Day 127
Exercise One, Part 4: Stress and Chronic Pain 129
Call to Action for the Fifth Chapter 135

Chapter Six: Effects of Prescription and/or Other Drugs ... 136
Pain Relief versus Euphoria 136
Exercise Two: Effects of Prescription and/or Other Drugs ... 141
Exercise Two, Part 2: Side Effects and Problems 143
Exercise Three: Decision Making about Pain Medication 146
Exercise Four: Moving into the Solution 155
Call to Action for the Sixth Chapter 165

**Chapter Seven: Utilizing Nonpharmacological/Holistic
Treatment Processes 166**
Denial Management Counseling 167
More about Nonpharmacological Treatment Approaches 169
Developmental Model of Recovery Transition and
    Stabilization Tasks 181
Nutrition and Healing 183
Exercise and Healing 187
Call to Action for the Seventh Chapter 192

Chapter Eight: Reciprocal Relapse Prevention 193
The CENAPS® Model of Relapse Prevention 193
Redefining Relapse 194
Relapse Prevention Planning 195
Exercise Five: Identifying and Personalizing Your
    High-Risk Situations 197

Exercise Six: High-Risk Situation Mapping 208
Call to Action for the Eighth Chapter 210

Chapter Nine: The TFUAR Process and Recovery Planning 211
Exercise Seven: Analyzing and Managing
   High-Risk Situations 211
Exercise Eight: Recovery Planning 238
The Importance of a Pain Medication Management Plan 241
Call to Action for the Ninth Chapter 243

Chapter Ten: Measuring Treatment Effectiveness 244
Benchmarks for Effective Treatment 244
Evaluating Your Pain and Addiction Management Skills 245
A New Beginning 249
The Final Call to Action for the APM® Recovery Guide 250

Appendix 251
Medical Marijuana Controversy Update 255
Recovery and Smoking Just Don't Mix 256
Brief Red Flags Checklist for Pain Medication Addiction ... 260
From Denial to Effective Pain Management 262
Pain Management Reference List and Recommended
   Reading List 267
Useful Internet Resources 272

Foreword

*By Terence T. Gorski
President, The CENAPS Corporation*

When I first started working with Stephen Grinstead on integrating the concepts of the CENAPS® Model with the concepts of Pain Management in 1996, I was doing it because I had seen so many people suffering from pain disorders. I saw many people with long-term quality sobriety relapse over mismanaged chronic pain. I believed that with the proper expert help the basic principles of the CENAPS® Model could be adapted to help those suffering from chronic pain. I never thought I would benefit directly—as a recipient—from the principles in this collaboration, but I have. I believe that you can as well.

Chronic pain can be a problem for everyone. I know. I became trapped in a chronic pain cycle that nearly destroyed my life and my ability to keep working. The combination of old sports injuries, a lifestyle of high stress, and the gradual development of severe arthritis and other joint problems left me nearly incapacitated. It made everything I did more difficult and stressful.

As a result, I moved on to using the principles and exercises in the original version of the *Addiction-Free Pain Management® (APM®) Recovery Guide* and *APM Workbook*. I'm not pain free all of the time, but as long as I consistently practice the pain management principles described in the *Addiction-Free Pain Management® Recovery Guide* (www.relapse.org) and the exercises in the *APM Workbook*, I am able to function normally and am pain free much of the time.

I'm excited about the second edition of the *Addiction-Free Pain Management® Recovery Guide,* because it introduces the evolution of the Gorski-CENAPS® *Relapse Prevention Counseling Workbook* as well as Stephen Grinstead's past eleven years of innovative growth and improvements in the Addiction-Free Pain Management® System. Some of the changes in this book include the latest additions to the Relapse Prevention Counseling process as well as the following APM modifications:

- Updated explanations of pain and the pain system
- Explanation of the improved exercise to help you differentiate

between the biological and psychological/emotional components of pain
- The addition of craving and pain flare-up planning
- A revised APM High-Risk Situation List
- The transition from Abstinence Contracting to a more appropriate APM Medication Management Agreement
- An improved Pain Medication Problem Checklist exercise

As you read this book, remember—the journey to effective pain management is not easy, but it is worth the effort. No matter how much pain you are experiencing today, if you learn to do the right things, you can help yourself feel a little bit better—and in some cases a lot better. If you allow yourself to give in and keep using ineffective pain management and problematic use of pain medication, you will feel a little bit worse—or in some cases a lot worse. *The choice is yours!* This, to me, is the most important message of this book. You don't have to stay trapped in a never-ending cycle of pain. This book gives you the information and practical skills that you need to help yourself make better choices.

Preface

The Recovery Guide Road Map

Some of you are reading this book because you have a chronic pain condition and are looking for help. Others may be family members who are living with someone in chronic pain and want to learn how to help your loved ones. Some of you are in recovery from an addictive disorder and are afraid you might relapse over a pain condition. Some of you may not be in recovery, but you have chronic pain and want to avoid becoming chemically dependent. Or some of you are in chronic pain and have begun to either abuse or become dependent on your pain medication, which could be causing a variety of problems in your life.

Whoever you are, I want you to know there is hope if you suffer from chronic pain and fear ineffective pain management, addictive disorders, or relapse. It is possible to escape the bonds of pain and addiction. That is the main reason I am writing this book—to help you recognize any potential problems and develop effective solutions.

Your Call to Action

The best way to get the greatest benefit from this book is to start by thoroughly reading and understanding the first four chapters. As you read these chapters, be aware of your thinking and your feelings. It is also helpful to keep a notebook or journal close by as you read so you can write about your reactions to what you are learning.

Freedom from Bondage

When you get to the end of Chapter Four, you should have a copy of the *Addiction-Free Pain Management® (APM®) Workbook* to use as you read the remainder of this book. Starting with Chapter Five, I explain the APM process by describing each exercise in the workbook. In the original *APM Recovery Guide* I used two of my former patients, Donna and Matt, to illustrate the various APM exercises. However, since the model has significantly grown since that time, in this second edition I will be introducing two new patients, Jean and Dean. They experienced what I hope you can obtain by doing this work—*freedom from bondage!*

I personally have seen many recovering people relapse and even die as a result of untreated—or mistreated—chronic pain conditions. I decided to do something about it and have spent the past eleven years developing and updating the Addiction-Free Pain Management® System. The goal of this second edition of the *APM Recovery Guide* is to share what I have learned since the first edition was published in 2002.

I propose that effective treatment for someone with an addictive disorder and chronic pain requires a three-part approach: (1) a medication management plan—in consultation with an addiction medicine specialist; (2) a cognitive-behavioral treatment plan—addressing the psychological/emotional components of pain and changing self-defeating behaviors; and (3) a nonpharmacological pain management plan—developing safer, chemical-free ways to manage chronic pain and pain flare-ups. The Addiction-Free Pain Management® System is a strategic combination of all three of these components working together, implementing a multidisciplinary integrated pain management approach.

> Be an active participant, not a passive recipient.

Recovery and avoiding relapse is possible if you are willing to do the footwork and follow this type of plan using a collaborative multidisciplinary treatment team. With the proper treatment plan and positive support, you can have successful pain management. You can become a proactive participant in your healing process instead of being a passive recipient (i.e., victim). This shift allows you to be empowered and experience a much better quality of life.

> At the end of each chapter you will be asked to complete an additional "Call to Action" where you will be asked to answer three simple questions before moving on to reading the next chapter.

Acknowledgments

I am excited to present the second edition of the *Addiction-Free Pain Management® (APM®) Recovery Guide*. The advances and improvements I have made to the APM System since the original *Recovery Guide* was first published in 2002 are now incorporated, as well as updates from the recently revised *APM Workbook*. I am confident this work will continue to make a significant contribution to people suffering with chronic pain, and I want to acknowledge all those individuals who have helped to make this publication possible.

First, I want to thank Terence T. Gorski, president of the Gorski-CENAPS® Corporation, for his generosity in allowing me to adapt the Relapse Prevention Counseling (RPC) model for use with people living with chronic pain and coexisting addictive disorders. Mr. Gorski's RPC model has also significantly evolved since the *APM Recovery Guide* was first published, and those changes are also reflected in this second edition. Mr. Gorski has not only been my mentor over the years, he has become a close friend, and I look forward to our continued collaboration.

This second edition would not be possible without several major contributors:
- All of the pain patients that I have been fortunate enough to work with since the first edition of the *APM Recovery Guide* came out in 2002.
- The healthcare professionals who attended my Addiction-Free Pain Management® trainings and/or have used my APM books with their own patients and provided me with their valuable feedback.
- One of the healthcare professionals that I want to single out for special thanks is Dr. Jennifer Messier. Dr. Messier not only uses my work, but she has been APM certified and has also assisted me in conducting the *Addiction-Free Pain Management® Certification Schools*. Thanks Jen!
- My wife and partner in life as well as business, Ellen Gruber-Grinstead, for her assistance in analyzing, editing, and formatting this book, as well as her encouragement and emotional support the past twenty years.

- Finally, I want to especially thank all of the healthcare agencies who have sponsored my pain management trainings. They have allowed me to receive up close and personal feedback that has assisted my ongoing commitment to modify and enhance the Addiction-Free Pain Management® System. Just as it takes a village to raise a successful child, it takes a team to write a successful book—a special thank-you to my team! I just wish I had the space to mention all of the individuals who have been an important part of the ongoing development of the Addiction-Free Pain Management® System. You know who you are—thanks!

> Most of all,
> I want to thank my own pain.

I now consider pain my friend. Without the ongoing positive relationship I have learned to develop with my pain, I would not have been able to write this book, nor share my hope with those who might be feeling hopeless and helpless because of their pain.

Stephen F. Grinstead
January 2008
Palm Springs, California

Turn to the next page to begin Chapter One in the
Addiction-Free Pain Management® Recovery Guide.

Chapter One
The Road to Empowerment

Exploring the Problem

> Moving Out of the Problem
> and into the Solution

Before I can explain what *empowerment* is in relationship to *the solution*, you must first come to terms with the problems associated with living with chronic pain that you may be experiencing. Chronic pain is a serious health condition confronting many people today. Those of you living with chronic pain know firsthand that your pain is often disabling, and, for many of you, there are few safe alternatives when seeking help. As a result, you may end up suffering or developing an addiction to the medications you are using to help manage your pain. Many people in chemical dependency recovery can relapse and may even die from their addiction as a result of untreated—or mistreated—chronic pain conditions.

Please know that if you have chronic pain and think you may be experiencing problems with your medication, you are not alone. As you see in the following chart, there were more than 117 million people with chronic pain in the United States in 2003 and at least 11.7 million people experienced either abuse or addiction problems with their prescription medications. An April 2005 poll conducted by ABC News, USA Today, and the Stanford University Medical Center estimated that as many as 150 million people were living with chronic pain at that time—and the numbers keep rising. As I mentioned earlier, people in addiction recovery who relapse could be facing death.

> **Pain and Rx Abuse/Addiction**
>
> - 57% of adults experiences level 4 + chronic pain, nearly 117 million people
> - 40% say they have pain all the time
> - 66% expect to have pain all their lives
> - 18–34-year-olds are as likely to experience chronic pain as aging baby boomers
> - 10% conservative estimate, 11.7 million with abuse/addiction issues in 2003
>
> **Source: Peter D. Hart Research Associates, August 2003**

The Roadblock Called Denial

If you do not know whether or not you have a problem, it can be extremely difficult to find a solution. Many people I have worked with have the mistaken belief that "they can't be addicted because they're in pain and a doctor gave them the medication." This can be one of the four levels of denial if, in fact, they have been abusing or are addicted to their medication and experiencing life-damaging consequences. I will provide an in-depth explanation of addiction in the following chapter. You will also learn the difference between abuse, addiction, dependency, and pseudoaddiction.

> **Four Levels of Denial**
> - Lack of Information
> - Conscious Defensiveness
> - Unconscious Defense Mechanism
> - Delusional System

There are four levels of denial. The first level is *a lack of information* about addiction, pain, and recovery. The previously mentioned example shows this first level. The solution here is for you to be open to education and information about addiction, pain, and recovery. It is important for you to learn as much as you possibly can about chemical dependency and effective pain management.

The second level of denial is *conscious defensiveness*. You know that something is wrong, but you don't want to look at the problem and face the pain of knowing. You tend to vigorously defend yourself and deny a problem even though you know you have one. The solution for this level of denial is to recognize that you are experiencing an inner conflict where one part of you knows there's a problem, but another part doesn't want to admit it. To resolve this conflict you must be willing to listen to the part that knows the truth and take authentic action. The old saying, "The truth will set you free," is certainly relevant in this case.

The third level is denial as *an unconscious defense mechanism*. You get to this level when you have stayed in the inner conflict, mentioned above, and the defensive voice keeps winning. Once this happens, denial then becomes an unconscious defense mechanism. The solution is much more difficult. It usually takes outside interventions, or what is called a motivational crisis, to break through this defense and allow you to know the truth and start addressing the problem. For some of my patients this motivational crisis was generated when their treating physicians became concerned about their use/abuse of pain medication. For others it was family members intervening and urging them to seek help.

The fourth level is denial as *a delusional system*—this is the toughest level to address. Terence Gorski describes this delusion as "a mistaken belief that is firmly held to be true despite convincing evidence that it is not true." Sometimes this fourth level is exacerbated by brain damage caused by the use of psychoactive substances, such as prescription medication and/or alcohol and other drugs. If your denial is at this level, you probably would not be reading this book. People at this level of denial usually need psychotherapy and probably medication management to resolve their delusional system.

I will discuss more about denial management in a later chapter. For an excellent resource on denial, you can read the article in the Appendix of this book—"From Denial to Effective Pain Management." If you want an even more in-depth focus, you can obtain the *Denial Management Counseling for Effective Pain Management Workbook* by Stephen F. Grinstead and Terence T. Gorski, with Jennifer C. Messier.

Hitting the Wall Called Depression

Many people with chronic pain frequently become depressed due to living with undertreated or mistreated pain symptoms. This process starts when your thinking and emotions become problematic. This is when your thinking becomes irrational or dysfunctional and you start mismanaging your feelings; you often have urges to indulge in self-defeating, impulsive, or compulsive behaviors to cope with your depression. This in turn affects your relationships with others.

There are several types of clinical depression that involve disturbances in mood, concentration, self-confidence, sleep, appetite, activity, and behavior as well as disruptions in friendships, family, work, and/or school. A clinical depression is different than the experiences of sadness, disappointment, and grief familiar to everyone, and sometimes makes it difficult to determine when professional help is necessary. The following information is intended to provide you with a brief overview of the symptoms, causes, and treatment of clinical depression and offers you tools to assess the severity of any symptoms you may be experiencing to determine whether you should consider seeking professional help for treating your depression at this time.

Feeling Down versus Being Depressed

A period of depressed mood that lasts for several days or a few weeks is often just a normal part of life and is not necessarily a cause for concern. Although these feelings are often referred to as depression, they typically do not constitute a clinical depression, because the symptoms are relatively mild and only last for a short period of time. Moreover, milder periods of depression are often related to specific, stressful life events, and improvement frequently coincides with the reduction or elimination of the stressor.

If you are experiencing a clinical depression, however, you would be experiencing substantial changes in your mood, thinking, behaviors, activities, and self-perceptions. If you are depressed, you might often have difficulty making decisions. Even the day-to-day tasks of paying bills, attending classes, reading assignments, and returning phone calls might seem overwhelming.

If depressed, you might also dwell on negative thoughts, focus on unpleasant experiences, describe yourself as a failure, report that things are hopeless, and feel as though you are a burden to others. The changes in mood brought on by depression frequently result in feelings of sadness, irritability, anger, emptiness, and/or anxiety and may eventually lead to thoughts of suicide.

There are different types of depression, including *bipolar disorder*, where depressive episodes alternate with mania (extremely elevated mood, energy, and unusual thought patterns) or hypomania (generally a less destructive state than full mania). These episodes may include feelings of agitation and euphoria. A severe or long-term depressive episode can substantially wear down self-esteem and may result in thoughts of death and even attempts at suicide.

Please review the following information on a depression rating scale. The assessment and ratings are from the work of Terence T. Gorski (2006) and his book, *Depression and Relapse: A Guide to Recovery,* and are used here with his generous permission. If you have an addictive disorder and co-occurring depression, you may want to consider obtaining Mr. Gorski's book for a more in-depth look at depression that is beyond the scope of this book.

Gorski's Depression Rating Instrument

Please be honest with yourself as you complete the following:

- How depressed are you?
  Please rate 0–10 _____, where:

1 = When I get depressed, my depression is a nuisance, but I can always function normally with extra effort.
5 = When I get depressed, I can sometimes function normally with extra effort and at other times I can't.
10 = When I get depressed, I usually can't function normally even with extra effort.

- How often do you feel depressed?
  Please rate 0–10 _____, where:

1 = Almost never
5 = Almost half the time
10 = Almost all of the time

- How long does each episode of depression last?
  Please rate 0–10 _____, where:

1 = Less than an hour
5 = Several days

10 = I'm depressed all of the time with no break between episodes.
- How severe are the negative consequences caused by your depression? **Please rate 0–10** _____**, where:**
1 = **Mild:** I feel bad but there are no negative consequences.
5 = **Moderate:** My depression causes some serious problems in my life
10 = **Severe:** My depression causes serious damage to my health, emotional well-being, and lifestyle.

Suicide Checklist

- I sometimes feel that life isn't worth living.
  ❑ Yes   ❑ No   ❑ Unsure
- I sometimes think I would be better off dead.
  ❑ Yes   ❑ No   ❑ Unsure
- I sometimes think about killing myself.
  ❑ Yes   ❑ No   ❑ Unsure
- I have a plan to kill myself.
  ❑ Yes   ❑ No   ❑ Unsure
- I have recently tried to kill myself.
  ❑ Yes   ❑ No   ❑ Unsure
- I will probably try to kill myself some time in the future.
  ❑ Yes   ❑ No   ❑ Unsure

Note: If you answered "yes" or "unsure" to any of the last six questions, you may be seriously depressed enough that you need professional help immediately.

In the following table you will see a checklist that includes many of the symptoms typical for clinical depression. Note, however, that only some of these symptoms are necessary for a diagnosis of depression. Some of you will be more comfortable with the depression rating instrument on pages 18 and 19, while others may benefit more from the following symptom list. Sometimes my patients use both.

Symptoms of Depression

- **A significantly depressed mood or general absence of mood:** You may sometimes find yourself feeling overly negative and down or at other times emotionally cut off.
- **Inability to experience pleasure or feel interest in daily life:** Things that used to excite or interest you now hold no attraction at all. Sometimes it hardly seems worth getting up.
- **Inexplicable crying spells, sadness, and/or irritability:** You may find yourself crying for no reason or having a temper tantrum and lashing out without any provocation.
- **Insomnia (difficulty sleeping) or hypersomnia (over-sleeping) nearly every day:** You either can't get to sleep or stay asleep and/or find yourself spending most of your time sleeping, to the point of missing important events in your life.
- **A substantial change in appetite, eating patterns, or weight:** You find you have no appetite and nothing sounds good so you just don't eat, or in an effort to feel better you discover that eating certain types of foods seems to soothe you. You either lose or gain a significant amount of weight.
- **Fatigue or energy loss:** You seem to be always tired or don't have enough energy to accomplish even simple tasks of daily living.
- **Diminished ability to concentrate:** You find that paying attention is very difficult. You may even find yourself reading the same page over and over or forgetting the plot of a movie you are watching.
- **Difficulty making decisions:** You can't seem to decide what to do even in simple areas that used to be easy for you. You tend to procrastinate or put off having to decide.
- **Feelings of hopelessness or worthlessness:** At times you feel like your life is always going to be unbearable or you don't deserve to be happy or successful.
- **Inappropriate feelings of guilt or self-criticism:** You find yourself putting yourself down for little things and feel bad about things that might not even be your fault.

- **A lack of sexual desire:** You have lost your interest and passion for being a sexual being. It either seems like too much of a hassle or you just don't care anymore.
- **Suicidal thoughts, feelings, or behaviors:** You start having thoughts like "maybe I'd be better off dead," or "I feel that life isn't worth living." You may start thinking about ways you could kill yourself and even start developing a plan.

Problems Treating Depression

One of the biggest problems in treating depression in people with chronic pain is a misdiagnosis—you or others do not realize that you are depressed. This occurs for two reasons: (1) when you live with chronic pain, you often do not realize you may also be suffering from a major depression, and (2) your healthcare provider is not looking for it. People living with chronic pain will often define their problem as strictly medical and related to the pain. Therefore, being alert to see if depression is present and being willing to develop a treatment strategy becomes a crucial component of an effective pain management treatment plan.

There are currently a variety of highly effective interventions available for the treatment of depression. The majority of depressive conditions can be treated with either psychotherapy (especially cognitive behavioral therapy) or medication, but research studies have indicated that a combination of these interventions is usually the most effective form of treatment for moderate to severe depression. There are also some types of depression that have a seasonal patterning where intensive *Full Spectrum Lighting* therapy is often effective in reducing symptoms. It should be emphasized that the majority of depressive conditions can be treated without hospitalization.

The Pitfalls of Isolation and Enabling

Some people living with chronic pain and depression become isolated and start to believe they can handle life without any help, or they may go to the other extreme and become increasingly dependent on others to take care of them. Either style can worsen their depression. Caretaking by others may be enabling the depressed person to continue ineffective behaviors and continue his or her role as a victim. Some of you may need to have treatment for depression. An effective depression management treatment plan should include cognitive behavioral therapy and possibly an antidepressant medication. The roles of antidepressant medication are discussed in a later chapter where I describe the *APM Medication Management Components*.

The important thing to remember is that you need to be able to recognize and admit that you have a problem before you can work on an effective solution. Typically you are going to need help—a support network for instance—to work through any denial or depression issues in order to develop an effective recovery and pain management program. But be careful who you choose to help you. Sometimes self-help support people and healthcare providers can become part of the problem.

Misguided "Helpers"

> Don't take nothin'—no matter what!

This statement can be heard frequently if you attend Alcoholics Anonymous (AA) or Narcotic Anonymous (NA) meetings. The message is, if you don't use any alcohol or other drugs, you are clean and sober and will experience the promises of recovery, but if you take *anything*, "you've blown it."

In most cases those words are good counsel for people recovering from an addictive disorder. However, when the *nothin'* includes appropriate medication prescribed by a knowledgeable physician for a legitimate condition, those words could actually lead you to a relapse. Some examples of medications that are often prescribed for people in recovery include antidepressants, antianxiety medication, or pain medication. AA's central office produced a pamphlet written by recovering physicians warning AA members "not to play doctor," and that sometimes people in recovery need to take *appropriate* medication. NA also has similar published information available for their members.

> You're just drug seeking.

Problems with healthcare providers usually occur in one of two ways. One example is when the treatment provider decides you are an *addict,* and they won't prescribe any narcotic medication, which results in them treating you as if you were *drug seeking.* When consulting with other treatment professionals, I try to explain to them that the person in pain is not *drug seeking;* he or she is really *seeking relief.*

Another example is when the doctor thanks you for your honesty and is willing to prescribe narcotic medication, but does not fully understand addiction or recovery. This doctor might say something like, "I appreciate you being honest with me, but rest assured, I'll be careful—just let me take care of this." If this doctor does not have training or a good understanding of addiction and recovery, his or her lack of knowledge can very well be a setup for disaster. You need to have an effective medication management plan in place that will prevent serious problems.

> You must have a plan.

What is especially true—if you are in recovery for prescription medication, alcohol, or other drug dependency—is that you must be very careful when using any mood-altering (psychoactive) medication. The most common problems occur with pain medication. You need to use caution, have a plan, and, most importantly, have support.

Over the past twenty-four years I've seen many people relapse and die because they mismanaged their pain medication. Frequently the relapse starts with an acute pain episode such as dental work or a car accident that requires pain medication. Some people experience problems when they develop a chronic pain condition that does not respond to non-narcotic interventions. In either case, the person failed to develop an effective medication management plan.

Managing pain medication is an issue that every person dealing with chronic pain must face at some point in their journey. Yet most people don't know how to develop an effective plan of action. When you are in recovery for chemical dependency—whether the substance is prescription drugs, alcohol, marijuana, etc.—the risk of relapse is always present. It is unrealistic to expect you will never have a medical or dental situation where pain management is needed. In addition, if you also suffer from a chronic pain condition, relapse prevention becomes even more crucial.

> **Two Major Pain Management Roadblocks**
> - Overmedicating Pain
> - Undermedicating Pain

There are two major problems when you are in recovery and experiencing a pain condition that requires medication—taking the wrong thing (or too much of the right thing) and not taking anything (or not taking enough). Even a seemingly benign condition such as minor dental pain may lead to relapse or medication management problems. When you are overmedicated, you can develop substance-induced problems or even addiction. When you are undermedicated, you may decide to use self-defeating behaviors such as alcohol, other drug use, or even suicide to cope with your pain. I devoted a significant section of Chapter Nine to help you develop a plan for managing pain medication in recovery.

Discovering the Solution

Knowledge Is Power

To effectively manage a pain condition it's important that you understand exactly what is going on with your body. When you are in pain, you experience both physical and psychological symptoms. To understand the language of pain, you must learn to listen to how the pain echoes and reverberates between the physical, psychological, and social dimensions of your human condition. Pain is truly a total human experience that affects all aspects of human functioning.

> Personal empowerment is
> the best—and only—way out.

When you are in pain for a long period of time, you can begin feeling victimized by your pain. You hate your pain. You want to escape from your pain and are willing to do anything to obtain relief. Unfortunately, the way out for many people leads to self-defeating behaviors, including abusing pain medication.

> You will manage your pain better when you are proactive in your own treatment and recovery process.

Most of the chronic pain research I have reviewed over the past two decades has been very clear about treatment outcomes. The best prognosis occurs when you are very proactive in your own treatment process. One way to do this is to learn as much as you can about your pain and effective pain management. The next chapter will help you do this by explaining the *Addiction Pain Syndrome*® and the biopsychosocial nature of pain. Future chapters will describe an effective *Addiction-Free Pain Management*® protocol and show you how two of my patients, Jean and Dean, used the APM process in their recovery.

> Pain is your friend.

Knowledge is power. Once you know what is really going on with your body and mind, you can start taking action to effectively manage your pain. In fact, it is vital that you begin to see pain as your friend, instead of your enemy. I know this is much easier said than done.

Many of my patients have looked at me like I'm crazy when I tell them they must make peace with their pain, and pain can be their friend. Some even tell me—very strongly—they can't buy that, but nevertheless it is true.

Pain sensations are essential for human survival as you will see in the next chapter. Without pain you would have no way of knowing that something was wrong with your body. So without pain you would be unable to take action to correct the problem or situation causing the condition. However, with chronic pain management it is crucial that you take the correct type of action or you could end up in an addiction trap.

Coping with Anticipatory Pain

When you live with chronic pain, you hurt. Doing certain *things* can make you hurt worse. So you come to believe that these things will *always* cause you to hurt. In other words, you associate those *things* with pain. You believe that every time you do those *things*, you will have pain. Because you believe you are going to hurt, you activate the physiological pain system just by thinking about doing something you believe will cause you to hurt. This is called *anticipatory pain*. You expect that something will make you hurt. That, in turn, activates the physiological pain system. This makes you start hurting even before you begin doing whatever it is you believe will cause you to hurt. All you have to do is to start thinking about doing that *thing*.

> This is horrible, awful, and terrible!

Once the physical pain system is activated, the anticipatory pain reaction actually makes the pain symptoms worse. Whenever you feel the pain, you *interpret* it in a way that makes it feel worse. You *start thinking* about the pain in a way that makes it worse. You *tell yourself* that the pain is "awful and terrible and you can't handle it." You *convince yourself* that "it's hopeless, you'll always hurt, and there's nothing you can do about it." This way of thinking causes you to develop emotional reactions that further intensify or amplify the pain response. The increased perception of pain causes you to keep changing your behavior in ways that create even more unnecessary limitations and more emotional discomfort. This can make you feel trapped in a progressive cycle of disability.

> *You get the level of pain and dysfunction that you expect!*

Your expectations—what you believe it will be like when you experience pain—affect your brain chemistry. Your brain chemistry can either intensify or reduce the amount of physical pain that you experience. What you think and how you manage your feelings in anticipation of feeling pain can make your pain either more severe or less severe. In other words, you usually get the level of pain and dysfunction that you expect—a self-fulfilling prophecy.

The anticipation of an expected pain level can influence the degree to which you experience pain. When your self-talk is saying, "this is horrible, awful, and terrible," the brain tends to amplify the pain signals. When this occurs, the level of distress increases and you suffer, remaining a victim to your pain.

Fortunately, you can learn how to change your anticipatory response to pain. You can lower the amount of pain that you anticipate by changing what you believe will happen when you start to hurt. You can also change your thinking—your self-talk—and learn how to better manage your emotions. You can learn new ways of responding to old situations that used to cause or intensify your pain. As you come to believe you really can do things that will make your pain sensations bearable and manageable, your brain responds by influencing special neurons that reduce the intensity of your pain. Your brain becomes less responsive to an incoming pain signal.

There are things you can do that will make you habitually less responsive to incoming pain signals. Herein lies the rationale for including biofeedback, positive self-talk, meditation, and relaxation response training as part of your pain management treatment plan. In any event, both ascending (pain signals coming from the point of injury to the brain) and descending nerve pathways (signals from the brain to the point of injury) influence or modify the effects of pain on your body.

As mentioned earlier, anticipation of an expected pain level (i.e., anticipatory pain) can influence the degree that pain is experienced. The good news is that in some cases, when the anticipatory level of pain expectation is lowered, the brain responds by influencing special neurons. This renders your brain less responsive to an incoming pain signal. This is the reason for the effectiveness of biofeedback and meditation as pain control methods.

When a negative *anticipation effect* is coupled with the *cascade effect* (intense and prolonged pain that you will learn more about in the next chapter), you can experience a downward spiral and begin to think like a victim. This results in feeling hopeless and helpless, which often leads to grief and depression.

Remember, the cumulative biopsychosocial effects of chronic pain can lead to this pain spiral. When you try to cope with this condition using addictive medications, the downward addiction spiral is intensified—although you may be so medicated you really don't notice the spiral. In addition, the brain is attempting to adapt by telling other parts of the body to produce additional chemicals as it tries to manage the situation.

While it is important to realize that pain communicates there is something wrong with the body and is part of the healthy defense system, the fact that pain can sometimes be maladaptive, as well, is not always as obvious. Once again, knowledge is power, so it is crucial to learn how to identify your patterns of anticipation to stop the downward spiral and break the cycle of pain. See the following charts to review the problematic anticipatory pain cycle followed by the solution—anticipatory relief.

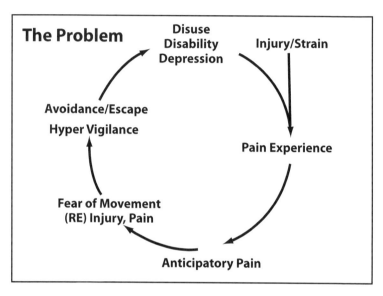

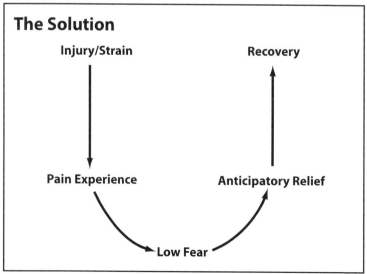

There Are No Magic Fixes

Don't forget, treatment for chronic pain does *not* include magical interventions or quick fixes; rather, it is a combination of proven psychological treatment approaches in addition to medication management and other nonpharmacological—holistic—interventions that address all the issues people in chronic pain experience. These are the three core components of the Addiction-Free Pain Management® System, which I explain in depth in Chapter Three. Before I review the core components, you need to understand the *Addiction Pain Syndrome*®, which is explained in the next chapter.

- **Call to Action for the First Chapter**

It is time to summarize what you have learned so far now that you have come to the end of the first chapter. Please answer the questions below.

1. What is the most important thing you have learned about yourself and your ability to help yourself as a result of completing Chapter One?

2. What are you willing to commit to do differently as a result of what you have learned by completing this chapter?

3. What obstacles might get in the way of making these changes and what can you do to overcome these roadblocks?

Take time to pause and reflect, then
go to the next page to review Chapter Two.

Chapter Two
The Addiction Pain Syndrome®

Exploring Addiction and Pain

Addiction-Free Pain Management® (APM®) is a system that can help you manage your chronic pain without abusing or becoming addicted to pain medication. To fully understand APM®, three major concepts need to be clearly understood: (1) addiction, (2) pain, and (3) the pain system.

This chapter focuses on understanding addiction, pain, and the human pain system. The following chapter will discuss and define the Addiction-Free Pain Management® recovery process. Let's look at the first concept—addiction.

Understanding Addictive Disorders

This book uses the terms *addictive disorders* and *addiction* to discuss what the DSM-IV-TR™ (*Diagnostic and Statistical Manual of Mental Disorders; Fourth Edition, Text Revision*) classifies as *substance use disorders* and is also referred to as *chemical dependency,* or *psychological dependence.*

In this book I define addictive disorder as: *A collection of symptoms (i.e., a syndrome) that is caused by a pathological response to the ingestion of mood-altering substances and has ten major characteristics*. These characteristics are shown in the following table, which is followed by a brief explanation of each characteristic.

Addictive Disorder Symptoms

1. Euphoria	6. Inability to Abstain
2. Craving	7. Addiction-Centered Lifestyle
3. Tolerance	8. Addictive Lifestyle Losses
4. Loss of Control	9. Continued Use Despite Problems
5. Withdrawal	10. Substance-Induced Organic Mental Disorders

Let's look at each of these characteristics in more detail.

Euphoria

People use drugs because they work—they meet some kind of *need*. This is true of pain medications as well as for alcohol and other potential drugs of abuse. In addition to blocking physical pain, one side effect of some pain medications is a sense of euphoria. If you experience this unique sense of well-being or euphoria when you use a drug or medication, you are at high risk of becoming psychologically dependent and may even become addicted to that substance.

Positive Reinforcement for Use

Recent research shows that when you are genetically susceptible to being addicted to a specific drug, your brain will release large amounts of brain reward chemicals whenever that drug is used. It's this high level of brain-reward chemicals that causes the unique feeling of well-being many people who become addicted experience when using their drug of choice. In this book we will call this unique feeling of well-being—*euphoria*.

Euphoria versus Intoxication

It is essential to distinguish between *euphoria* (the unique sense of well-being experienced when using your drug of choice) and *intoxication* (the symptoms of dysfunction that occur when your use exceeds the limits of your tolerance to a drug). Most people who become addicted do not use their drug of choice to get intoxicated and become dysfunctional. The opposite is true. For instance, people who become addicted to prescription medication, at first, use it to manage their physical pain. They eventually can begin to use it to feel good and experience a unique feeling of well-being that will allow them to function better—or in many cases experience the illusion of functioning better.

You can actually become addicted to the feeling of euphoria and start to crave this unique sense of well-being. You feel somehow empty and incomplete when you can't feel this way and even deprived without it. You may even experience deprivation anxiety, which is a fear that if you can't get your drug of choice (or are deprived of it), you mistakenly believe you won't ever be able to feel good or function normally again.

> Positive reinforcement leads to cravings.

This positive reinforcement is biopsychosocial in nature. Biologically, the drug of choice causes a release of pleasure chemicals that create a unique sense of well-being. Psychologically, you come to believe the drug is good for you because it makes you feel good in the moment. This is called emotional reasoning ("if it feels good, it must be good for me"). You then begin adjusting your social network to accommodate these beliefs. "Anyone who supports the use of my drug of choice is my friend. Anyone who challenges the use of my drug of choice is my enemy." The result is the development of a drug-centered lifestyle.

The stronger the positive reinforcement experienced when you use your medication, the greater the risk you will become addicted to that drug. This is true because strong biological reinforcement from drug use creates a craving cycle.

Craving

The addictive process starts when you receive a reward, payoff, or gratification from taking a psychoactive (mood altering) drug. This reward may be the relief of pain or the creation of a sense of euphoria. Because the drug provides a quick positive reward, you continue to use it.

With a pattern of consistent drug use some people come to overly rely upon the drug to provide that reward. This leads to an addictive disorder, or what DSM-IV-TR calls a substance dependence. At this point you need to use the drug to successfully accomplish one or more life tasks. Once you become addicted, you experience psychological distress when the thing you are dependent upon is removed. So when you become addicted to medication for relief or euphoria, you experience anxiety when the drug is no longer available. This is also known as *deprivation anxiety*. You are anxious because you have been deprived of a drug you believe you need in order to function normally.

This deprivation anxiety then causes you to start thinking about the drug. *Obsession* is the out-of-control thinking about the reward that could be achieved by using the substance. Obsession can lead to *compulsion*—the irrational desire for the drug. Obsession and compulsion combine together to create a powerful *craving* or feeling of need for the drug.

> Obsession + Compulsion = Craving

This cycle of obsession, compulsion, and craving creates a strong urge or pressure to seek out and use the medication even if you consciously know it's not in your best interest to do so. Over time this reward continues to be reinforced, leading to an increased need for the drug. This leads to *tolerance*.

Tolerance

There is a definite biological component to developing tolerance. The increased need for the substance leads to drug-seeking behavior. There are also psychological and social components to this developmental process.

On the biological level, after this drug-seeking behavior has been established, your brain undergoes certain adaptive changes to continue functioning despite the presence of the drug. This adaptation is called *tolerance*. When tolerance occurs, your brain chemistry actually changes, including the development of more receptor sites.

Psychologically you start believing you need the drug. When you start to experience difficulty obtaining enough of the drug, you begin to feel anxious and afraid. Socially you begin to experience difficulty with other people because of the time and energy you are expending—experiencing a *loss of control*.

Loss of Control

The final stage of the craving cycle and development of tolerance is a loss of control over medication use and/or your behavior while using the drug. You begin to develop an even higher tolerance for the drug. In other words, it takes more of the drug to get the same effect. If you keep using the same amount of the drug, you experience less of an effect. So you begin using more of the medication or seeking out stronger drugs, including alcohol, that will give you the same—or better—reinforcing effect.

At times the medication and/or other drugs are taken in such large quantities that you become intoxicated or dysfunctional. This dysfunction creates biopsychosocial life problems. At this point, if you stop using the drug, you will experience uncomfortable physical and emotional problems. This leads to lowered motivation to stop the drug use.

Withdrawal

Withdrawal is marked by the development of a specific clinical syndrome when the medication is stopped. In some cases you might use the same or a similar drug to relieve or avoid the withdrawal syndrome.

> **Withdrawal as Negative Reinforcement (Mental Anguish or Dysphoria)**

Once tolerance and loss of control take place, further abnormalities occur in the brain when drugs are removed. In other words, the brain loses its capacity to function normally when drugs are not present.

- Low-grade abstinence-based brain dysfunction is distinct and different from the traditional acute withdrawal syndromes.
- Low-grade abstinence-based brain dysfunction is marked by feelings of discomfort, increased cravings, and difficulty finding gratification from other behaviors.
- Low-grade abstinence-based brain dysfunction creates a desire to avoid the unpleasant sensations that occur in abstinence.
- The desire to avoid painful stimuli is called *negative reinforcement*.

> - People who experience biological reinforcement are more likely to use drugs regularly and heavily.
> - People who use drugs regularly and heavily are more likely to develop an addictive disorder.

Inability to Abstain

As a result of experiences created by biological reinforcement and high tolerance, you come to believe your drug of choice is good for you and will magically fix you or make you better. You could then start to develop an addictive belief system. When this happens, you come to view people who support your drug use as friends and people who fail to support it as your enemies.

Addictive Beliefs

At this point you are experiencing both positive and negative reinforcement to keep using. If you continue to use, you experience euphoria and pain relief. This occurs because the brain releases large amounts of *reward chemicals* when you use your drug of choice. At this point you are totally unable and/or unwilling to adhere to a medication management agreement you agreed to follow with your healthcare provider.

If you stop using, you experience dysphoria—generally characterized as an unpleasant or uncomfortable mood, such as sadness (depressed mood), anxiety, irritability, or restlessness. You may start to experience a sense of anhedonia—an inability to experience pleasure from normally pleasurable life events such as eating, exercise, and social/sexual interactions. You begin to believe you have no choice but to keep using your drug of choice.

Addiction-Centered Lifestyle

An *addiction-centered lifestyle* develops when you attract, and are attracted to, other individuals who share strong positive attitudes toward the continued use of drugs, like problematic pain medication. You usually have an enabling support system that condones and encourages your continued use. You become immersed in an addiction-centered system.

Addictive Lifestyle Losses

As this cycle progresses, you distance yourself from people who support sobriety or effective medication management and surround yourself with people who support problematic medication use and/or alcohol and other drug use. The pattern of biological reinforcement has motivated you to build a belief system and lifestyle that supports heavy and regular use.

A Pattern of Heavy and Regular Use

You are now in a position where you will voluntarily use larger amounts with greater frequency until progressive addiction and the accompanying physical, psychological, and social degeneration occur. Your life becomes unbearable and unmanageable. You start experiencing a downward spiral of problems—*addictive lifestyle losses*.

Continued Use Despite Problems

Unfortunately, this downward spiral leads to continued drug use despite the consequences. This inability to control drug use causes problems. The problems cause pain. The pain activates a craving. The craving drives you to start using the drug to get the relief that you believe you need.

As a result, when you experience adverse consequences from your addiction, the adverse consequences cause cravings instead of correction. As a result, you keep using drugs to gain the immediate reward or relief despite experiencing serious life problems.

Substance-Induced Organic Mental Disorders

The progressive damage of pain medication and/or alcohol and other drugs on the brain create growing problems with judgment and impulse control. As a result, behavior begins to spiral out of control. Your cognitive capacities, necessary to think abstractly about your problems, have also been impaired, and you are now locked into a pattern marked by denial and circular systems of reasoning. You will read more about denial in a later chapter.

> Progressive neurological and neuropsychological impairments will lead to denial.

At this stage you are now unable to recognize the pattern of problems related to your drug of choice. When problems are experienced, you begin to experience physical, psychological, and social deterioration. Unless you develop an unexpected insight or are confronted by motivational crisis or by concerned people in your life, the progressive problems are likely to continue until serious damage results.

Defining Misunderstood Terms

There needs to be clarification when choosing words to describe people on long-term pain medication use. Many of these people are identified or labeled as "addicts" when in fact they are definitely not—they do not meet the criteria previously listed. To help clarify this issue a consensus document was developed by the American Academy of Pain Medicine, the American Pain Society, and the American Society of Addiction Medicine in 2004. They have agreed upon the following definitions for addiction, physical dependence, tolerance, and pseudoaddiction:

Addiction

Addiction is a primary, chronic, neurobiological disease, with genetic, psychosocial, and environmental factors influencing its development and manifestations. It is characterized by behaviors that include one or more of the following: impaired control over drug use, compulsive use, continued use despite harm, and craving.

Physical Dependence

Physical dependence is a state of adaptation manifested by a drug class-specific withdrawal syndrome that can be produced by abrupt cessation, rapid dose reduction, decreasing blood level of the drug, and/or administration of an antagonist.

Tolerance

Tolerance is a state of adaptation where exposure to a drug induces changes resulting in a diminution (lessening) of one or more of the drug's effects over time.

Addiction versus Pseudoaddiction

Pseudoaddiction

The term pseudoaddiction has developed over the past several years in an attempt to explain and understand how some chronic pain patients exhibit many of the red flags that look like addiction. Pseudoaddiction is a term that has been used to describe patient behaviors that may occur when pain is undertreated. Patients with unrelieved pain may become focused on obtaining medications, may *clock watch*, and may otherwise seem inappropriately *drug seeking*. Even such behaviors as illicit drug use and deception can occur in the patient's efforts to obtain relief. Pseudoaddiction can be distinguished from true addiction. In pseudoaddiction the behaviors resolve when the pain is effectively treated.

Pseudotolerance

Dr. William W. Deardorff (2004) advocates the importance of differentiating tolerance (described previously) and pseudotolerance. He describes pseudotolerance as the need to increase dosage not due to tolerance but due to other factors such as changes in the disease, inadequate pain relief, change in other medication, increased physical activity, drug interactions, lack of compliance, etc. Examples of pseudotolerance in a patients' behavior may include drug seeking, "clock watching" for dosing, and even illicit drug use in an effort to obtain relief. Like pseudoaddiction, pseudotolerance can be distinguished from addiction when the behaviors resolve once the pain is effectively treated.

Physical Dependency versus Addiction

Not everyone who uses pain medication on an ongoing basis will become addicted. You may in fact become physically dependent to the medication, but may not experience the addiction cycle covered previously. In a later chapter I will discuss the *Recovery and Relapse Indicators* for those of you needing to take psychoactive medication on a continuing basis.

Now that you have a better understanding of addictive disorders, you must also learn more about your pain and the biopsychosocial processes that influence it. This is important in order for you to gain the most benefit from the APM recovery process.

Learning More about Pain Disorders

An Overview of the Biopsychosocial Components of Pain

In order to understand pain management you need to first understand the concept of pain. Pain is a signal from the body to the brain that tells you that something is wrong. There are three components of pain—biological, psychological, and social/cultural.

Deardorff (2004) emphasizes that pain is not easy to define. But in 1979, the International Association for the Study of Pain (IASP) published its first working definition of pain: "An unpleasant sensory and emotional experience associated with actual or potential tissue damage, or described in terms of such damage."

This definition was reaffirmed in 1994 along with an extensive footnote discussion regarding its implications. The IASP definition acknowledges that, for most people, tissue damage is the *gold standard* by which pain is understood. However, the definition also recognizes that pain may occur in the absence of tissue damage and is impacted by emotional (psychological) factors. In a footnote explaining the definition, the authors point out that pain is not equivalent to the process by which the signal of tissue damage is passed through the nervous system to the brain (this is called nociception); rather, pain is always a psychological state that cannot be reduced to objective signs. In other words, pain is always subjective—there is no test or instrument that can measure anyone's personal experience of pain.

> Pain is a signal from the body to the brain that communicates that something is wrong.

Pain is a total biopsychosocial experience. You hurt physically. You psychologically respond to the pain by thinking, feeling, and acting. You think about the pain and try to figure out what is causing it and why you're hurting. You experience emotional reactions to the pain. You may get angry, frightened, or frustrated by your pain. You talk about your pain with family, friends, and coworkers who help you to develop a social and cultural context for assigning meaning to your personal pain experience, which leads to taking appropriate action.

The Gate-Control Theory of Pain

The *gate-control theory of pain* was developed originally by Melzack and Wall in the early 1960s. It changed the way pain perception was viewed. The basis of this theory is that physical pain is not a direct result of the activation of pain receptor neurons, but rather its perception is modulated by the interaction between different neurons. This theory also proposes that cognitive and emotional factors influence the perception of pain—there are more than just physiological factors involved.

How This Theory of Chronic Pain Works

Your brain commonly blocks out sensations it knows are not dangerous, such as the discomfort of tight-fitting shoes put on in the morning, then feeling OK a short time later. A similar process is at work in processing some moderately painful experiences.

In the gate control theory, the experience of pain depends on a complex interplay of two systems as they each process pain signals in their own way. Upon injury, pain messages originate in nerves associated with the damaged tissue and flow along the peripheral nerves to the spinal cord and on up to the brain. The gate control theory asserts that before the pain messages can reach the brain they encounter *nerve gates* in the spinal cord that open or close depending upon a number of factors (including instructions coming down from the brain). When the gates are opening, pain messages *get through* more or less easily and pain can be intense. When the gates close, pain messages are prevented from reaching the brain and pain may not be experienced. This theory attempts to explain the experience of pain (including psychological factors) on a physiological level.

Deardorff (2004) states that when living with chronic pain, it is important to understand the gate control theory, which provides an excellent foundation about what factors can open and close the spinal nerve gates. An in-depth explanation of this theory is beyond the scope of this book. If you seek additional information, please refer to the bibliography in the Appendix of this book under Melzack and Wall (1965 & 1982) and Deardorff (1997 & 2004).

Three Essential Levels of Pain Management

Successful pain management systematically approaches the treatment of pain at three levels simultaneously—biological, psychological, and social. This means using physical treatments to reduce the intensity of the physical pain. It also means using psychological treatments to identify and change the thoughts, feelings, and behaviors making the pain more intense or distressing and replacing them with positive thinking, as well as using feeling and behavior management skills to reduce the intensity of the pain.

In addition, effective pain management must involve not only you, but also the significant people in your life who can help you develop a social and cultural context to experience your pain in a way that reduces any suffering.

The Biological Component of Pain

Biological pain is a signal something is going wrong with your body. The biological, or physical, pain sensations are critical to human survival. Without pain you would have no way of knowing something was wrong with your body. You would be unable to take action to correct the problem or deal with the situation that is causing the pain. There are people who are born with a compromised pain system, and most of them suffer serious problems as a result. Imagine that you have no pain receptors in your hand and you put that hand on a hot stove. Your first indication of a problem would be when you smelled burned flesh. By then the damage to your hand would be extensive.

The Psychological Component of Pain

Psychological pain results from the meaning that you assign to a pain signal. The psychological symptoms include both cognitive (thinking changes) and emotional (uncomfortable feelings) that often lead to suffering. Most people are not able to differentiate between the physical and psychological symptoms. All they know is "they hurt." For effective pain management you need to learn all you can about your pain.

The Social/Cultural Component of Pain

Social and cultural pain result from the social and cultural meaning assigned by other people (or your culture/society as a whole) to the pain you are experiencing, and whether or not the pain is recognized as being severe enough to warrant a socially approved sick/injured role. These three components determine whether the signal from the body to the brain is interpreted as pain or suffering.

Imagine the following vignette: Bob is his college's star football player. In the previous week's homecoming game Bob scored the winning touchdown but broke his arm in the process. This week Bob is sitting on the bench with a cast on his arm that everyone has signed. This cast and how he earned it are seen as an honorable reason for him sitting on the bench instead of being out on the field helping his team. But, in that same game, Karl, a big hulking lineman, "tweaked" his back and was also sitting on the bench. Unlike Bob, Karl doesn't have an observable injury, and people keep asking him why he isn't out on the field helping his team. Karl is much more apt to experience shame/guilt than Bob, which could amplify his pain symptoms.

Pain versus Suffering

The psychological meaning you assign to a physical pain signal will determine whether you simply feel pain ("Ouch, this hurts!") or experience suffering ("Because I hurt, something awful or terrible is happening!"). Although pain and suffering are often used interchangeably, there is an important distinction that needs to be made. Pain is an unpleasant signal telling you something is wrong with your body. Suffering results from the meaning or interpretation your brain assigns to the pain signal.

Pain is "biopsychosocial."

Biological Pain:
A signal that something is going wrong with the body

Psychological Pain:
The meaning that people assign to the pain signal

Social/Cultural Pain:
The approved "sick" role assigned to people by society concerning their pain

---

Many people irrationally say, "I shouldn't have pain!" or "Because I have pain and I'm having trouble managing my pain, there must be something wrong with me." A big step toward effective pain management occurs when you can reduce your level of suffering by identifying and changing your irrational thinking and beliefs about the pain, which in turn decreases your stress and overall suffering.

Using a Two-Part Approach: Physiological and Psychological

Because of the two parts—pain and suffering—pain management must also have two components: physical and psychological. The way you sense or experience pain—its intensity and duration—will affect how well you are able to manage it. *Anticipatory Pain*, covered earlier, is also a major psychological factor that must be addressed. The research on recovery from chronic pain is very clear. The people most likely to successfully manage their pain do so by becoming proactively involved in their own treatment process. Your chances of success go up as you learn as much as possible about your pain and effective pain management.

> You will manage your pain more effectively when you stop being a passive recipient and become an active participant in your treatment.

Psychological treatment for chronic pain is meant to supplement medication treatment, not replace it. Emotional stress and negative thinking can increase the intensity of your pain, but the presence of psychological factors doesn't mean that your pain is imaginary. Psychological treatment goals are designed to help you learn how to understand, predict, and manage your pain cycles; use coping skills to minimize your pain; and maximize active involvement in positive life experiences despite the presence of chronic pain.

Breaking the pain cycle involves addressing the physiological as well as the psychological/emotional components of the pain. Stress, discussed in a later chapter, also plays a role in keeping a pain cycle going. Stress causes muscle tension that leads to increased pain sensation. At the same time your cognition (thinking) and emotions (feelings) can also amplify the cycle. Breaking the cycle requires concurrent treatment of the physiological and psychological/emotional condition. See the following diagram for a visual of this pain cycle.

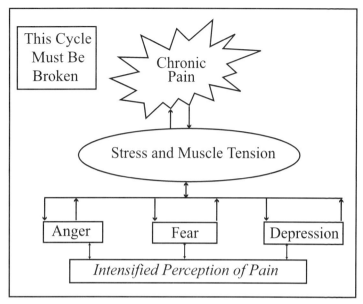

Additionally, psychological treatment for chronic pain focuses on the emotional toll you experience, living with pain on a daily basis. Factors such as disability, financial stress, or loss of work are also a part of the pain picture, and psychological treatment is designed to address all relevant issues. The treatment for chronic pain does not include magical interventions; rather, it includes a combination of proven psychological treatment approaches combined with medication management and other nonpharmacological interventions that addresses all the issues people in chronic pain experience. As you can see in the following chart, your pain cycle can be broken by dealing with the biological stress component using relaxation tools for stress management. You can cope with the psychological perception of pain by using cognitive behavioral therapy (CBT) tools. When you relax, there is a reduction of stress and muscle tension, leading to a more peaceful acceptance; this leads to the decreased perception of pain.

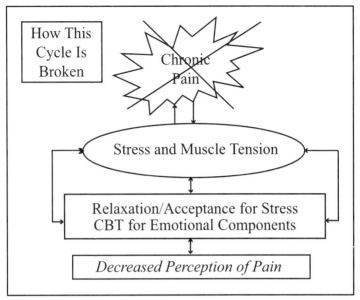

Because of the two parts—pain and suffering—pain management must also have two components: physical and psychological. The way you sense or experience pain—its intensity and duration—will affect how well you are able to manage it. In addition, there are three major classifications of pain that need clarification: acute pain, chronic pain, and recurrent acute pain.

Acute Pain, Chronic Pain, and Recurrent Acute Pain

When there is a need to manage pain with potentially addictive medication, it is important to understand the difference between acute pain and chronic pain. Acute pain tells your body something has gone wrong or damage to your system has occurred. The source of the pain can usually be easily identified and typically does not last very long—less than three to six months. When you touch a hot burner on the stove or cut your hand with a knife or razor, you feel acute pain.

> **Acute pain** is short lived, but **chronic pain** lasts three to six months or more.

A chronic pain condition will linger long after the initial injury, sometimes for years. In many cases chronic pain no longer serves a useful purpose. To be considered a chronic pain condition some say that the symptoms should continue for at least six months, while others look at three months as the transition time. Some examples of chronic pain are ongoing back pain, fibromyalgia, and frequent cluster headaches.

Deardorff (2004) states, "There are at least three types of chronic pain problems: (1) chronic pain that is due to a clearly identifiable cause or process, (2) chronic pain that is 'nonspecific' and there is no clearly identifiable pain generator that explains the pain, and (3) chronic pain that is due to some type of nerve damage or abnormal nervous system reaction." He also discusses how tissue damage is a major factor in acute pain but not so much with chronic pain, where the thoughts and emotions play a more significant role. See Dr. Deardorff's diagrams in the following table.

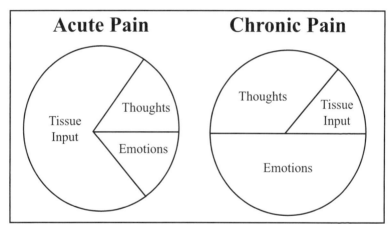

Effective pain management requires accurate identification of the physical and psychological components of the pain disorder. This is where the *Addiction-Free Pain Management® Workbook* should be used. As you will see later in this book, there are ways to determine whether your pain condition is related more to physiological factors (tissue input) or psychological/emotional reasons. There is also another classification of pain stated in the following table that Dr. Deardorff (2004) calls *acute recurrent pain.*

> Acute recurrent pain is when the individual suffers from pain episodes with pain-free periods in between. The pain episodes are usually brief (less than three months) and associated with an identifiable physical process (such as migraine headaches, sickle cell anemia, back sprain, etc.).

Neuropathic Pain

Neuropathic pain is a complex chronic pain state that is usually accompanied by tissue injury. With this type of pain the nerve fibers themselves may be damaged, dysfunctional, or injured. These damaged nerve fibers send erroneous signals to other pain centers in your brain. The impact of nerve fiber injury includes a change in nerve function both at the site of injury and areas around the injury. According to the *Neuropathic Pain Network*, in the United States there are between 5 and 23 million people (that's 1.5 percent to 7.7 percent of our population) living with neuropathic pain. Unfortunately, it is a syndrome that is often underdiagnosed and undertreated.

One striking example of neuropathic pain is called *phantom limb syndrome*. This occurs when an arm or a leg has been removed because of illness or injury, but the brain still receives (or perceives) pain messages from the nerves that originally carried impulses from the missing limb. These nerves now misfire and cause pain. Some symptoms of neuropathic pain include shooting pain, burning pain, tingling, and numbness. Neuropathic pain often seems to have no obvious cause; however, some common causes can include those listed in the following table.

- Alcoholism
- Back, leg, and hip problems (sciatica)
- Diabetes
- HIV infection or AIDS
- Shingles (herpes zoster virus infection)
- Amputation (phantom limb pain)
- Cancer chemotherapy
- Facial nerve problems
- Multiple sclerosis
- Spine surgery

Neuropathic pain responds poorly to standard pain treatment and may get worse instead of better over time. For some people, it can also last indefinitely and lead to serious disability. This type of nerve pain is often puzzling and frustrating for people and their caregivers, as it seems to respond poorly to standard pain therapies.

Neuropathic problems are not fully reversible for many people. However, some improvement is possible with proper treatment. Some neuropathic pain studies suggest the use of NSAIDs (Nonsteroidal anti-inflammatory drugs), or an analgesic with morphine, which can be effective. Anticonvulsant (e.g., Neurontin and Lyrica) and antidepressant drugs and various pain relievers seem to work in some cases. You will learn more about medication management and nonpharmacological approaches in a later chapter. It is worth noting that electrical stimulation of the nerves involved in neuropathic pain generation (i.e., using a TENS Unit, which is also covered later) might significantly control the pain symptoms.

The Neurophysiology of Pain

As discussed earlier, pain is a complex combination of biopsychosocial phenomena. In a part of this section you are exposed to the work of Dr. Mark Stanford (1998 with updates for this revision) in order to better understand the neurophysiology of pain.

Let's start by examining the word *neurophysiology*. The root *neuro* refers to the nerves or more precisely how the actions of the brain and nerves are involved in the pain response. The word *physiology* refers to the physical aspects of pain or, more precisely, how the total human organism responds and adapts to pain.

This section gives you an accurate yet easy-to-understand model for explaining the complex biopsychosocial symptoms that chronic pain patients experience. It will also prepare you to understand why many of the treatment methodologies described later in this book are both necessary and effective.

Despite a significant effort to simplify this section, the information covered is rather complex. My goal is not to describe the technical details of pain neurophysiology, but to present some basic theories and concepts that form the basis of many current pain management approaches.

Pain as a Signal That Communicates Information

The easiest way to understand pain is to recognize that every time you feel pain your body is attempting to tell you that something is wrong. Pain sensations are critical to human survival. Without pain you would have no way of knowing that something was wrong with your body. So without pain you would be unable to take action to correct the problem or situation that is causing your pain.

> What is your pain trying to tell you?

Whenever you are experiencing pain, it is always appropriate to ask, "What is my pain trying to tell me?" Remember, the pain is trying to tell you that something is wrong, and you should find out exactly what it is and a way to fix it.

To understand the language of pain, you must understand how the pain echoes and reverberates between the physical, psychological, and social dimensions of the human condition. Pain is truly a total human experience that affects all aspects of human functioning.

The Pain System

Every human being has a pain system that is a combination of pain receptors and pain circuits. As you continue reading, it may be useful for you to refer to the following *Pain System Diagram*. This diagram shows some of the pain receptor sites and pain circuits that make up the human pain system.

You also have specialized and general pain receptors and circuits. These receptors and circuits usually function very well, alerting you when something is wrong.

- Pain is a signal or warning that something is wrong.
- Pain receptors are nerve cells that detect when something is wrong.
- Pain circuits are a series of nerve cells that transmit the message that something is wrong.

Physically, the experience of pain originates in receptors located throughout the body. Some of these receptors are located deep within the body, providing sensations about muscle aches, pulled tendons, and fluid-filled, swollen joints.

Other receptors, such as in the skin, provide pain sensations when cuts, burns, or abrasions have occurred near the surface of the body. Many times the skin receptors will respond to the signal generated from the localized damage to tissue. For example, a skin cut will essentially cause various cells to produce and release a variety of chemical messengers that stimulate pain receptors into action from the area of injury.

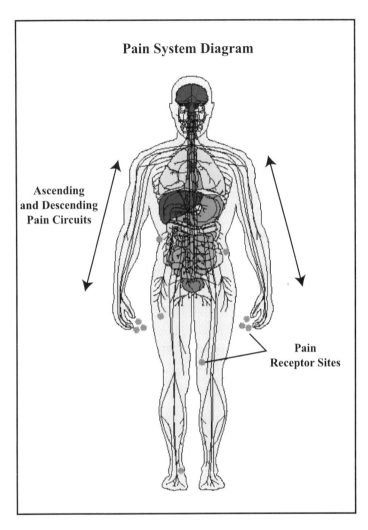

Pain Receptors and Circuits

The human brain and nervous system have *pain receptors* that respond to the pain where it occurs in the body. There are also *pain circuits* (sometimes called neuropathways) that transmit pain signals from the local site of the pain to the spinal cord, and then to the brain itself. As the pain signal moves along its primary circuit or pathway, other secondary pain neurons are activated creating a wide variety of different types of pain signals.

Some of these signals simply report the presence of pain (I hurt or I don't hurt). Other signals report the intensity of the pain (I hurt a little or I hurt a lot). Still other pain signals report the location of the pain (my stomach hurts) and whether the pain is associated with an internal or external injury (my stomach hurts deep in my gut or the skin on my stomach hurts). Other pain signals report the type of pain (my pain burns or it throbs).

All of these different pain signals are transmitted into the spinal cord through nerve pathways. The nerve pathways transmit the pain signal information to other specialized pain neurons, which in turn send the information to different areas of the brain.

Certain types of pain will activate an automatic protective reflex (you suddenly pull your hand away from the hot handle of a frying pan without thinking about it). Other types of pain burst into conscious awareness, prompting you to try and figure out what is wrong.

Specialized and General Purpose Pain Receptors and Circuits

The human body has *specialty pain receptors and circuits* dedicated exclusively to recognizing and transmitting information about pain. There are, for example, separate pain receptors and circuits that respond to skin cuts. This provides you with the ability to recognize and respond to certain types of pain quickly.

You also have *general purpose receptors and circuits* that are capable of detecting and transmitting pain signals and other sensations that give information about other physiological processes.

- Specialty Pain Receptors and Circuits
- General Purpose Receptors and Circuits

Because pain is an indication of threat or emergency, these general-purpose receptors and circuits give your pain signals top priority. When an emergency pain signal competes with other routine nonemergency sensations, the routine sensations are temporarily shut down or distorted so the transmission of the pain signal can be given a top priority.

As a result, there can be a *generalized nonspecific response* to pain signals. In other words pain signals can disrupt other systems of your body not directly affected by the injury or illness causing the pain. This occurs by disrupting the routine flow of sensation.

Pain and the Cascade Effect

As you can see, the process of experiencing pain is very complex and has the potential of affecting all areas of your brain and body. When your pain is intense and prolonged, there is a widespread *cascade effect* that results in an extensive disruption in your normal functioning.

To understand this cascade effect let's look at what happens when you accidentally cut your hand with a sharp piece of glass. The cut activates specific pain receptors, which in turn begin sending pain signals down a pain circuit or pathway. As the signal moves along the pain circuit, a variety of signals related to the pain are activated. These signals are transmitted through the spinal chord to your brain. One part of your brain's cortex receives the information about the sudden pain that has just happened. Another part determines where your body has been hurt. Another part determines what type of pain you are experiencing, and still another part determines how severe (intense) your pain is.

The Immediate Reflex Response

While the various parts of the brain are communicating about your pain, another part of the nervous system activates an immediate reflex response. This reflex causes a quick withdrawal from the point of the pain-producing situation (in this case the piece of glass).

The rapid behavioral withdrawal reflex is a response based largely in your spinal cord and less so in your brain. Other areas within your brain begin activating the autonomic nervous system that, among other things, increases heart rate. Still another part of the brain signals the hypothalamus to start secreting a cascade of chemical reactions.

Meanwhile, your brain overrides a number of routine neurological circuits and reroutes available body resources to respond to the pain. You quickly enter into a high stress response that prepares you to fight, freeze, or flee from the danger.

This cascade of effects from the original pain sensation occurs on many levels and involves a variety of different areas within your nervous system. As a result, a wide variety of nervous system chemicals are produced and dumped into your blood while other brain chemicals are rapidly absorbed or depleted. Pain doesn't just hurt. It changes your most basic neurophysiological processes.

Anticipation of Pain Affects How Pain Is Experienced

The anticipation of an expected pain level can influence the degree to which you experience your pain. In some cases, when your anticipatory level of pain expectation is lowered, your brain responds by influencing special neurons. As you saw in the last chapter, this renders your brain less responsive to an incoming pain signal and your sensation of pain decreases. This is the rationale for utilizing biofeedback and meditation as pain control methods. In any event, both ascending (pain signals coming from the point of injury and going to the brain) and descending nerve pathways (signals from the brain going to the point of injury) will influence or modify the effects on your body.

The Pain Spiral

You can begin a downward spiral when the *cascade effect* occurs and is coupled with a negative *anticipation effect*. You begin to think like a victim. You start feeling hopeless and helpless, which often leads to grief and depression.

This condition is covered in a later chapter, but for now remember that the cumulative biopsychosocial effects of chronic pain lead to this pain spiral. When you try to cope with this condition by using addictive medications, the downward addiction spiral is intensified. In addition, your brain is attempting to adapt by telling other parts of your body to produce additional chemicals as it tries to manage the situation.

It is important to grasp that most of the time your pain is telling you there is something wrong with your body and is part of your defense system. Sometimes, however, your pain is not serving a useful purpose and may not always be obvious.

An Impaired Pain System Leads to Chronic Pain

As with any sensory system, pain receptors and circuits can become impaired, resulting in chronic pain that cannot be attributed to any identifiable physical problem. The greatest challenge with regard to understanding the biological aspects of pain is why it sometimes continues even after a painful stimulus has been removed. To help clarify pain further it is necessary to briefly describe the following three types of pain.

Three Types of Pain

Pain can be organized depending on the type of pain. The experience of pain, regardless of the pain-producing source, has the single physical feature of discomfort. However, pain can be categorized into three types.

Three Types of Pain
- Type One: Direct Pain
- Type Two: Indirect Pain
- Type Three: Systemic Pain

Type One pain is directly related to a pain source. This type of pain is well known and easily understood. There is a direct cause and effect relationship between the pain source and the sensation of painful stimulation. Burns, abrasions, and cuts are examples of this type of pain.

Type Two pain is indirectly related to a pain source. This type of pain includes the pain of inflammation: such as in a sprained ankle or swollen knee, where there is swelling, redness, and the skin around the affected area is hot to the touch. These two types of pain and their treatments are well understood by the medical community and usually treated effectively.

Type Three pain is not related to a pain source and is systemic or universal. It still remains somewhat of a mystery to the medical and scientific communities and does not possess the clear and distinct cause-effect relationships between source of pain and pain sensation.

Chronic pain is often Type-Three pain.

Type Three pain includes the condition of neuropathy. This is a condition where the pain nerve receptors and circuitry are super sensitive and interpret ordinary input to the brain as painful sensations. It is like putting an electrical signal through an unnecessary amplifier and the high voltage burns out or damages the appliance.

Since there is no pain source, per se, for Type Three pain, surgery is not useful and alternative treatment methods need to be considered. Chronic pain is often a result of the pain signal being turned on, but unable to be turned off.

Unanswered Questions

While the physiology of pain can be explained to a large extent, this sensory experience is a very complex phenomenon. There are still many unanswered questions about the various types of pain sensation.

For example, many of you have experienced the muscle aches and pains after a full day of strenuous physical work, such as in a backyard garden. Your muscles can get tight, sore, and aching due to excessive lifting, digging, and stretching. However, if you apply some light massage or bodywork to this type of pain, the intensity of your pain decreases and sometimes disappears altogether. This example appears initially contradictory. If your muscles are aching, you might think that the last thing to help alleviate the pain would be to apply pressure through bodywork.

On the other hand, pain sensation will also result when a sensory experience is pushed to the extreme. That is, when the pain receptor limit is reached and surpassed, sensory experience can change from pleasant to painful. An example is when heat receptors in the skin are stimulated by warm sunlight. The results are usually experienced as pleasurable sensations. However, these same receptors also signal a painful sensation if overstimulated (pushed past a certain threshold) such as in the case of severe sunburn.

The Addiction Pain Syndrome® Defined

The Chronic Pain and Addiction Connection

In 1996 I conducted research to begin developing the first clinical skills training for Addiction Free Pain Management®. What I looked for was information on people who had chronic pain and coexisting addiction. What I found was disturbing. There was nothing there! What I did find was a large quantity of data on people with addiction and an abundance of information about people who had chronic pain. But I couldn't find anything that addressed someone who suffered with both conditions.

During my research I surveyed addiction and pain programs to find out what happened to these people when they tried to seek help. What I discovered was when they went into an addiction treatment program, the entire focus was on the addictive disorder. Unfortunately, their pain was *not* adequately addressed. The addiction programs really struggled with what to do about the chronic pain. Now, when that same person went into a pain clinic, the entire focus was on the chronic pain, the physiological pain. The pain clinic struggled with what to do when people were acting out with the addiction.

I realized that the focus needed to be on concurrent treatment for both pain and addiction. That is why I developed the Addiction Free Pain Management® System so treatment providers could learn how to effectively deal with both conditions concurrently. What I also discovered during my research was that when the person had both conditions, there was amplification, or a synergism, of their symptoms present. I coined that condition the Addiction Pain Syndrome®.

The final task in this chapter is to understand this connection between pain and addiction. Physical pain is the reason many people start using potentially addictive substances. Chronic medication use plus genetic or environmental susceptibility can lead to increased tolerance as a result of searching for pain relief. Eventually the addictive substance no longer manages the pain symptoms. In fact, it often increases or amplifies the pain signals—a condition called *hyperalgesia* (an extreme sensitivity to pain) can also develop. The end result is severe biopsychosocial pain and problems.

As you can see from the *Addiction Pain Syndrome®* diagram that follows, addiction treatment programs cover about a third of the problem (the *Addictive Disorder Zone*) when dealing with a chronic pain patient. The pain clinics cover a different third of the problem (the *Pain Disorder Zone*). Each of the above modalities when implemented independently miss about two thirds of the problem.

Sometimes addiction treatment centers recognize the need to refer you to a pain specialist or the pain clinics refer you to an addiction specialist. This is definitely an improvement. Now about two-thirds of your needs are being addressed (both the Addictive Disorder Zone and the Pain Disorder Zone). But what about the third zone?

The center area in the diagram is the *Addiction Pain Syndrome Zone*. This is why I developed the Addiction-Free Pain Management® (APM) System that is described in the next chapter.

APM concurrently addresses the addictive disorder, the pain disorder, and the Addiction Pain Syndrome. All three zones are addressed—the Addictive Disorder Zone, the Pain Disorder Zone, and the Addiction Pain Syndrome Zone.

Addiction Pain Syndrome® Diagram

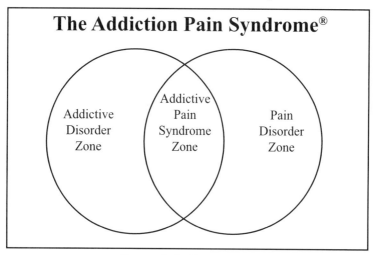

Synergistic Symptoms

The negative consequences more than double when you experience both addictive disorders and pain disorders. Addictive disorders lead to one universe of biopsychosocial problems, and the pain disorders lead to a different set of problems. One plus one no longer equals two; rather, one plus one now equals three or more. This is called *synergism*. Synergism is a condition where the combined action is greater in total effect than the sum of the individual effects.

> Synergism: 1 + 1 = 3 or More

Now take another look at the Addiction Pain Syndrome diagram, and notice the area labeled the Addictive Disorder Zone. Now look at the Pain Disorder Zone. When these two zones are added together, we have the sum of both zones plus a new zone—the Addiction Pain Syndrome Zone. A new universe of symptoms occurs due to the synergistic effect.

APM®— A Synergistic Treatment System

The APM System uses three different types of components to treat the synergistic symptoms, which include all three of the Addiction Pain Syndrome Zones. The first treatment component includes eight Core Clinical Exercises using cognitive behavioral and rational emotive approaches, which are the foundation of the *Addiction-Free Pain Management® Workbook*. Second are the Medication Management Components, and third are the Nonpharmacological Treatment Processes. These three APM components are described fully in the next chapter.

Synergistic Treatment System
1. Core Clinical Exercises
2. Medication Management Components
3. Nonpharmacological Treatment Processes

Developing an effective treatment plan depends upon knowing which stage of the problem you are in. You need to recognize how much damage has been done by the inappropriate use of pain medication and at which stage of the addiction process you are in. Additionally, it is crucial to know what type of pain management skills you have already learned. As you move into a recovery process, it is also essential to differentiate which stage of the developmental recovery process you are in.

Historically, addictive disorders and pain disorders have been treated as separate issues. In the next chapter you will learn that to effectively implement the Addiction-Free Pain Management® System, both the addictive disorder and the pain disorder must be addressed concurrently. Finally, the physical, psychological, and social implications of these disorders must also be dealt with.

> Addressing both the pain disorder and the addictive disorder concurrently is crucial.

In the following chapter you will learn about the Developmental Model of Recovery and Addiction-Free Pain Management®. I will show you how the APM System effectively addresses an addictive disorder and a pain disorder at the same time.

- **Call to Action for the Second Chapter**

It is time to summarize what you have learned so far now that you have come to the end of the second chapter. Please answer the questions below.

1. What is the most important thing you have learned about yourself and your ability to help yourself as a result of completing Chapter Two?

2. What are you willing to commit to do differently as a result of what you have learned by completing this chapter?

3. What obstacles might get in the way of making these changes and what can you do to overcome these roadblocks?

> Take time to pause and reflect, then go to the next page to review Chapter Three.

Chapter Three
The Addiction-Free Pain Management® System

The Developmental Model of Recovery

Once the progression of your addiction or mismanaged chronic pain has been halted, the next step is to determine what stage of the recovery process you're in. This is where an understanding of the CENAPS® Developmental Model of Recovery is essential. I'm going to present a brief overview here. If you want to explore this model further, please refer to *Passages through Recovery* by Terence T. Gorski.

The GORSKI-CENAPS® Developmental Model of Recovery for addictive disorders is based on the premise that addiction and its related mental and personality disorders are chronic, lifestyle-related conditions that require a long-term developmental process of recovery. The CENAPS® developmental recovery process is conceptualized as moving through a series of seven stages.

The Seven Stages of Recovery

Stage 0: Active Abuse/Addiction

Stage 1: Transition

Stage 2: Stabilization

Stage 3: Early Recovery

Stage 4: Middle Recovery

Stage 5: Late Recovery

Stage 6: Maintenance

Stage 0: Active Abuse/Addiction

Before you get to the first stage, you're in *Stage 0* (also known as pretreatment or precontemplation). If you are in this stage, you're actively abusing (or are addicted to) your pain medication, receiving substantial *perceived* benefits from your use, experiencing few *perceived* adverse consequences, and as a result you see no reason to seek help. It usually takes some type of motivational crisis (medical problem, family problem, job problem, etc.) to halt this cycle.

Stage 1: Transition

During the *Transition Stage* (also known as contemplation) the primary focus is on interrupting denial and treatment resistance. If you are in this stage, you're usually experiencing a motivating crisis, coupled with failure of your usual coping tools (i.e., your pain medication no longer works like you want it to or you are receiving too much aggravation from others). The primary task is to help you recognize and accept the need to move out of the problem and into the solution.

Stage 2: Stabilization

During the *Stabilization Stage* the primary focus is on breaking the addiction cycle, managing withdrawal, stabilizing mental status (thinking and feelings), and managing situational life crisis. If you experience an addictive disorder and have chronic pain, this stage requires that you develop safer pain management tools while developing hope—moving from victim to empowerment. Stress and craving management are key tasks to resolve at this stage so you can move into early recovery—covered in Chapter Five.

Stage 3: Early Recovery

During the *Early Recovery Stage* the primary focus is on learning about your addictive disorder and pain disorder, as well as any related mental and personality disorders. If you are in this stage, you need to learn about the recovery process, establish a structured recovery program, and integrate basic skills for identifying and changing addictive thoughts, feelings, and behaviors. You also need to continue learning nonpharmacological pain management and develop an appropriate and safe medication management plan (these are covered in depth later in this chapter).

Stage 4: Middle Recovery

During the *Middle Recovery Stage* the primary focus is on repairing any damage to significant others and to career, social, intimate, and friendship systems caused by your addictive disorder or mismanaged chronic pain. Middle recovery is also the time for you to fully resolve the grief and loss issues caused by your pain disorder and/or your addictive disorder. It is a time to establish a balanced lifestyle, as well as developing effective pain management plans and a solid recovery program.

Stage 5: Late Recovery

During the *Late Recovery Stage* the focus is on helping you make changes in self-defeating personality styles and self-destructive lifestyle structures that interfere with maintaining sobriety, effective pain management, and responsibility. Since many people with chronic pain disorders have also experienced past physical and/or emotional trauma, those issues need to be processed and resolved.

Stage 6: Maintenance

During the *Maintenance Stage* the primary focus is on the continuance of sobriety, effective pain management—especially in ways to manage pain flare-ups—and increasing personal responsibility. In this stage you are learning how to obtain a better quality of life while actively participating in your developmental life process. Understanding and implementing the developmental model of recovery is crucial for helping you recover from the *Addiction Pain Syndrome*.

APM®: The Concurrent Treatment of Pain and Addictive Disorders

---

In the previous chapter you saw how addictive disorders and pain disorders interact—*The Addiction Pain Syndrome®*. Now that you understand how these two conditions overlap, I'll use the remainder of this chapter to define and explain the overlapping synergistic treatment system—*Addiction-Free Pain Management®*.

Addiction-Free Pain Management® Defined

First of all, let me define the term *addiction free*. To understand this term you need to be able to differentiate between addiction, pseudoaddiction, and dependency. Also remember the earlier definition of an addictive disorder, which includes biological rewards, craving cycles, loss of control, and negative consequences.

Many people living with chronic pain are physically dependent upon their medication, but they do not exhibit the addictive biopsychosocial tendencies described in the previous chapter—this is called physical dependency. To be considered addiction free you must be free of inappropriate psychoactive substances and using additional nonpharmacological treatment modalities to manage your pain, such as some of the ones described later in this chapter.

In some instances addiction free may mean that you must take mood-altering (psychoactive) medication, but you are able to take it exactly as prescribed. You use the medication for physical pain relief, but *do not* use the medication to achieve a state of euphoria or mood alteration or to cope emotionally. You do not obsess about the medication or become compulsive about taking it. You are not using it to manage psychological/emotional pain, and you do not experience negative consequences from using it. This is a fairly simple description of *Addiction-Free Pain Management*®, which will be expanded upon later in this book.

> Addiction-Free Pain Management® is the ability to manage a chronic pain condition without experiencing the negative consequences of addiction.

The Development of Addiction-Free Pain Management®

Now that addiction and Addiction-Free Pain Management® have been defined, it's time to look at the developmental process of the APM System. This is accomplished by exploring the five developmental stages that APM has undergone over the past few decades. My hope is that by reading this book you will become a part of its ongoing evolution.

> **APM Stage One:** A Personal Recovery Experience
> **APM Stage Two:** Working with Chronic Pain Patients
> **APM Stage Three:** Applying the CENAPS® Model
> **APM Stage Four:** Field Testing the System
> **APM Stage Five:** Transferring the Technology

APM Stage One
Pain Management—A Personal Recovery Experience

An elementary school accident and the opiate pain medication I received for it in 1962 was the beginning of my journey towards the development of the Addiction-Free Pain Management® System (APM). That first incident and repeated exposure to opiate-based pain medications, as I continued to grow, resulted in many problems that followed me throughout my adolescence and early adult life. Of course, I did not know it at the time, but the seeds for APM were being planted.

During my personal recovery in the early 1980s I experienced a severe workplace accident for which surgery was recommended by all of the surgeons I consulted. Here the APM seeds were beginning to germinate as I became determined to find a way to heal myself and be free of the inappropriate use of psychoactive medication that had plagued me most of my life.

The developmental process or evolution began as I desperately tried to find other alternatives and struggled with healthcare providers over recommendations for operations, pain medication, and physical therapy. We all grappled with the question of "What do we do next?"

My purpose in writing this book is to share the answers to that question. My main goal has been to provide a system demonstrating that successful treatment outcomes are possible by creatively combining existing addiction treatment and chronic pain treatment methods along with the CENAPS® Model of Relapse Prevention Counseling and Denial Management Counseling as part of its foundation. APM did not develop overnight and is continually being improved with each training I do and every client that I consult with. In fact, it remains an ongoing "work in progress" as research in the pain management and addiction fields continues.

> Chronic pain can be successfully treated by creatively combining existing chemical dependency and chronic pain treatment methods.

The maturing process began with the pioneering work of Dr. Jerry Callaway and Dr. Philip Mac. These two addiction medicine specialists had a vision ahead of its time. They were sure that someone with a chronic pain disorder who developed an addictive disorder due to using pain medication needed to be treated for both conditions at the same time.

Because of my own chronic pain condition and my interest in helping this population, they asked me to take on the role of primary therapist for their addiction pain treatment program. I was now working with patients who had lost almost all hope of ever having a normal life. Some of these people came into our program in wheelchairs or using crutches and canes. As a result of this program, many of them walked out under their own power in a relatively short time. I began to develop my own vision of addiction-free treatment, and the APM System continued to grow.

APM Stage Two
Working with Chronic Pain Patients

APM continued to mature as the result of a team approach that included all disciplines. The basic approach was pragmatic—we looked for methods that worked. I developed and promoted special treatment plans for patients, some of which were quite unheard of in an addiction treatment program at that time.

On-site chiropractic visits were arranged. Two to three massage therapy sessions per week became an integral part of the patients' treatment plans. One of the more memorable activities included trips to a hydrotherapy treatment facility. In such a relaxed and nurturing environment patients were much more open and willing to share. In addition, exercising in water was much more beneficial than land-based workouts for many chronic pain conditions.

> The APM System continued to grow with many challenges still ahead.

Within the first few years that I worked in the pain program, I noticed that many patients who were not in the pain program—and even some of the treatment staff—began to complain about the "special" treatment pain patients were receiving. Other staff members thought the pain patients were complaining and "drug-seeking." At a time when teamwork was most needed, the staff was in constant conflict. I began to ask myself, "Now what?"

Fortunately, Drs. Callaway and Mac advocated for the pain program and helped me develop a plan to address these issues and facilitate a team approach. It wasn't easy. At times the specialized alternative treatments were not allowed. The rationale was that they were too disruptive to the treatment milieu. By educating the staff, we were able to help them understand that the pain patients were not receiving special treatment, but had special treatment requirements that had to be addressed if they were to succeed.

> A major challenge for APM® was the onset of managed care.

Another major challenge for APM was the onset of insurance reform and the initial introduction of a managed care approach. What started in the name of cost containment, resulted in patients no longer receiving adequate treatment. When chemically dependent chronic pain patients did not receive effective treatment, they continued to overutilize the healthcare system and their health problems became even worse. Instead of containing costs, expenses grew even higher, and some people died as a result of these misguided cutbacks.

Another challenge was that a high percentage of the pain patients were dropping out of treatment at a much higher rate than other patients. During this time I was introduced to new relapse prevention tools that one of the hospital's counselors, Molly Burke, brought back from a Gorski-CENAPS® relapse prevention training. The one thing that made a significant difference in discouraging patients from leaving against medical advice (AMA) was the *Relapse Prevention Early Intervention Plan*, which became the hospital's AMA intervention plan.

We interviewed patients and asked them to answer three questions:

- What are you going to do if you want to leave treatment?
- What should we (as your treatment providers) do if you attempt, or ask, to leave treatment?
- What significant people in your life can we involve to help you get through the moments of craving and despair without your leaving treatment?

Out of these questions we developed a concrete and specific plan of action that could be used to proactively intervene should patients want to leave treatment against medical advice. This plan allowed early identification and effective responses rather than patient management by crisis.

The more I learned about the Gorski-CENAPS® Model, the more intrigued I became. I realized this could be the way to increase the effectiveness of the pain program. As you will see in the following chapters, it turned out I was right.

Another problem that impacted long-term success with this population developed after they left primary treatment and went into the continuing care program. Many of the patients did not last more than three or four weeks before dropping out. Some of them ended up experiencing painful relapses and returning to treatment even more hopeless than before.

We looked at the questions of "Why this was happening?" and "What can we do about it?" The answer was simple—but not easy to implement. The pain patients needed their own continuing care program. The objections were loud, but I was not about to give up. So I volunteered to facilitate the first continuing care group for the pain patients.

> Relapse prevention tools are a crucial part of APM® development.

While facilitating that continuing care group, I learned the importance of ongoing warning sign and high-risk situation identification and management. I realized I needed to understand even more about relapse prevention to make a difference with this population. I didn't know it at the time, but my search for more relapse prevention tools was a crucial transition for the APM System and myself.

APM® Stage Three
Applying the CENAPS® Model

The big turning point for the APM System was a trip to Chicago to participate in training with Terence T. Gorski at his Advanced Relapse Prevention Therapy Certification School. I was very excited when I first got there, but when I discovered what the next seven days were going to look like, I almost returned home. This was the most intense experiential training I had ever participated in.

We attended lectures, practiced clinical techniques in role-play simulations, and worked on treatment applications in small groups. We had four primary jobs: learn the clinical model, integrate it with our clinical style, develop a plan to integrate it into our clinical programs, and learn how to appropriately adapt it to the needs of each individual patient. By completing this rigorous training program and the optional competency certification, I learned how to competently apply relapse prevention therapy to the treatment of patients with addictive disorders and coexisting chronic pain conditions.

In going through the rigorous case study process, I discovered ways to use these new skills with pain patients. I also realized I had to make a dramatic change in my career if I wanted to really help people with chronic pain. Shortly after this training I resigned from my job and went back to school to complete my college degrees. It was then that I began researching and writing about what was to become the Addiction-Free Pain Management® System.

> Addiction-Free Pain Management® grew from personal experience and the integration of treatment methods for addiction treatment, relapse prevention, and chronic pain.

While attending classes at the university, I offered consultation services for other treatment professionals and started training people to work with pain and coexisting addictive disorders. I assisted one of the local addiction treatment hospitals to develop their own pain management program.

By this time I was implementing even more CENAPS® tools: such as identifying and managing high-risk situations, warning sign identification, and warning sign management. I was also using other ideas that I had discovered in my research of pain clinic treatment programs. I started helping my patients to access eclectic pain management approaches: acupuncture, trigger point injections, hypnotherapy, chiropractic, etc. These approaches are covered more in a later chapter.

> Combining the CENAPS® tools and nonpharmacological pain management approaches helped form the foundation for the existing APM model.

Combining the CENAPS® tools with effective medication management and nonpharmacological pain management approaches was a big step for APM—one that would help develop a firm foundation for the evolving model. I knew I was on the right path now. People I worked with in my private practice were receiving effective treatment and avoiding relapse in growing numbers. I envisioned the APM program growing and knew there was a long way to go yet. Part of that vision was how to encourage other people to learn about and use the model.

Here is where fate intervened. I was now part of the Gorski-CENAPS® faculty and participating in an advanced relapse prevention certification training school. I had just published a journal article about my vision of an effective treatment approach for people with chronic pain and coexisting addictive disorders and asked Terry Gorski for his feedback.

This interaction proved to be the beginning of our joint effort to first write a relapse prevention workbook for this population, then to collaborate and design a system that would provide effective treatment. *Addiction-Free Pain Management®: Relapse Prevention Counseling Workbook* was published in April 1997. Again a team approach was crucial to the process. Many other treatment professionals were needed to help the APM System through the next stage of development.

APM® Stage Four
Field-Testing the System

In addition to developing the workbook, I also created a training process based on my research and practice with this population. The treatment model was transitioning from a vision in my mind to a real world application for other people to use. In fact, my doctoral dissertation focused on "Managing Pain and Coexisting Addictive Disorders."

The more I write and train others, the more I learn myself. The evolution of APM is an ongoing process that becomes richer every time I teach a class, write an article, or work with my patients. The process is indeed coming of age. I envision the second edition of this book as another of the major milestones in the development of the APM System.

> APM becomes richer every time I conduct a training, write an article, or work with a pain patient.

In December 1999, right after the *Addiction-Free Pain Management® Professional Guide* manuscript was sent to Herald House/Independence Press, Terry Gorski and I discussed the next project in the development of Addiction-Free Pain Management®. We decided I should write a book for pain patients that would serve two purposes: (1) to define and explain Addiction-Free Pain Management® and (2) to explain to people how they could get the full benefit of using the *Addiction-Free Pain Management® Workbook*. The development of the original *APM Recovery Guide* began.

APM Stage Five
Transferring the Technology

As a result of my personal and professional experiences, I know that successful treatment for people with substance use disorders and chronic pain can be achieved. By reading this book and integrating the ideas and processes into your life, you are all now a part of this journey. By creatively combining the addiction and chronic pain treatment methods presented in this *APM Recovery Guide* and the *Addiction-Free Pain Management® Workbook* you can learn to more effectively manage your chronic pain and be hopeful once more for a higher quality of life.

The Addiction-Free Pain Management® System consists of eight *Core Clinical Exercises* that can be used with most people in chronic pain. Some of you will also need the *Medication Management Components*, while others need one or more of the *Nonpharmacological Treatment Processes*. Most of you will probably need a strategic combination of all three components.

APM® Core Clinical Exercises

Addiction-Free Pain Management® (APM) has an eight-part core clinical protocol for treating chemically dependent people who have coexisting chronic pain disorders. We call each part of the APM protocol a *clinical exercise*. To make consistent implementation of the process easier, faster, and more effective, the *Addiction-Free Pain Management® Workbook* was developed. It provides exercises related to each core clinical component. What follows is a brief description of each of these eight exercises. Chapters Five through Nine of this book are devoted to exploring how to use these clinical exercises more effectively and explaining how two of my patients, Dean and Jean, completed these workbook exercises.

> External awareness leads to internal cognitive/affective restructuring.

As you go through the remainder of this book and learn how the *Addiction-Free Pain Management*® *Workbook* is used, please remember one important point. The major goal of the workbook exercises is to increase your understanding about your condition and learn what it takes to heal all of the biopsychosocial areas of your life. Please do not just "fill out the forms." Get the most you can out of these exercises; answer as completely and truthfully as possible.

Exercise One: Understanding Your Pain

Many of you may not have the words necessary to accurately describe the symptoms you are experiencing. Therefore, in this exercise you have an opportunity to review and analyze a list of common symptoms that people who live with chronic pain experience. You are asked to identify the symptoms that affect your own life and rate your intensity (severity) on a 0-to-10 pain scale. Next, you learn to differentiate between your physical (*ascending*) pain symptoms and your psychological/emotional (*descending*) pain symptoms. You also examine your TFUARs (**T**houghts, **F**eelings, **U**rges, **A**ctions, and **R**eactions of others) and how they change when you experience a bad pain day.

Exercise Two: Effects of Prescription and/or Other Drugs

Many people living with chronic pain use a variety of different medications to treat the pain and the underlying medical disorders that are causing the pain. In *Exercise Two* you explore the benefits you experienced from using problematic pain medication (including alcohol) and other drugs and what you wanted to get from using the chemicals. You also identify the problems you experienced as a result of problematic pain medication (including alcohol) and other drug use.

Exercise Three: Decision Making about Pain Medication

In this exercise you explore the reasons why you started using problematic pain medication (including alcohol) and other drugs, make an assessment of life-damaging problems you experienced as a result of using chemicals, and explore reasons for deciding to do something different.

Exercise Four: Moving into the Solution

In this clinical exercise you are asked to define what your medication management and recovery plan will include. You complete and sign a medication management agreement that details your adherence to this commitment. Next, you develop a relapse prevention intervention plan that describes the responsibilities for you, your counselor, and three significant others to stop a relapse process quickly should it occur. Finally, you develop a personal craving management plan and a pain flare-up plan to support you if you feel tempted to deviate from your medication management agreement.

Exercise Five: Identifying and Personalizing Your High-Risk Situations

In this clinical exercise you learn to identify the immediate high-risk situations that can cause chemical use and ineffective pain management despite your commitment. You review a list of common high-risk situations that can activate the urge to use/abuse problematic pain medication (including alcohol or other drugs) and/or sabotage your effective pain management program. Next you are asked to identify and personalize your own most important (critical) high-risk situation and write a personal title and description for use in self-monitoring.

Exercise Six: High-Risk Situation Mapping

In this exercise you are asked to describe one past situation where you experienced your immediate high-risk situation and managed it poorly. This situation map is used to help you identify the pattern of self-defeating behaviors that drive a relapse or self-defeating process. Next you identify one past situation where you experienced your immediate high-risk situation and managed it effectively. This situation is used to identify new and more effective ways of coping with your high-risk situation. These new behaviors will become the foundation for your future high-risk situation management and recovery planning.

Exercise Seven: Analyzing and Managing High-Risk Situations

Here you are asked to analyze the immediate high-risk situation you are learning to manage. You get to identify the irrational (addictive) *thoughts*, unmanageable *feelings*, self-destructive *urges*, self-defeating (addictive) *actions*, and *reactions* of others (TFUARs) that drive your high-risk situation. You learn how to manage this kind of high-risk situation more appropriately by identifying three points where you can use more effective ways of thinking, feeling, and acting to avoid relapse. You are encouraged to apply these new ways of coping to future high-risk situations.

Exercise Eight: Recovery Planning

In this exercise you develop a schedule of recovery activities that support the ongoing identification and effective management of your high-risk situations. You are instructed to write a schedule of recovery activities and explore how each activity can be adapted to help you identify and manage your personal high-risk situations.

Summarizing the Core Clinical Exercises

The first two exercises in the workbook are data gathering or assessment instruments focusing on pain. The third and the fourth are motivational with a goal to help you make better choices with your pain management and develop a plan to implement more effective pain management strategies. The fifth, sixth, seventh, and eighth are relapse prevention counseling exercises, and the goal of *Exercise Eight* is to develop a recovery plan to address future high-risk situations for pain and addiction. Look at the following chart to see a final summary of all of these Core Clinical Exercises.

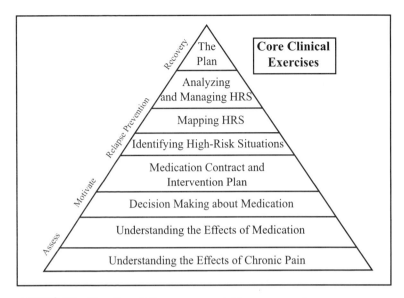

APM® Medication Management Components

Some pain disorders require pharmacological (prescription drug) interventions. Other conditions may respond to over-the-counter medications like aspirin or ibuprofen. Still other conditions may need a combination of both.

However, some pain disorders can be effectively treated without any chemical interventions at all. These nonchemical interventions are called *Nonpharmacological Treatment Processes* and will be discussed at the end of this chapter. However, the focus of this section is the medication management components of the APM System. Review the brief overview of typical medication management in the following table.

Typical Medication Management Approaches

- Acetaminophen and nonsteroidal anti-inflammatory medications can be used alone to treat mild to moderate pain symptoms.

- Acetaminophen and nonsteroidal anti-inflammatory medications can be used with opioids to treat more severe pain.

- SSRIs—like Prozac, Effexor, Lexapro, or Celexa—improve mood as well as help relieve pain, reduce fatigue, and improve sleep problems. There have been reports about SSRIs being helpful for some types of *neuropathic* pain symptoms. Using an SSRI and a tricyclic antidepressant (such as amitriptyline) together may be more successful at breaking the cycle of pain, depression, and sleep problems caused by chronic pain than using either one alone.

- Adjuvant medication—such as antidepressants, anticonvulsants, steroids, anxiolytics, and muscle relaxants—can also be considered for pain relief to boost and/or assist other pain medication.

Remember that any psychoactive medication could be problematic for people with a genetic or personal history of an addictive disorder. Unfortunately, there may be times when opiate (or opioid) medication management is needed, but there are risks. Please see the following table for an overview.

Efficacy and Risks of Opioid Medication Management

- Opioids have been shown to effectively reduce cancer and acute pain conditions, and they can also share a role in the management of chronic pain.

- Opioids may be inappropriate for patients with substance use disorders or a history of those problems. If any psychoactive medications are used, providers must take special precautions.

- Concerns about side effects, such as functional impairment and physical inactivity, as well as concerns about physical or psychological dependence, must be taken into consideration when using opioids for chronic pain management.

- Physical dependence is a physiological adaptation to a substance, defined by a growing tolerance for its effects and/or withdrawal symptoms when use is reduced or ends.

- Psychological dependence (often called addiction) is a primary, chronic, neurobiological disease with genetic, psychosocial, and environmental factors influencing its development and manifestations.

- Psychological dependence may occur with or without physical dependence and is conceptually characterized by impaired control over drug use, compulsive use, continued use despite harm, and craving for the psychic effects of the drug.

- What appears to be psychological dependence may be due to pain that is under treated. This is also known as *pseudoaddiction*.

Please review the information in the following table (provided by Dr. Mark Stanford and updated for this revision). In this table you will see the medications, how they work, and for which conditions they are typically used to treat. In addition, some of the other medication and medical procedures to consider are covered in the following pages.

Medication	Mechanism of Action (How They Work)	Treatment Uses
Non-Narcotic Analgesics: aspirin, acetaminophen (Tylenol), ibuprofen	Acts mostly on the peripheral nervous system. Inhibits prostaglandin E, a substance that sensitizes pain receptors, and increases body pain receptors, inflammation, and body temperature.	Headaches, muscle pain analgesia, anti-inflammatory, anti-pyretic (fever reducer)
Narcotic Analgesics: codeine, morphine, Demerol	Acts in central nervous system to block pain messages. Activates pain modulating systems in the brain that project to the spinal cord. Blocks signals from descending nerve pathways that inhibit the neurons and thus reduce the intensity of pain sensation. There are many types of narcotic analgesics.	Postoperative pain, as well as other pain conditions
Narcotic and Non-Narcotic Combinations: Other pain reducing drugs	Acts on a variety of neurotransmitter systems. Sometimes it's a combination of narcotics with non-narcotic analgesics such as Percocet (percodan and acetaminophen) or vicoprofen (vicodan and ibuprofen).	Variety of pain conditions

Anti-Depressant Drugs (i.e., Tricyclics and SSRIs)	Increases activity of certain neurotransmitters.	Chronic pain, atypical pain syndromes
Epidural Injections	Reduces inflammation in the spine (usually surrounding a damaged spinal disc) reducing pain. Certain steroid drugs (drugs related to cortisone) contain strong anti-inflammatory properties.	Inflammatory pain from damaged spinal disc, arthritic spinal joints, acute strain of spinal muscles or ligaments, pain caused by degeneration of the spine as in osteoporosis
Trigger Point Injections	Local anesthetic, usually procaine and sometimes a corticosteroid, is injected directly into the site. With the injection, the trigger point (muscle knot) is made inactive and pain is alleviated.	Mainly used for fibromyalgia and tension headaches. Also used to alleviate myofascial pain syndrome

Non-Narcotic (Non-Opiate/Opioid) Analgesics

First of all, the term *narcotic* is a legal term, not a medical term. When used, it usually means an opioid or opiate-type medication. The non-opiate analgesics include medications such as aspirin, acetaminophen (Tylenol), and ibuprofen (Motrin, Advil). These medications relieve pain by acting on the peripheral nervous system.

These analgesics inhibit the production of a chemical substance called prostaglandin E. Prostaglandin E is released in response to an initial pain stimulus and intensifies pain in four ways:

1. It makes your pain receptors more sensitive.
2. It increases the number of your pain receptors.
3. It causes inflammation, which in turn creates a new source of pain.
4. It elevates your body temperature, creating pain and discomfort that goes along with having a fever.

Since these types of analgesics inhibit the production of prostaglandin E, they reduce these pain-inducing reactions. As a result, they are a medication of choice for the treatment of headaches, muscle pain, inflammation, and fever.

Opiate Analgesics

The opiate analgesics act within the central nervous system to block pain messages. Opiates activate pain-modulating systems in the brain that communicate with the spinal cord and block signals from descending nerve pathways that inhibit specific neurons, thereby reducing the intensity of pain sensation. There are many types of opiate analgesics; the best known include *codeine, morphine, and Demerol.*

The opiate analgesics are used for the treatment of intense pain. They are ideal for treating postoperative pain and severe pain conditions caused by acute injury. Most people develop tolerance to their pain killing effects within eight to twelve weeks and require an increased dosage. As a result, these medications can be highly addictive. They should be used with extreme caution and are not usually the medication of choice for the treatment of mild to moderate long-term chronic pain conditions.

Opiate and Non-Opiate Combinations

There are a variety of other pain-reducing drugs—many of which are a combination of opiates with non-opiate analgesics. These combinations can provide the pain-relieving benefits of both types of painkillers and act on a variety of neurotransmitter systems. Some of the common combinations of opiates with non-opiate analgesics include Percocet (a combination of percodan and acetaminophen), Vicodin (a combination of hydrocodone and acetaminophen), Vicoprofen (a combination of hydrocodone and ibuprofen), and Tylenol 3 (a combination of acetaminophen with codeine).

Because of the wide variety of pain-relieving effects, the opiate non-opiate combinations are used for a wide variety of pain conditions that exhibit a combination of Type 1 and Type 2 pain characteristics.

Antidepressant Medication

Antidepressant medication may be indicated for several reasons; one is that many patients with chronic pain disorders become clinically depressed. Once again the APM approach suggests that a full biopsychosocial evaluation is necessary to determine the severity of the problem.

Some types of depression (situational) respond best to cognitive behavioral therapy. Other types (bipolar) may need a medical intervention in addition to therapy. There are many different types or classifications of antidepressants to choose from; therefore, a specialist should be consulted to determine the most effective medication for each patient.

Pain reduction is another reason for using an antidepressant. The use of *tricyclic* antidepressants has been an effective tool in pain management for years. For example, the tricyclic Elavil (amitriptyline) is frequently used to treat and help prevent migraine headaches. These antidepressants have been able to provide relief for nerve pain and often result in lowering the dose of opiate medications.

Another class of newer antidepressants is the SSRIs (selective serotonin reuptake inhibitors). Many pain management specialists utilize this type of medication for chronic pain treatment particularly for people who live with constant debilitating chronic pain, as their serotonin system becomes depleted. This type of medication is good for both depression as well as improving pain management.

SSRIs—like Prozac, Effexor, Lexapro, or Celexa—improve mood as well as help relieve pain, reduce fatigue, and improve sleep problems. There have been reports about SSRIs being helpful for some types of *neuropathic* pain symptoms. Some studies also suggest that using an SSRI and a tricyclic antidepressant (such as amitriptyline) together may be more successful at breaking the cycle of pain, depression, and sleep problems caused by fibromyalgia than using either one alone.

In addition, three antidepressant medications can also be very helpful: Cymbalta and Effexor, which block the reuptake of *serotonin* and *norepenepherine,* and Wellbutrin, which alters the levels of *norepenepherine* and *dopamine*. Cymbalta is a versatile medication approved to treat depression and certain types of pain. Norepenepherine, serotonin, and dopamine are neurotransmitters that not only affect depression but also pain management. Many pain management specialists recognize that combining different medications creates a synergistic effect for both pain management and improving depression.

Epidural Injections

Epidural injection is the process of administering a drug into the outer covering of the central nervous system, usually in the spine. The use of epidural steroid injections can lead to a reduction of inflammation in the spine (usually surrounding a damaged spinal disc). Certain steroid drugs (those related to cortisone) contain strong anti-inflammatory properties. This reduction in inflammation leads to a decrease in pain.

Spinal injections are not new—their use to treat low back pain was first documented in 1901. In 1952 epidural steroid injections were first used to treat low back pain with associated sciatica (pain in the sciatic nerve due to lumbar or sciatic disc herniation). Today, epidural steroid injections have become an integral part of the non-surgical management of low back pain.

An epidural injection is typically used to alleviate chronic low back and/or leg pain. While the effects of the injection are temporary—providing relief from pain for one week up to one year—an epidural can be very beneficial for patients during an episode of severe back pain. More importantly, it can provide sufficient pain relief to allow the patient to make progress with their rehabilitation program.

An epidural is effective in significantly reducing pain for approximately 50 percent of patients. It works by delivering steroids directly to the painful area to help decrease the inflammation that may be causing the pain. It is thought that there is also a flushing effect from the injection that helps remove or *flush out* inflammatory proteins from around the structures that may be causing the pain.

The use of opioids injected epidurally can lead to significant pain relief for severe pain conditions. This technique uses a lower dose of opioid, which has a longer duration and low risk of sedation. However, side effects may sometimes occur. So this procedure is usually reserved for serious conditions where the patient is in a specialized care center.

Trigger Point Injections

Trigger point injection (TPI) is used to treat extremely painful areas of muscle. Normal muscle contracts and relaxes when it is active. A trigger point is a knot or tight, ropey band of muscle that forms when muscle fails to relax. The knot can often be felt under the skin and may twitch involuntarily when touched (called a jump sign). The trigger point can trap or irritate surrounding nerves and cause referred pain—pain felt in another part of the body. As a result, scar tissue, loss of range of motion, and weakness may develop over time.

TPI is used to alleviate myofascial pain syndrome (chronic pain involving tissue that surrounds muscle) that does not respond to other treatment, although there is some debate over its effectiveness. Many muscle groups, especially those in the arms, legs, lower back, and neck, are treated by this method. TPI can also be used to treat fibromyalgia and tension headaches.

Two Types of Trigger-Point Injection Therapy

There are two main types of trigger point injections: injection by *manual palpation* and *needle EMG-guided injection*. The manual palpation type of trigger point therapy involves the physician manually locating the trigger point by massaging the skin. A trained physician can usually tell where a trigger point is located, how big it is, and how deep it is lying within the muscle. However, it is sometimes difficult to estimate the exact location of a trigger point.

Needle EMG-guided injection uses both manual palpation and guided imagery to locate the trigger point. First, the physician will feel around for the trigger point. A needle is then inserted into the area and relays information back to a monitor. The doctor can then see how to guide the needle directly into the trigger point; this is a much more accurate method.

Physical therapy is recommended within minutes or a few hours immediately after a TPI procedure. Stretching of the muscles enhances the effects of trigger point injections, leading to longer lasting pain relief. Whenever possible, refer patients to a physiotherapist or to massage therapy after the TPI procedure.

Prolotherapy

Prolotherapy treatment is useful for many different types of musculoskeletal pain: arthritis, back pain, neck pain, fibromyalgia, sports injuries, unresolved whiplash injuries, carpal tunnel syndrome, and chronic tendonitis. It is also useful for partially torn tendons, ligaments, and cartilage; degenerated or herniated discs; TMJ; and sciatica. The information in the following table is from the Web site *http://www.prolotherapy.org/*. As you will see, prolotherapy may be an appropriate nonsurgical intervention for people who meet the criteria for this type of procedure. Although it is not *medication* per se, it is a medical procedure.

Prolotherapy Defined

Prolotherapy is a simple, natural technique that stimulates the body to repair the painful area when the natural healing process needs a little assistance. That's all the body needs; the rest it can take care of on its own. In most cases, commonly prescribed anti-inflammatory medications, and more drastic measures like surgery and joint replacement, may not help and often hinder or even prevent the healing process. The basic mechanism of prolotherapy is simple. A substance is injected into the affected ligaments or tendons, which leads to local inflammation. The localized inflammation triggers a wound healing cascade, resulting in the deposition of new collagen—the material that ligaments and tendons are made of. New collagen shrinks as it matures. The shrinking collagen tightens the ligament that was injected and makes it stronger. Prolotherapy has the potential of being 100 percent effective at eliminating chronic pain due to ligament and tendon weakness, but depends on the technique of the individual prolotherapist. The most important aspect is injecting enough of the solution into the injured and weakened area. If this is done, the likelihood of success is excellent.

Prolotherapy involves the treatment of two specific kinds of tissue: tendons and ligaments. A tendon attaches a muscle to the bone and involves movement of the joint. A ligament connects two bones and is involved in the stability of the joint. A strain is defined as a stretched or injured tendon; a sprain is a stretched or injured ligament. Once these structures are injured, the immune system is stimulated to repair the injured area. Because ligaments and tendons generally have a poor blood supply, incomplete healing is common after injury. This incomplete healing results in these normally taut, strong bands of fibrous or connective tissue becoming relaxed and weak. The relaxed and inefficient ligament or tendon then becomes the source of chronic pain and weakness.

Prolotherapy works by exactly the same process the human body naturally uses to stimulate the body's healing system—a process called inflammation. The technique involves the injection of a proliferant (a mild irritant solution) that causes an inflammatory response which "turns on" the healing process. The growth of new ligament and tendon tissue is then stimulated. The ligaments and tendons produced after prolotherapy appear much the same as normal tissues, except that they are thicker, stronger, and contain fibers of varying thickness, testifying to the new and ongoing creation of tissue. The ligament and tendon tissue which forms as a result of prolotherapy is up to 40 percent stronger in some cases.

There are obviously many more medication and medical type procedures available than those listed previously, but this was only meant to be a brief overview of what is available. One of the procedures already described was epidural injection. This procedure is one of several called *Interventional Pain Management* procedures. In the following table is a partial list of these procedures.

Interventional Pain Management

1. **Epidural injections (in all areas of the spine):** The use of anesthetic and steroid medications injected into the epidural space to relieve pain or diagnose a specific condition.
2. **Nerve, root, and medial branch blocks:** Injections done to determine if a specific spinal nerve root is the source of pain. Blocks also can be used to reduce inflammation and pain.
3. **Facet joint injections:** An injection used to determine if the facet joints are the source of pain. These injections can also provide pain relief.
4. **Discography:** An "inside" look into the discs to determine if they are the source of a patient's pain. This procedure involves the use of a dye that is injected into a disc and then examined using X-ray or CT scan.
5. **Pulsed radiofrequency neurotomy (PRFN):** A minimally invasive procedure that disables spinal nerves and prevents them from transmitting pain signals to the brain.
6. **Rhizotomy:** A procedure where pain signals are "turned off" through the use of heated electrodes that are applied to specific nerves that carry pain signals to the brain.
7. **Spinal cord stimulation:** The use of electrical impulses that are used to block pain from being perceived in the brain.
8. **Intrathecal pumps:** A surgically implanted pump that delivers pain medications to the precise location in the spine where the pain is located.
9. **Percutaneous discectomy/nucleoplasty:** A procedure in which tissue is removed from the disc in order to decompress and relieve pressure.

Migraine-Specific Medication Management

Medications used to combat migraines fall into two broad categories:
- *Pain-relieving medications:* Also known as acute or abortive treatment, these types of drugs are taken during migraine attacks and are designed to stop symptoms that have already begun.
- *Preventive medications:* These types of drugs are taken regularly, often on a daily basis, to reduce the severity or frequency of migraines.

The following information is from an early 2007 online survey of *migraineurs* (migraine headache sufferers) and physicians commissioned by the National Headache Foundation (NHF) and conducted by Harris Interactive. The following information in this *migraine* section can also be found on the *www.healthcentral.com* Web site. The actual survey is titled: *NHF Survey—Migraine-Specific Medications vs. Nonspecific Medications for Acute Treatment*. The NHF survey shows that 20 percent of migraine patients are currently taking potentially addictive medications that contain barbiturates or opioids and have not been approved by the U.S. Food and Drug Administration (FDA) for the relief of migraines.

The survey also shows that patients taking prescription medications not approved by the FDA to treat migraines are more likely to experience drug-related side effects than patients taking prescription medications that have been approved by the FDA as migraine treatments. Although barbiturates and opioids are sometimes considered effective for short-term migraine relief, many doctors recommend against prescribing them for long-term use because of the potential for dependence and abuse and the very real danger of developing medication overuse headaches (this is sometimes called *pain rebound*). The pros and cons of opioid medication management were also covered earlier in this chapter.

In the realm of migraine treatment, little emphasis is placed on whether the medications have been specifically FDA approved for the treatment of migraine, since so few are FDA approved for their prevention. In fact, there is not a single medication that was originally developed for migraine prevention. All were originally developed for other purposes. When it comes to treating migraine attacks (acute treatment), however, this is not the case. There are seven *triptans* (Imitrex, Maxalt, Zomig, Amerge, Axert, Frova, and Relpax) that were developed for and FDA approved as migraine abortive (management) medications. These medications work to actually stop the migrainous process in the brain and stop the migraine attack and its associated symptoms.

Ergotamine medications are used as vasoconstrictors for migraine prevention and are sometimes mixed with caffeine. DHE and Migrana are also FDA approved for Migraine treatment as is Midrin (a combination of acetaminophen, dichloralphenazone, and isometheptene). In addition to the ergotamine medications the

NHF study also involved the *triptans* as well as prescription pain-relieving medications that cannot abort a migraine. Thus, the issue here is not so much FDA approval of acute medications, but the difference between using "generic pain medications" as opposed to migraine-specific medications.

Findings from the NHF survey of 502 patients and 201 primary care physicians and neurologists, conducted in early 2007, are reproduced in the following table. This table is followed by the APM *Nonpharmacological Treatment Processes* section. These approaches are meant to work collaboratively with the medication management components, along with the APM *Core Clinical Exercises* covered earlier.

NHF Survey Results

- Fifty-three percent of migraine patients take triptans as the primary prescription medication for their condition
- Twenty percent take barbiturates or opioids
- Another 27 percent take other medications
- Patients taking triptans are significantly more likely than those taking barbiturates or opioids to report that their medication works well at relieving migraine symptoms.
- Sixty percent of triptan patients report their medication worked "extremely" or "very" well to relieve their migraine symptoms completely
- Only 42 percent of patients taking barbiturates and opioids report their medication worked "extremely" or "very" well to relieve their migraine symptoms completely.
- Four out of five patients (82%) have taken more than one prescription medication for their migraines.
- The average number of medications a patient has taken to treat migraine attacks is four (treatment for attacks, not prevention).
- Patients taking opioids and barbiturates for their migraines also reported a lower quality of life than patients taking triptans. They were twice as likely as patients taking triptans to say that migraines "always" limited their ability to: exercise

> or play sports (35% vs. 14%); engage in sexual activity (33% vs. 17%); drive a car (28% vs. 14%); spend time with family and friends (28% vs. 8%); or simply get out of the house (33% vs. 15%).

APM® Nonpharmacological Treatment Processes

Nonpharmacological treatments have proved to be effective for many pain conditions. For example, recent studies have shown that endorphins mediate the analgesic effects of acupuncture and placebos as well. Still to be discovered is the mechanism by which hypnosis accomplishes its analgesic effects.

Addiction-Free Pain Management® uses both of the components described earlier along with the nonpharmacological processes briefly described on the following pages. You will be provided with a more extensive overview of these and more nonpharmacological approaches in a later chapter. Since each of you has your own unique problems, different combinations will be needed for each person. The remainder of this book describes how to effectively implement both the core and optional components to obtain the best treatment outcomes.

Meditation and Relaxation

For decades addiction treatment (addictive disorders) research literature has established the effectiveness of teaching meditation and relaxation techniques to people with addictive disorders. Pain literature also indicates the importance of using relaxation to help reduce the level of pain that people living with chronic pain experience. For example, Dr. Margaret Caudill (2001) explains in her book, *Managing Pain before It Manages You,* how to evoke what she calls the *relaxation response* in order to reduce stress and pain.

There are many books and audiocassettes that can be used to teach you how to use meditation and relaxation exercises to reduce stress and anxiety. Later you will learn about the stress-pain connection. But remember, in most cases, if you can learn to lower your stress level, you will also experience a decrease in your level of pain.

Emotional Management

Most addiction treatment professionals realize the importance of teaching their patients how to appropriately deal with emotional issues to reduce their stress and anxiety. The CENAPS® Model is based in part on the belief that masking or avoiding painful emotions will often lead a recovering chemically dependent person to relapse.

One of the most difficult and crucial emotional issues that must be resolved is the grief and loss of your health and/or prior level of functioning. Obtaining support to work through a painful grieving process improves your chances of a successful treatment outcome with chronic pain.

Massage Therapy and Physical Therapy

As we saw earlier, direct pressure can sometimes change the way you experience pain. When using massage therapy, you need to understand there will be some immediate pain relief and reduced muscle tension, but it will be short-lived if not followed with other measures. This is understandable since there are many precursors or triggers for muscle tension that often resurface soon after a massage session. Therefore, other interventions must be implemented that are specific to each individual person and must be used in the proper sequence.

Many healthcare providers combine physical therapy and hydrotherapy for support in helping you strengthen and recondition your body—allowing you to become an active participant in your healing process.

Chiropractic Treatment

Many chronic pain patients receive long-term pain reduction when undergoing chiropractic treatment. Chiropractic adjustments restore proper motion and function to damaged joints, thereby reducing irritation to associated muscles and nerves.

Most chiropractors are also trained in nutrition and may include dietary changes and nutrient supplementation in their treatment plans. This process helps to build up the immune system while at the same time raising one's pain threshold. A later chapter discusses the importance of using supplements as part of the healing process. Some chiropractors are also using *cold laser therapy,* which is covered later.

Acupuncture

Acupuncture is one of the oldest, most commonly used medical procedures in the world. Originating in China more than 2,000 years ago, acupuncture became better known in the United States in 1971, when *New York Times* reporter James Reston wrote about how doctors in China used needles to ease his pain after surgery. The term "acupuncture" describes a family of procedures involving stimulation of anatomical points on the body by a variety of techniques. The acupuncture technique most studied scientifically involves penetrating the skin with thin, solid, metallic needles manipulated by the hands or by electrical stimulation.

Acupuncture is often effective in managing certain types of pain. It stimulates the large and small nerve fibers that inhibit pain signaling and may produce a placebo effect through the release of endorphins and enkephalins. Acupuncture is often used in the treatment of back pain, minor surgery, and other pain conditions.

Biofeedback

Biofeedback is a treatment technique where people are trained to improve their health by recognizing and using signals from their own bodies. Physical therapists use biofeedback to help stroke victims regain movement in paralyzed muscles. Psychologists use it to help tense and anxious clients learn to relax. Specialists in many different fields use biofeedback to help their patients cope with pain.

Biofeedback has proved to be another effective method you can learn in order to participate more actively in your own treatment. This procedure teaches you how to minimize or eliminate the physical symptoms of stress and tension.

Effective biofeedback treatment is progressive and includes several steps. It starts with an accurate diagnosis of the problem followed by implementation of the appropriate treatment modality specified for you. It also includes time for you to practice situations that simulate instances where symptoms most often arise. Learning to use meditation and relaxation techniques to reduce stress is a helpful complement to the biofeedback process.

Hypnosis

Hypnosis can be an effective treatment for various pain conditions. There is some evidence that certain people are more susceptible to the effects of hypnosis than others. The effects of hypnosis are definitely biopsychosocial. Although it is not certain how hypnosis biologically mediates pain, there is growing evidence it may activate pain-inhibitory descending nerve pathways from brain to spinal cord. It appears, however, that hypnosis does not affect the opioid pathways.

Hypnosis also creates an altered state of consciousness usually marked by a slowing of brain-wave patterns. As a result, people under the influence of hypnosis often experience a state of consciousness associated with alpha and theta brain-wave activity. These states of consciousness bypass normal cognitive processes and, hence, can prevent many expectations and beliefs about the pain experience (e.g., anticipatory pain) from coming to mind.

Psychologically, hypnosis may act in the brain to shift attention away from pain sensation. Hypnosis is commonly used in conjunction with dental procedures, childbirth, burns, and headaches.

Socially, hypnosis may create a cultural expectation through suggestion that the pain will be minimal and manageable. The social context of hypnotic suggestion may also distract from the pain.

The following table lists an even wider variety of nonpharmacological interventions. As you review this table, you may find that you are already utilizing some of these tools.

Nonpharmacological Approaches

- Emotional Management
- Massage Therapy
- Physical Therapy
- Chiropractic Treatment
- Acupuncture
- Biofeedback
- Hypnosis
- Meditation and Relaxation
- Yoga/Tai Chi
- Gardening
- Humor
- NLP
- Journaling
- Art Therapy
- Reiki Therapy/Energy
- Twelve-Step/Self-Help Groups
- Pilates

- Diet/Nutrition
- Prayer
- Tribal Healing
- Sweat Lodges
- Talking Circles
- Pet Therapy
- Self-Help Groups
- TENS Units
- Reflexology
- Cranial Sacral
- Aerobics
- Rolfing/Hellar
- Nature
- Hobbies
- EMDR (Eye Movement Desensitization and Reprocessing Therapy)
- Infrared Heat
- Visualization
- Avoidance/Distraction
- Sleep Hygiene
- Music
- Aroma Therapy
- Smudging
- Sex Therapy
- Swim/Hydrotherapy
- Movies
- Arts and Crafts
- Shiatsu/Watsu Therapy
- Play Therapy
- Reading
- Wisdom Groups
- Infrared Sauna
- Retail Therapy
- Trager Therapy
- Sensory Meditation
- Nature Walks
- Psychodrama
- Cold-Laser Therapy
- Acupressure
- Travel
- Sand-Tray Therapy
- Spiritual Retreat
- Dance/Movement
- Hot Tubs
- Going to School
- Guided Imagery
- Stargazing
- Equine Therapy
- Cooking
- Healing Touch
- Empty-Chair Therapy
- Karaoke
- Ice/Heat
- Singing
- Thought-Field Therapy
- Assertiveness Training
- Rebirthing
- Knitting
- Reflexology

> Use This Information in the Real World

The challenge now is to understand how to adapt the information in this chapter to implement what you are learning in the real world. The remainder of this book takes you through the APM Core Clinical Exercises with two actual patients, Jean and Dean, whose names and other identifying information were changed to protect their confidentiality.

- **Call to Action for the Third Chapter**

It is time to summarize what you have learned so far now that you have come to the end of the third chapter. Please answer the questions below.

1. What is the most important thing you have learned about yourself and your ability to help yourself as a result of completing Chapter Three?

2. What are you willing to commit to do differently as a result of what you have learned by completing this chapter?

3. What obstacles might get in the way of making these changes and what can you do to overcome these roadblocks?

> **Take time to pause and reflect, then
> go to the next page to review Chapter Four.**

Chapter Four
Learning to Live Again

Understanding Your Chronic Pain

Chronic pain can be difficult to manage. Your pain is real. You may also be at a high risk of becoming addicted to your pain medications. Your need for relief is urgent. The typical treatment involves the use of pain-killing medications. When undergoing pain management treatment, you are forced to answer a series of difficult questions.

- What if traditional medication management doesn't work?
- What if you quickly develop tolerance to your pain medication and require progressively larger doses to gain relief from your pain?
- What do you do if you find yourself consistently abusing your pain medication by using more or taking it more often than prescribed?
- How can you distinguish between the legitimate need for more pain medication (over a longer period of time) and the possibility that you may have become addicted to it?
- How do you deal with feeling helpless and hopeless because you are in pain and/or addicted to your pain medications and can see no way out?

The Addiction-Free Pain Management® (APM) System provides a way to answer these and many more difficult questions routinely asked by people with chronic pain. As I mentioned previously, the APM System is a treatment approach that also incorporates components of the GORSKI-CENAPS® Developmental Model of Recovery.

The APM System integrates the most advanced pain management methods, developed at the nation's leading pain clinics, with the most effective treatment methods for addiction, developed at the nation's leading chemical dependency treatment programs. The result is a unique integration of treatment methods that combines proper medication management with nonpharmacological techniques. This can lead to pain relief, while lowering or eliminating your risk of addiction or relapse.

How Jean and Dean Deal with Their Pain

I will be using two former patients, Jean and Dean, to illustrate the various exercises in the *Addiction-Free Pain Management® Workbook*. This *Recovery Guide* is designed to help you accomplish the following:
- Understand the APM treatment philosophy.
- Integrate APM into your personal recovery program.
- Adapt APM to meet the unique needs of your personal life.

I will explain each concept from the workbook exercises and then describe how the exercises were completed by these two different patients. By doing this you can see some of the ways you can apply APM for yourself.

The following chapters explore the separate elements of APM by showing how Jean and Dean completed the APM treatment process and by discussing the exercises in the *APM Workbook*. Jean and Dean are typical of the many people who suffer from the combination of chemical dependency and chronic pain. Now I would like to briefly introduce you to Jean and Dean.

Introducing Jean

People in chronic pain often seek treatment as a result of a complex combination of physical, psychological, and social problems. Many people have serious coexisting problems that must also be addressed to appropriately manage a pain disorder or risk sabotaging successful treatment. Jean is no exception.

Jean is a thirty-year-old married woman and a mother of four children under ten years of age. Jean's oldest daughter found her mother unconscious at the bottom of the stairs, which was the motivation for her family to seek help. Jean was unconscious because she had taken too large a dose of her medication—Demerol. The family contacted an intervention specialist to conduct a family intervention, which included Jean's husband, mother, father, sisters, and brothers. All shared their love and concern. As a result, Jean accepted the treatment recommendations and enrolled in a program that utilized the APM model.

Jean suffered from ongoing headache pain. It started when she was a young adolescent, shortly after she was repeatedly sexually abused by a trusted middle-school teacher. She never told anyone about the abuse and continued to have troubling flashbacks of those abusive incidents.

Jean exhibited obsessive compulsive tendencies that served her very well in the past. Unfortunately she also developed repetitive patterns of self-defeating compulsive and/or impulsive behaviors. Because of this, one central focus of treatment was to help her pause when facing a stressful situation and select new relevant responses that could support her in solving problems, rather than acting out old self-defeating behaviors.

Jean's father, now in recovery from prescription drug dependency, as well as alcoholism, often encouraged Jean to take addictive medications for her headaches. Like many people who have been sexually abused, Jean had an extremely difficult time with trust and was very resistant to seeking help, which was compounded by the fact her first serious boyfriend was also abusive to her.

> It is crucial to be aware of your intial motivation for treatment and build on it.

Jean's major motivation for treatment originated with the family intervention. She was in a place to hear from her family that she was hurting not only herself, but her children as well. In fact, her primary motivation for treatment, at least at the beginning, was for her children. Jean's husband enabled her quite a bit and needed his own intervention to educate him about the ways he was sabotaging his wife's treatment. For example, in the middle of her first week in the program Jean asked him to come and take her home. It was fortunate that when he tried to do so, another family member called to warn the staff, and they were able to intercept him and intervene. You will learn more about Jean and how she completed the APM process as you go through the remainder of the book, but right now let's take a look at Dean's story.

Introducing Dean

Dean is a forty-five-year-old married male who had a long history of addictive pain medication use, which also included alcohol and other drugs. He was treated in several addiction treatment programs for both alcohol and pain medication over a five-year period. In his early adolescence he was molested by an older male cousin and still experienced shame and trauma flashbacks, as well as difficulty being emotionally intimate with his current wife. Dean acted out sexually with strangers in order to avoid emotional intimacy. As a result of his addiction, as well as affairs and his inability to share emotional intimacy with his ex-wife, his previous marriage ended. In his early twenties Dean started using alcohol and several illicit drugs, including speed (methamphetamine) and marijuana. Dean also had several medical problems: the most critical was a serious knee injury resulting from a construction accident that happened more than ten years before.

After being confronted by his wife and learning she spoke with his doctor, Dean finally admitted to his doctor and himself that he was once again out of control with his pain medication (at that time he was using over seventy Vicodin per day). Later in treatment he realized that in addition to helping him manage his knee pain, he used the medication to help him cope with uncomfortable feelings and to get high (to experience a pleasant state of euphoria), which would help him forget about his problems—at least for a little while.

Dean also suffered from extreme guilt and shame about having several affairs, which he believed would lead to a divorce if his wife found out. He did not want to destroy his marriage and blamed the high amount of pain medication he was taking for making those bad decisions. He would later admit he also felt free and uninhibited with his sexual partners, because there were no demands to be emotionally present with them.

> Isolation tendencies are common with chronic pain and addictive disorders.

Like many people living with chronic pain, Dean developed a tendency to isolate when in legitimate pain (either physically or emotionally) and would eventually go to an urgent-care clinic. Once there it was easy for him to persuade the staff to give him opiate medication for his multiple physical pain conditions, since his records indicated medical necessity for that type of medication. The frequency of these visits eventually became hard to hide, until he found someone who was selling *black-market* Vicodin. At that point his use really escalated.

Dean's motivation for treatment was the result of his wife finding several hundred Vicodin tablets in his work vehicle and reporting his increased drug use to his primary care physician. Dean's doctor refused to care for him unless he went into an addiction treatment program. In addition to Dean's addictive use of alcohol and Vicodin, his doctor was concerned about his impaired liver functions because of the high amount of acetaminophen in the Vicodin and the synergistic effect of the alcohol. Dean's use was well over the recommended ceiling dose of 4,000 mgs per day of acetaminophen. Dean's wife, who was working a very good Al-Anon program, also informed him that she was going to leave him unless he got help—because she couldn't watch him slowly killing himself. In the following chapters you will learn more about Dean and how he completed the APM process.

Learning to Connect

Both Jean and Dean shared the lack of trust found in many chemically dependent chronic pain patients. Some of you may have been given negative messages by your caregivers, such as: "It's all in your head." "You need to try harder." "You're making yourself hurt so you can get drugs." Many of you may believe that no one can possibly understand what you are going through until eventually you think, "Why should I even try to convince them anymore?"

I asked one patient why she believed she kept relapsing with pain medication and she told me, "My psychiatrist says it's because I'm a *Borderline*." It took some time, but I was able to help her understand that she was *not* a Borderline. But because of her prolonged use of psychoactive medication, she had developed some traits that were similar to the diagnostic criteria for a Borderline Personality Disorder. She finally realized that she was *not* her diagnosis—which, as it turned out, was true, because her diagnosis was inaccurate.

Jean and Dean were both extremely guarded when they first began APM treatment. They were defensive and angry because they had been *forced* into treatment. Dean had just come from a major intervention with his doctor and was also feeling ashamed that he had cheated on his wife. Jean had been steadily increasing her pain medications for a number of months before her family finally arranged an intervention—after her daughter found her passed out on the floor. Up until that point she did not think that her escalation of Demerol use was a problem—even though she often obtained many of her refills in an illegal manner.

You, also, may be feeling guarded, defensive, hopeless, and helpless due to a lack of understanding about addiction and pain management—in addition to some of the negative messages mentioned previously. Finding an effective way to connect is a crucial part of the APM treatment process. In the intervention and recovery planning sections you will learn how to incorporate other people into your APM team in a healthy way that supports and encourages you.

Making an Important Decision

Your initial decision to seek help is the most crucial point in your treatment process. Finding treatment providers who are willing to work with you—*not on you*—is also important. It is crucial to find doctors, therapists, or counselors who are willing to see you as a whole person, and not just your pain condition.

> Making an Empowered Decision

Asking yourself the five questions below and answering as completely and truthfully as possible will help you make your decision to start the APM process. Share your answers to these questions with someone you trust—as well as someone who will be honest with you—to obtain an accurate reality check.

1. What is the best that will happen if I continue using my pain medication and/or managing my pain the way I have been doing?
2. What is the worst that will happen if I continue using my pain medication and/or managing my pain the way I have been doing?
3. What is the worst that will happen if I decide to start on this APM recovery journey?
4. What is the best that will happen if I decide to start on this APM recovery journey?
5. Am I willing to make a commitment to complete this APM process and develop a plan to overcome any resistance or obstacles? Please explain why or why not.

Once you fully answer these five questions, you will have the information you need to make an empowered decision and the beginning of an action plan to move you forward. It is imperative you not do this work alone for many reasons. The most important is that many people in chronic pain, or who suffer from substance abuse/dependency, often isolate themselves. Another reason is you deserve to have support when dealing with this problem. The APM treatment process requires a tremendous amount of hard work and self-honesty, as well as allowing other people on your *team* who are willing—and able—to support you in a healthy way.

If you are currently using your pain medication problematically or experiencing negative consequences from your medication, you may need detoxification treatment or a medication taper before starting the APM process. Some of you may not have reached the abuse or dependency stages yet, but you, too, can benefit from the APM process so you don't have to experience the painful ramifications of a full-blown addictive disorder.

Detoxification Issues

Neurotransmitters and Pain Suppression

Stimulation of certain areas of the brain can cause pain suppression. In the brain there are a variety of chemicals called neurotransmitters—substances that transmit information to the brain and body. Three neurotransmitters—enkephalins, serotonin, and endorphins—are known to be associated with pain suppression.

Analgesic treatments—treatments that prevent pain—are believed to be assisted by endorphins and enkephalins. Consistent with this understanding, it is now believed that opiates relieve pain because they are similar in structure to endorphins and enkephalins. They act on the same sites in your brain and spinal cord as do these neurotransmitters.

The concern about using opiates repeatedly over a period of time is that they can ultimately reduce your brain's own natural pain suppressant neurotransmitters, since they are so chemically similar in structure. With repeated use of many opiates, your brain responds and adapts by slowing down production of its own natural opiates (the endorphins/enkephalins). In a sense, the brain begins to adapt to the presence of an opiate drug by reducing its own natural source of pain suppressing neurotransmitters. The result is that opiate drugs can ultimately increase the sensation of pain via the brain's adaptive response—this is sometimes called a pain-rebound effect or a condition called *hyperalgesia* (hypersensitivity to pain).

Neurotransmitters and Withdrawal

When someone who abuses narcotic analgesics abruptly stops taking these drugs, they often experience a very hypersensitive and painful physical reaction. This is why the narcotic withdrawal syndrome can be so uncomfortable and painful. It takes approximately two weeks for the brain to de-adapt from opiate medication, which has essentially replaced its own pain-reducing capacity, and go back to its natural ability to make and use endorphins.

Because of the potential for physical dependency (meaning that the drug produces tolerance and a characteristic withdrawal syndrome upon abrupt cessation of use), opiate medications should only be used with the highest degree of caution in persons suffering with chronic pain and coexisting disorders.

How and where to start treatment varies depending on the results of the identification and assessment process discussed earlier. However, effective treatment cannot be obtained if you remain on problematic pain medication (including alcohol). In the APM treatment process the first approach is usually detoxification (or medication taper) and stabilization.

Inpatient versus Outpatient

Sometimes this stage of treatment needs to incorporate a medically supervised inpatient program due to the quantity and/or types of medication being used. In other situations an outpatient detoxification or taper protocol can be effectively implemented. Whatever method is used, it should be implemented with the team approach in mind. Please remember that you need to be an integral part of this team, because empowering yourself is essential in order to obtain a positive treatment outcome.

In early treatment a major difference between pain clinics and addiction treatment centers involves medication and detoxification issues. Although many pain clinics will withdraw their *problem* patients from most narcotic medication, some do not. Meanwhile, most addiction treatment professionals believe that addiction is a chronic, life-threatening disease. Therefore, they conclude that the removal of all psychoactive chemicals is imperative for effective treatment. If the progression of the addictive disorder is not too advanced, an outpatient detoxification protocol could be used.

Even when there is agreement that detoxification is the starting point for recovery treatment, ways of accomplishing that task may vary. In many situations it can be dangerous to suddenly quit taking a medication without following medical precautions. Often those precautions include other medication to ensure a safe withdrawal. If you need to be medically detoxified, make sure you learn as much about the process as possible so you can give what is called informed consent. Two examples of detoxification follow.

Two Common Approaches for Detoxification

In addiction treatment centers there are basically two methods typically used for administering detoxification medication: (a) an *as-needed* (or PRN) basis and (b) a *regular interval* administration. One drawback of the PRN method is that you can still self-medicate, while a drawback of regular interval administration is that it may result in experiencing high levels of pain before each dose is due. Although a physician prescription of analgesics in sufficient doses may be preferable, a compromise solution would consist of an as-needed order with a range of doses, depending on your level of pain.

In many pain clinics the *pain cocktail* method is used for withdrawing people from the problem drug(s). This technique allows the gradual and systematic withdrawal of analgesics, narcotics, or benzodiazepines.

The process involves combining the detoxification medication into a single mix, which is given in a disguising mixture (such as cherry syrup). The mix is given only at fixed time intervals on an ongoing basis. The decrease in medication is achieved by gradually withdrawing the active ingredients, while keeping the total volume the same.

> You need to be proactive
> in your own healing process.

However, one difficulty with the pain cocktail approach is that it enables you to remain a passive participant. The APM approach encourages you to take a proactive part in your treatment, which includes being informed about the exact parameters of your detoxification protocol.

Detox for Jean and Dean

Now, we will look at the approaches used when Jean and Dean went through their detoxification.

> Dean needed inpatient detoxification.
> Jean needed a medication taper protocol.

Dean's last relapse started with abusing a nonsteroid, anti-inflammatory medication—Ultram®. This medication is contraindicated for patients with a history of opiate dependency/abuse, and in Dean's case it retriggered his addiction. In fact, it was shortly after starting the Ultram® (Tramadol) that he began to search out and use Vicodin again.

This retriggering effect for Dean resulted in visits to urgent care clinics to receive Vicodin, which he started abusing over a very short period of time and eventually buying on the street again in large quantities. He was also using a benzodiazepine (Xanax) medication for his anxiety, as well as experiencing a return to alcohol. While in treatment after this relapse episode, Dean realized and admitted for the first time that he was using his medication for emotional pain in addition to his physical pain symptoms.

Dean's early treatment plan included not only detoxification and stabilization, but also training in emotional management skills. With Dean's combination and quantity of drug use, an addiction medicine practitioner determined that inpatient treatment was the appropriate and safest protocol.

> Jean's case was different.

Jean's motivation for treatment was also an external intervention by her family, who insisted that she be in pain management treatment. Since she was not on that high a dose of medication, Jean's healthcare providers were open to a medication taper while in the residential treatment program, instead of completing a detoxification protocol first. One of her primary treatment goals was to eliminate opiate pain medication completely before leaving treatment.

This was very frightening for Jean, who did not believe she could ever function without at least periodic access to her pain medication—especially during a major pain flare-up. Since Jean's pain symptoms were amplified by a toxic and stressful abuse history, one early approach included teaching Jean how to manage her stress and contain her PTSD symptoms more effectively.

> Finding safer medication is crucial.

Ongoing use of pain medication can be a necessary treatment alternative for some patients. However, psychoactive medication such as opiates may be contraindicated for many chronic pain conditions due to the tendency for the user to develop tolerance. Earlier you learned about the importance of understanding the pharmacological implications that determine the proper medication to use for ongoing chronic pain conditions. Once again, I cannot emphasize enough that a team approach is crucial.

Finding the safest medication protocol possible cannot be overemphasized. When the narcotic medication is taken in increasingly larger doses due to tolerance, the side effects from the medication may become physically and/or psychologically damaging and, in some cases, even life threatening.

> Buprenorphine: A New Pain Management and Detoxification Treatment Alternative

There is now an effective medication for both opiate addiction treatment and/or maintenance pain management that was FDA (Food and Drug Administration) approved since the original publication of this book. The new medication is *buprenorphine*, which is an opiate agonist/antagonist and a very effective pain medication for appropriate patients. It has been used in pain management for many years—mostly in its injectable form. Buprenorphine is now available in the United States as sublingual (dissolved under the tongue) medication and is many times more potent than injected morphine. Buprenorphine is different from other opiates because the patient usually feels more "clear headed" when taking it.

Being the first oral medication that has been approved in the United States, physicians can now prescribe buprenorphine in their offices for people who are dependent or addicted to opiates, such as opiate pain medication, heroin, or methadone. Buprenorphine is an effective medication for opiate addiction that does not require daily or weekly visits to a clinic. It blocks the effects of other opiates and eliminates cravings and prevents withdrawal symptoms such as pain and nausea. Patients can be maintained on buprenorphine or go through detoxification.

Subutex and Suboxone are the brand names that buprenorphine is being marketed under for the treatment of opiate dependence. Both medications contain the active ingredient buprenorphine hydrochloride, which works to reduce the symptoms of opiate dependence. Subutex contains only buprenorphine hydrochloride, which was developed as the initial product. The second medication, Suboxone, contains an additional ingredient called Naloxone to guard against misuse or abuse. Subutex is usually given during the first few days of treatment, while Suboxone is used during the maintenance phase of treatment. Both medications come in 2 mg and 8 mg strengths as sublingual tablets.

However, medication is not the only component of detoxification and treatment. At the same time that medication management issues are being decided, other treatment protocols must be developed. One major treatment intervention concerns the importance of developing an appropriate support system.

Developing Support Systems

Building Trust and Safety

Another potential block to effective treatment for Jean was her difficulty in trusting others and her resistance to using self-help groups. Finding the correct type of support system was not easy, but she finally chose a women's church group. Once she got to know the other women in the group, she reported feeling like she finally found a family-like group she might be able to trust.

Building trust and safety is a key part of any therapeutic process, but with the APM population it is even more important. You might have learned that it was not safe to trust your healthcare providers, since many of them did not listen to your complaints or take your concerns seriously.

On the other hand, well meaning sympathetic healthcare providers can sometimes come across as patronizing to you. These types of interactions support the perception of you as being a victim of your condition. Jean was especially hypervigilant in this regard. Dean had his own issues with trust and safety, as well as isolation tendencies when his life became difficult.

Using Twelve-Step Support

While Dean was willing, and even eager, to use Twelve-Step support groups, Jean was reluctant and believed she did not fit in at *those* meetings. Instead she chose a group for recovering Christian women. At first she was unable to open up and share. Later, when she felt safe and trusted the group, she actively participated.

On the other hand, Dean attended his Twelve-Step support groups, but he also avoided them when he needed them the most. This resistance to trust was an obstacle that needed to be overcome in order for Dean and Jean to be successful with their treatment.

Dean and Jean are not unique among addicted chronic pain patients who avoid Twelve-Step support groups. Many of you reading this book may believe that you are not *real addicts* and do not belong in Twelve-Step groups. While this may be true, it could also be a type of denial or a way of fooling yourself. Also, although I firmly support the Twelve-Step concept, I realize that some people may need other self-help, social, or a religious type of support systems. The point to remember is that we all need, and deserve, to have support. You must do it yourself, but you do not have to do it alone.

Well Intentioned but Dangerous Messages

Another obstacle facing some of you who choose to attend Twelve-Step meetings, but especially for those who must remain on some type of medication, is the confusing and conflicting messages heard at AA (Alcoholics Anonymous) or NA (Narcotics Anonymous) meetings. You may hear or be told directly that to *belong,* you must stop using everything, no matter what—although this is not the official position of either program. Advice from well-meaning recovering alcoholics and addicts can sometimes sabotage a patient's recovery process with all-or-nothing messages.

Precautions When Using Twelve-Step Support

This inappropriate advice giving from self-help recovery programs can be frustrating for both patients and treatment providers and, in some cases, has led people to relapse and even die. You need to know that when you attend Twelve-Step groups, this might happen. You need to be prepared to deal with *well-meaning* people in recovery. It is helpful to read the Alcoholics Anonymous and Narcotics Anonymous conference-approved literature that clearly explains the *appropriate* use of medication.

Taking medication is a serious concern for a person in recovery, but, as I explained earlier, medication may sometimes be necessary for certain chronic pain conditions. This is where the *Medication Management Components* of APM are extremely useful.

Using Pills Anonymous and Chronic Pain Support Groups

There are other Twelve-Step programs that are often more appropriate for chronic pain patients who develop problems due to pain medication use. One program is called Pills Anonymous (PA) and the other is called Chronic Pain Anonymous (CPA).

Other communities may have other chronic pain support groups that are also beneficial for APM patients. Group therapy and peer support have proven to be effective components for successful treatment outcomes and should be sought out.

Support groups and therapy groups also provide another essential component—nonpharmacological pain management suggestions and stress reduction tools. Both Jean and Dean were finally able to join and stay connected with appropriate peer support groups.

Another useful tool for someone in recovery from pain and chemical dependency is a twelve-item protocol developed by myself and Sheila Thares, RN, MSN. This tool, which follows, was given to both Jean and Dean who eventually used it very effectively.

A Guide for Managing Chronic Pain in Recovery

By Dr. Stephen F. Grinstead, LMFT, ACRPS, and Sheila Thares, RN, MSN

1. During early recovery, postpone nonemergency dental work and elective surgical procedures that would require mind-altering medications. When you do need to be on medication, make sure that an addiction medicine practitioner/specialist is in charge of consulting about and/or prescribing that medication.
2. If you need to be on medication, have your sponsor, significant other, or an appropriate support person hold and dispense the medication. It would also be beneficial to only have a twenty-four-hour supply.
3. Consult with an addiction medicine practitioner/specialist about using nonaddictive medications such as anti-inflammatory Tylenol or other over-the-counter analgesics.
4. Be open to exploring all nonchemical pain management modalities. Some of the more common ones are acupuncture, chiropractic, physical therapy, massage therapy, and hydrotherapy. In addition, identifying and managing uncomfortable emotions may also decrease your pain significantly.
5. Be aware of your stress levels and have a stress management program in place, such as meditation, exercise, relaxation, music, etc. If you lower your stress, you will usually lower your pain as a result.
6. Take personal responsibility to augment your support group meetings in order to decrease isolation, as well as urges and cravings.
7. Inform all of your healthcare providers about being in recovery, and be aware of the importance of

consulting with an addiction medicine specialist in the event mind- altering medication is needed. There may be times you need to be on medication, but the risk of relapse can be minimized if open communication is maintained between the addiction medicine practitioner/specialist, yourself, and other healthcare providers.

8. Do not overwork, especially if you are in pain or sick. Take time off from work to heal and avoid fatigue.

9. Be open and aware of the cross-addiction concept. Any psychoactive chemical could trigger a relapse of your addiction.

10. As depression is common for people with chronic pain, be open to the possibility of taking appropriate antidepressants if needed.

11. Be aware of the importance of proper nutrition and exercise as an important part of chronic pain recovery. Stretch slowly at first, then structure progressive walking at least twice a day, increasing the distance as you are able. Add strengthening exercises if cleared by your healthcare provider. Remember, protein assists repair of injuries. It is, therefore, important to create a nutrition plan for tissue repair.

12. Explore your past beliefs and role models from childhood regarding pain and pain management. Look for healthy role models for pain management in recovery.

Getting Started: Transition and Stabilization Tasks

Once you are in treatment and have gone through detoxification, or are being withdrawn from the problem medication, you are in what the CENAPS® Developmental Model of Recovery refers to as the Transition and Stabilization Stages of Recovery that were mentioned earlier.

According to the CENAPS® Model there are five key tasks you need to accomplish during these stages:
1. Recover physically from the withdrawal effects of chemicals.
2. Work through resistance and denial.
3. Discontinue preoccupation with chemicals.
4. Learn to solve problems without using chemicals.
5. Develop hope and motivation for recovery.

Furthermore, to give yourself the best chance of accomplishing these transitional tasks, you need to quickly integrate into a recovery milieu. This is another point where identifying and managing your denial is important.

> Trust and safety are crucial.

As I discussed earlier, building trust and safety will help you fit in and bond. Many of you have learned to distrust others as a result of your interactions with healthcare providers. Some distrust may stem from dysfunctional family systems or other life-altering events. You may have become very isolated by the time you are ready to enter treatment. Some of you may even exhibit paranoid and/or agoraphobic (fear of going out) symptoms.

Letting go of your denial and other defenses through education and information, while at the same time learning to trust others, enables you to become capable of admitting and accepting your substance abuse or dependency. You can then identify with others in the treatment program or support groups, which will help you transition smoothly into recovery.

For some of you this process can be accomplished using group therapy followed by individual sessions on an as-needed basis. There is help available and a treatment process that can lead you out of the problem and into the solution. This solution is described in the following chapters, showing you how the APM process works.

At this point it would be helpful for you to obtain and start working in the *APM Workbook* as you go through the remainder of the *Recovery Guide*. What follows is an overview of the APM treatment process and how to get the most out of the workbook.

Now that you have an extensive overview of addiction, the Addiction Pain Syndrome®, and a better understanding of pain, please go on to the next chapter to begin the APM process.

- **Call to Action for the Fourth Chapter**

It is time to summarize what you have learned so far now that you have come to the end of the fourth chapter. Please answer the questions below.

1. What is the most important thing you have learned about yourself and your ability to help yourself as a result of completing Chapter Four?

2. What are you willing to commit to do differently as a result of what you have learned by completing this chapter?

3. What obstacles might get in the way of making these changes and what can you do to overcome these roadblocks?

Take time to pause and reflect, then
go to the next page to review Chapter Five.

Chapter Five
Beginning the APM® Treatment Process

APM Core Clinical Exercise One: Understanding Your Pain

When living with a pain disorder, you need to understand the difference between acute pain and chronic pain, especially when the pain may be managed with potentially addictive medication. It is also essential for you and your treatment professional to understand the biopsychosocial impact that a chronic pain condition can have on you.

In this section you will review the four parts of *Exercise One* in the *APM Workbook,* which will assist you in gathering this information.

Exercise One, Part 1: Acute Pain versus Chronic Pain

This first exercise explains the difference between acute pain and chronic pain as well as describing the biopsychosocial effects of pain. The goal of this exercise is to increase your knowledge and understanding of pain and its effects in order to help you shift from the perception of yourself as a victim of pain, to one of being empowered to successfully manage your health.

As noted earlier, pain can be classified as either acute or chronic. Because the conditions are dissimilar, the treatment for acute pain is very different than the treatment for chronic pain. Learn how to distinguish between the two and understand the difference.

Acute Pain

Acute pain tells your body that something has gone wrong or that damage to the system has occurred. The source of acute pain can usually be easily identified and typically does not last very long. Acute pain is a symptom of an immediate underlying problem.

An example of acute pain is when you touch a hot burner on the stove. Your first reaction is to pull your hand away. Contact with the heat will leave you with symptoms from minor redness to serious tissue damage, but in each case there is a predictable period of time for the burn to heal. There are also effective medical treatments that promote quick healing. Some other causes of acute pain include cuts and broken bones.

No matter what the source of acute pain, the result is to drive you to search for relief. Once the problem is identified, it is standard and usually safe to use analgesic and/or opiate medication for acute pain relief, unless you have a history of substance abuse or dependency. If you are in recovery for chemical dependency, an addiction medicine practitioner/specialist should be consulted before any opiate or other psychoactive medications are taken.

Acute Pain
- Gives an immediate signal to the brain
- Signals damage/dysfunction
- Is readily treatable
- Is of limited duration

Another example of an acute pain episode is when your pain worsens (also known as a pain flare-up). These flare-ups require different treatment than your typical day-to-day pain management plan. An upcoming section explains how to develop an effective pain flare-up plan.

Chronic Pain

Chronic pain, on the other hand, is a condition that frequently fails to respond to standard medical interventions. In some cases there is no easily recognizable reason for the pain, or the original acute condition seems to be resolved—but the pain signals keep firing. In addition, the pain has a duration of three to six months. The DSM-IV-TR criterion for a chronic condition is at least a six-month duration. In many cases chronic pain no longer serves a useful purpose; the pain system gets turned on and stays on well after the initial cause—or pain trigger—is resolved.

Dean and Jean present fairly typical examples of chronic pain conditions. Dean suffers from chronic knee pain. Although surgery and physical therapy have effectively treated the original injury, Dean's pain symptoms continued for years after his accident and long after his surgery. Like many chronic pain patients, Dean was often told that the pain was just in his head. But to him the pain was very real and he wanted relief.

> **Chronic Pain**
> - Fails to respond to typical treatments
> - Sometimes has no recognized source
> - Lasts at least three to six months
> - May no longer serve a useful purpose

Some other common chronic pain conditions include phantom limb pain, headaches, peripheral neuropathy, neck pain, and fibromyalgia. Chapter Two presented a more in-depth explanation of pain that was designed to help you more effectively complete the following exercises of the APM treatment process.

Biopsychosocial Effects of Chronic Pain

You can generally receive effective medical care for acute pain; however, treatment for chronic pain can be a confusing process of misunderstanding as well as incorrect diagnoses and inadequate treatment plans.

> What can you do when you are told that the pain is all in your head?

When you experience chronic pain and doctors are at a loss to define the exact nature of the problem, you might start to believe you are going crazy. Often treatment professionals will support that mistaken belief, because they find no observable or measurable reason for the symptoms. Nevertheless, chronic pain is real and often occurs for reasons that may not be identified easily. As explained earlier, chronic pain affects you physically, psychologically, socially, and spiritually—body, mind, and spirit.

- Physically, chronic pain raises stress and drains physical energy.
- Psychologically, chronic pain affects your ability to think clearly, logically, and rationally, and to manage feelings and emotions effectively.

- Socially, chronic pain affects your ability to use consistently responsible behaviors, thus affecting others.
- Spiritually, chronic pain can keep you separate from your inner self and/or Higher Power.

Chronic Pain Affects a Person's	
• Body	• Thoughts
• Emotions	• Behaviors
• Relationships	• Pain Management

In addition, the way you sense or experience pain—its intensity and duration—will affect how well you are able to manage it. This goes back to my original discussion on pain versus suffering. Pain is an unpleasant signal telling you something is wrong with your body. Suffering results from the meaning or interpretation you assign to the pain. Learning more positive ways of thinking about your pain will lead to more effective pain management.

When you experience chronic pain, it is usually accepted that something is physically wrong with your body. The symptoms of pain can range from mildly irritating, to somewhat annoying or uncomfortable, to moderately distressing, to severely horrible, to the worst possible excruciating suffering ever!

While you are affected biologically, other areas are also impacted. Your thought processes are impacted in several different ways. You might have difficulty thinking clearly or concentrating, which leads to being unable to solve problems that are normally easy for you. At times you may be unable to function very well in practically all areas of your life. Instead of thinking positively you may repress certain thoughts and blank out, or indulge in self-defeating, negative, or depressive thinking.

Chronic pain can also lead to difficulty in managing emotions. You may be cut off from your emotions, feel numb, or not know what you are feeling. At other times you may overreact to your emotions. The intensity of your feelings does not match the trigger situation. A third type of emotional dysfunction is when you experience *artifact emotions*—feelings that do not seem to have a clear cause or trigger (e.g., you cry, laugh, or even rage for no apparent reason).

> Chronic pain often leads to depression.

As you saw earlier, many people with chronic pain frequently become depressed. When your thinking is irrational or dysfunctional and you are mismanaging your feelings, you may have urges to indulge in self-defeating, impulsive, or compulsive behaviors to help cope with your distress. This, in turn, affects your relationships with others. You may become isolated and believe you can handle life without any help, or you may become overly dependent upon others to take care of you. This dysfunctional caretaking by others often enables you to continue ineffective behaviors that prolong a victim role.

The Biopsychosocial Sensation of Chronic Pain

Most people living with chronic pain do not have the words they need to describe their pain. The first step in accurately communicating with your caregivers is to develop a vocabulary that will help you describe the type and level of pain that you are experiencing. Remember that pain is a biopsychosocial experience. As a result, you need to learn to make a distinction between the physical sensation of pain, your psychological interpretation of the pain, and how you use your pain in relationships with other people.

Exercise One, Part 2-A: Identifying and Rating the Severity of Your Pain Symptoms

This exercise has significantly evolved since the *APM Recovery Guide* was first published in 2001. The original exercise was developed after reviewing several different pain assessment instruments (such as the McGuill Pain Assessment Questionnaire) that I have used with patients over the years. Through an active listening process I revised the original sixty-word list, which most patients found useful in describing pain, to the current list that uses fifty-four words. I call these words the *pain vocabulary.* This vocabulary has been revised and resequenced since the original work was published.

In order to help you quickly find the words to describe your pain, the list is now organized into eighteen categories with three words in each category that progress from less severe to more severe pain and/or distress. This new list has an equal blend of physiological and psychological/emotional symptoms.

When someone has chronic pain, their sensation of pain and its effects vary. *Exercise One, Part 2-A: Identifying and Rating the Severity of Your Pain Symptoms* in the *Addiction-Free Pain Management® Workbook* offers an assessment tool to determine the level and intensity of both psychological and physiological symptoms.

> **Goals for Exercise One, Part 2-A**
> - Building a pain vocabulary
> - Rating the severity of pain

The purpose of this exercise is twofold: to help you build a vocabulary for talking about your pain and to rate the severity of your pain. You need to explore your reactions to your pain in order to determine whether your condition is more physiological or psychological—pain versus suffering.

Look at the following table describing the types of pain many people experience. As you read through each set of descriptions, you are asked to circle the word (or words) in each set that describes your sensations. Write in the appropriate number (on a scale of 1 to 10, with 1 meaning *low pain* to 10 meaning *the worst pain ever*) that best describes the intensity level of your pain on a bad pain day.

The following exercise will provide you with increased vocabulary and insight to help you communicate more accurately about your symptoms. This exercise also gives you and your healthcare provides a deeper awareness of the issues that could influence successful treatment, as well as providing additional assessment information. You can see the directions listed in the table.

Instructions: When you have chronic pain, you are the only one that knows how it feels. Below are words (symptoms) that people with chronic pain can use to describe their pain. Not all will apply to you, but many of them will. The purpose of this worksheet is twofold: (1) to help you build a vocabulary for talking about your pain and (2) to rate the intensity or level of your pain. As you read through each three-word set, circle the **word(s)** and write in the **number** that best describes your pain level on a **bad pain day.**

The Pain Vocabulary
Symptoms (Sensations of Chronic Pain)   **Level**

1. aching — throbbing — pulsing
2. irritating — nagging — disturbing
3. splitting — piercing — pounding
4. dreadful — severe — awful
5. irritated — sore — sensitive
6. uncomfortable — troublesome — problematic
7. burning — stinging — lacerating
8. distressing — excruciating — agonizing
9. tender — painful — hurtful
10. worrisome — saddening — depressing
11. inflamed — sharp — swollen
12. torturing — grueling — punishing
13. hot — radiating — spreading
14. annoying — upsetting — aggravating
15. tearing — wrenching — slashing
16. frightening — terrifying — dreadful
17. numbing — tingling — shooting
18. exhausting — fatiguing — debilitating
19. Is your pain more (a) permanent, constant, ceaseless; (b) fleeting, brief, momentary; or (c) combination of both?
20. Why did you rate #19 that way?

When I talk with people, after they finish this exercise, I ask if there are any other words they might use to describe their pain. For example, Jean said *crushing* was a word she often used to describe her headaches, while Dean said the pain in his leg often felt like *squeezing* to him. As you look through the list of words, be thinking if there are any additional words you would use to describe your specific pain.

> *Please take a few minutes to complete this exercise in your* APM Workbook.

Exercise One, Part 2-B: Exploring Biological versus Psychological Pain Symptoms

Ascending and Descending Pain Signals

Once you have completed *Exercise One, Part 2-A,* go immediately to *Exercise One, Part 2-B,* to learn about the physiological versus psychological/emotional components of your pain. The physiological symptoms are the odd numbers, while the psychological/emotional symptoms are the even-numbered groups. The following table lists the directions for completing this exercise and is followed by the *Part 2-B* exercise.

Ascending pain signals, coming from the point of injury to the brain, and *descending* nerve pathways, signals from the brain to the point of injury, will influence or modify the effects of pain on your body.

Some of these ascending signals simply report the presence of pain (I hurt or I don't hurt). Other signals report the intensity of the pain (It hurts a little or it hurts a lot). Still other pain signals report the location of the pain (My stomach hurts) or whether the pain is associated with an internal or external injury (My stomach hurts deep in my gut, or the skin on my stomach hurts). Other pain signals report the type of pain (It burns or it throbs).

All of these different pain signals are transmitted into the spinal cord through nerve pathways to the hypothalamus section of the brain. There the brain transmits the pain signal information to other specialized pain neurons, which in turn send the information (descending signals) to different areas in the brain. One area that gets the message is your limbic system—this is the emotional center of the brain. It leads to a feeling or emotional response. Another signal goes to your frontal lobes—these are the cognition/thinking center of the brain. They lead to thoughts or judgments about your pain, including *anticipatory pain.*

Once the physical pain system is activated, the anticipatory pain reaction can actually make pain symptoms worse. Whenever you feel the pain, you *interpret it* in a way that makes it worse. You *start thinking* about the pain in a way that makes it worse. You *tell yourself* that the pain is "awful and terrible," and think, "I can't handle the pain." You *convince yourself*, "It's hopeless, I'll always hurt, and there's nothing that I can do about it."

Below are the same pain symptoms you identified and rated earlier in the previous exercise—*Identifying and Rating the Severity of Your Pain Symptoms*—but in a slightly different format. You will notice that the *odd-numbered* items from the worksheet are now in the left-hand (ascending) column, while the *even-numbered* items are in the right-hand (descending) column. This is where anticipatory pain is created.

Next you will have an opportunity to identify your ascending and descending pain signals. Take a few minutes to transpose the circled symptoms and numeric ratings from the previous exercise to the exercise on the next page. Then add up the total of the numbered ratings for each column. Remember that it really doesn't matter how you score as long as you are willing to use this as a self-monitoring system to help you better manage your pain.

Now let's look at the results of Jean and Dean's exercise results to see what can be learned.

Ascending/Biological Pain Signals	Descending/Psychological Pain Signals
1. aching, throbbing, pulsing Rating =	2. irritating, nagging, disturbing Rating =
3. splitting, piercing, pounding Rating =	4. dreadful, severe, awful Rating =
5. irritated, sore, sensitive Rating =	6. uncomfortable, troublesome, problematic Rating =
7. burning, stinging, lacerating Rating =	8. distressing, excruciating, agonizing Rating =
9. tender, painful, hurtful Rating =	10. worrisome, saddening, depressing Rating =
11. inflamed, sharp, swollen Rating =	12. torturing, grueling, punishing Rating =
13. hot, radiating, spreading Rating =	14. annoying, upsetting, aggravating Rating =
15. tearing, wrenching, slashing Rating =	16. frightening, terrifying, dreadful Rating =
17. numbing, tingling, shooting Rating =	18. exhausting, fatiguing, debilitating Rating =
Total Ascending = _____	**Total Descending** = _____

Let's start with how Dean and Jean completed *Exercise One, Part 2-A: Identifying and Rating the Severity of Your Pain Symptoms* and how they transposed their symptoms onto the worksheet below. The symptoms they circled are shown in the following table as **bold/underlined** and the level (or rating) is at the end of each row.

Dean's Pain Symptoms on a Bad Pain Day			
Ascending Symptoms	Rating	Descending Symptoms	Rating
1. **aching**, throbbing, pulsing	7	2. irritating, **nagging**, **disturbing**	8
3. splitting, **piercing**, pounding	6	4. dreadful, **severe**, **awful**	10
5. **irritated**, sore, sensitive	7	6. **uncomfortable**, **troublesome**, problematic	9
7. **burning**, stinging, **lacerating**	6	8. **distressing**, excruciating, **agonizing**	9
9. **tender**, **painful**, hurtful	7	10. **worrisome**, **saddening**, **depressing**	10
11. **inflamed**, **sharp**, swollen	7	12. torturing, grueling, **punishing**	10
13. **hot**, radiating, **spreading**	6	14. **annoying**, upsetting, **aggravating**	10
15. tearing, wrenching, **slashing**	7	16. **frightening**, terrifying, **dreadful**	10
17. numbing, tingling, **shooting**	7	18. **exhausting**, **fatiguing**, debilitating	10
Total Ascending = __60__		**Total Descending** = __86__	

Jean's Pain Symptoms on a Bad Pain Day			
Ascending Symptoms	Rating	Descending Symptoms	Rating
1. aching, **throbbing**, pulsing	10	2. **irritating**, nagging, **disturbing**	10
3. splitting, **piercing**, pounding	10	4. **dreadful, severe, awful**	10
5. irritated, **sore, sensitive**	8	6. uncomfortable, **troublesome, problematic**	10
7. **burning, stinging**, lacerating	6	8. **distressing, excruciating, agonizing**	10
9. tender, **painful, hurtful**	8	10. **worrisome, saddening, depressing**	10
11. **inflamed**, sharp, **swollen**	6	12. **torturing**, grueling, **punishing**	10
13. **hot**, radiating, spreading	6	14. annoying, **upsetting, aggravating**	10
15. tearing, wrenching, **slashing**	7	16. **frightening, terrifying, dreadful**	10
17. **numbing, tingling**, shooting	7	18. **exhausting**, fatiguing, **debilitating**	10
Total Ascending = 68		Total Descending = 90	

Please take a few minutes to complete this exercise in your APM Workbook.

Scoring the Ascending and Descending Pain Signals Exercise

After you are finished transposing the numbers from the first instrument (on page 117) to the one on page 119, you will have an opportunity to learn more about what your answers mean. Remember, it is normal to experience both physiological as well as psychological/emotional symptoms. Please see the remainder of the *Ascending/ Descending* exercise reproduced in the following table to learn more about what your answers mean.

You will get a chance to look at this exercise further on the following pages, especially when developing your *Pain Flare-Up Plan*. It is very important to remember that when you have pain, there are three components to that pain: (1) biological; (2) psychological/emotional; and (3) social/cultural. All three components need to be treated, but the treatment plan for each differs. An effective medication management plan coupled with nonpharmacological interventions is the best approach for the biological pain symptoms.

However, using medication for the psychological/emotional symptoms is like having an infected cut on your hand and the only thing you do for it is to find a color-coordinated bandage and slap it on. Using medication for the psychological/emotional symptoms puts you at risk for experiencing negative side effects from your medication, including potential addiction problems. The good news is there are ways you can learn to identify and cope with your psychological/emotional symptoms. It is also important to identify any social and/or cultural beliefs/biases that could potentially sabotage an effective pain management plan. Are you willing to make a commitment to learn more effective pain management tools?

❐ Yes ❐ No ❐ Unsure
Please explain:

What Do Dean and Jean's Answers Mean?

Several points stand out when reviewing Dean's completed exercise. Dean scored significantly higher in the *descending* area, which is not uncommon for someone living with chronic pain and a coexisting addictive disorder. Dean's first reaction was that he was being manipulated and tricked. This also is a common reaction, especially for patients who have trust issues. Dean eventually learned to use the ascending/descending process as a part of his daily pain journal work.

> Psychological/emotional pain is real!
> It needs appropriate interventions.

At this point in the *APM Workbook* process I want to mention again that everyone will have both *ascending* and *descending* pain symptoms. No matter which is more predominant—pain is pain and it needs appropriate intervention. Dean was very excited to hear that he could learn simple-to-implement nonmedication ways to help him cope with his *descending* pain symptoms. His interest increased as I told him he would be developing a nonpharmacological pain flare-up plan in a following exercise.

Now let's review Jean's answers for the same exercise. As with Dean, several points stand out when looking through Jean's completed exercise, including the fact that she scored higher in the *descending* area. The first important observation about Jean's *descending* symptoms is that she scored them **all** at a level 10. There are several reasons this happens for people; the most important is that they have not yet been taught how to understand and complete a pain-rating scale. Like Jean you will get a chance to learn more about how to accurately use both stress and pain scales in *Exercise One, Part 4: Stress and Chronic Pain.*

Another reason why many people, including Jean, score the descending symptoms so high is that they think no one will help them if they don't make their problem seem serious enough. In fact, that has proved to be true in research studies on pain behaviors impacting pain interventions by healthcare providers. Later in treatment, Jean also disclosed that rating her pain levels high was her justification for getting more, and taking more, pain medication. Once she convinced *herself* of this *need,* it was much easier to convince her doctor. When Jean completed this exercise and saw her scores and what they meant, she was shocked. After processing this exercise she became much more hopeful and eager to continue the APM process, especially when, like Dean, she looked ahead to the pain flare-up plan exercise.

The next stage of the work was to help Jean and Dean begin to notice how their thinking, emotions, and behaviors changed when they were experiencing a bad pain day. The following exercise is primarily focused on the problem; in *Exercise Seven* you will see how Dean and Jean learned to manage similar problematic thoughts, emotions, and behaviors that moved them into the solution.

Exercise One, Part 3: Exploring Your TFUARs on a Bad Pain Day

> The primary goal of *Exploring Your TFUARs* is to see how irrational thinking leads to emotional and social distress.

The acronym TFUAR means:

**T = Thoughts, F = Feelings, U = Urges,
A = Actions, R = Reactions**

This exercise is designed to explore addictive or irrational thinking (thinking errors) that occurs as a result of a chronic pain condition. This type of thinking often leads to uncomfortable emotions that trigger self-defeating urges, usually followed by self-destructive behaviors. The following table lists the questions asked in this *APM Workbook* exercise. Some of you may need coaching support in order to come up with answers in all the TFUAR categories. Sometimes it is helpful to do imagery exercises and try to reexperience a bad pain day and tell it like a story. This technique is explained in-depth in the *High-Risk Situation Mapping Exercise* later in the book.

Exploring Your TFUARs Exercise
When you experience a bad pain day, your TFUARs (thoughts, feelings, urges, actions, and reactions of others) often change. The purpose of this exercise is to explore your personal accounts in each of the above TFUAR areas when you experience pain on a bad pain day. You will do more with this TFUAR process later in the book.
Thoughts: Prolonged exposure to chronic pain leads to irrational thinking (thinking errors) and self-defeating decision making. List below three thinking problems that you've experienced as a result of your pain.
Feelings: Use the Feelings Chart below to describe how you feel when you're experiencing chronic pain at its worst, and how intense each feeling is on a scale of

			0 (lowest intensity) to 10 (highest intensity). Circle the appropriate feeling on each line.
		The Feelings Checklist Chart	
Strong	or	Weak	How strong is the feeling? (0–10) _____
Safe	or	Threatened	How strong is the feeling? (0–10) _____
Caring	or	Angry	How strong is the feeling? (0–10) _____
Fulfilled	or	Frustrated	How strong is the feeling? (0–10) _____
Happy	or	Sad	How strong is the feeling? (0–10) _____
Connected	or	Lonely	How strong is the feeling? (0–10) _____
Proud	or	Ashamed/Guilty	How strong is the feeling? (0–10) _____
Peaceful	or	Agitated	How strong is the feeling? (0–10) _____
Urges:			What do you have an urge (or impulse) to do when you're experiencing chronic pain at its worst?
Actions:			What do you usually do when you're experiencing chronic pain at its worst?
Reactions:			When you are experiencing chronic pain at its worst, how do other people usually react?
How do those reactions by other people affect your stress and/or pain levels?			

The purpose of this exercise is twofold. First, it gives you insight into your psychological (thoughts and feelings), behavioral, and social patterns. Second, it gives you a new way of looking at how your pain experiences often have a number of undesirable biopsychosocial consequences.

For example, Dean identified his three irrational thinking patterns: (1) I don't deserve this; (2) I have to do whatever it takes to stop this; and (3) I won't use meds next time, but this time I really need help. Dean tends to react in a *top-dog* (power) fashion. Jean, on the other hand, came up with three *under-dog* (victim) statements: (1) I'm such a bad mother; (2) Why won't they let me get relief?; and (3) This is too much to deal with.

Both Jean and Dean identified similar feelings: *weak, angry, sad, lonely, threatened,* and *frustrated.* Jean rated *weak* at level 10, while Dean rated it level 5. Jean rated *sad* at a level 8 and Dean rated it 4. Both rated *angry* and *frustrated* at a level 10, and Jean rated *ashamed* at level 10. While Dean did not rate either *proud* or *ashamed,* he later admitted he was in denial about his *shame*. Both rated *agitated* at a level 10.

Both Jean and Dean had urges to use inappropriate pain medication. Dean often over-used his pain medication on a bad pain day, and if there was not enough available, he would find other ways to distract himself. Recently he started having urges to drink again. Jean tended to cry or try to go to sleep to escape if she did not have enough pain medication.

Both Jean and Dean tended to isolate. Dean hid his pain with a *tough-guy* facade, and Jean reported that she was feeling too much shame and guilt to reach out. The result was that they closed themselves off from any support networks. Isolation is a common tendency for a chronic pain patient; this problem becomes much worse if they also have a coexisting addictive disorder.

> *Please take a few minutes to complete this exercise in your* APM Workbook.

Exercise One, Part 4: Stress and Chronic Pain

If you are asked to give up your problematic pain medication, an early treatment strategy is to learn alternative methods to manage your pain. As I mentioned earlier, you need to learn about the connection between stress levels and pain symptoms, and understand that stress management can also decrease your suffering. Learn simple stress reduction techniques and practice them during your early recovery period.

Learning to Identify Stress Levels

For Jean, this exercise gave her hope that freedom from her problematic medication was possible, but it would be a difficult journey. Stress identification and reduction is an important tool for anyone recovering from addiction and chronic pain.

When you are aware of your stress levels, you can then take action to reduce your stress, which, in turn, leads to a decrease in your pain symptoms.

In the *APM Workbook*, on page 17, the *TFUAR* exercise is followed by the *Stress and Chronic Pain* scales exercise.

Stress and Chronic Pain

It is important to know about the connection between stress levels and your pain symptoms, as well as understanding that stress management can also decrease your suffering. Physically, chronic pain raises your stress levels and drains physical energy, while psychologically, it affects your ability to think clearly, logically, and rationally, as well as to effectively manage your feelings or emotions. Remember, in most cases if you can learn to lower your stress levels, you will also experience a decrease in your perception of pain.

When you are more aware of your stress levels, you can take action to reduce your stress, which in turn leads to a decrease in your pain symptoms. One effective stress management strategy is exercise. In addition to lowering your stress levels, regular exercise can also be an important part of your pain management program. It is also important to reduce—or even eliminate—nicotine, caffeine, and sugar and implement a healthy eating plan. Other stress management tools could include focused breathing and relaxation exercises, meditation, Yoga, Tai Chi, soothing music, being in nature, soaking in a hot bath (or Jacuzzi), etc.

    Of course, before you learn to manage your stress, you need to be familiar with ways to assess your level of stress. It is important to learn how to accurately self-assess your levels of stress and then learn how to develop some simple but effective stress management tools. I like to use the Gorski-CENAPS® *Stress Thermometer* concept for stress identification. This concept proposes there are ten levels of stress. When you get to the upper moderate-to-severe levels of stress (6–10 range), your thinking, emotions, and behavior are impacted. Below are examples of stress scales and the stress thermometer for you to review.

General Stress Levels and the Stress Thermometer

General Stress Levels

Low Stress Level (stress score: 1–3)
    1 Very relaxed; vacation mode
    2 Stress is managed well; no discomfort
    3 No notable distress or dysfunction

Moderate Stress Levels (stress score: 4–6)
    4 Higher stress levels: normal operating level, no distress
    5 Stress managed poorly at times; some discomfort but no distress
    6 Some notable distress but minimal dysfunction

Severe Stress Levels (stress score: 7–10)
    7 Very high stress levels
    8 Stress is usually managed poorly
    9 Stress causes notable distress and dysfunction

        Score 7   =   I space out.
        Score 8   =   I get defensive.
        Score 9   =   I overreact.
        Score 10 =   I can't function (or I run away).

The Stress Thermometer

Trauma Reaction	10	**Loss of Control**
	9	**Overreact**
Stress Reaction	8	**Get Driven/Defensive**
	7	**Space Out**
	6	**Free Flow with Effort**
Functional Stress	5	**Free Flow with No Effort**
	4	**Focused and Active**
	3	**Relaxed—Focused**
Relaxation	2	**Relaxed—Not Focused**
	1	**Relaxed—Nearly Asleep**

Learning to Measure Pain Levels

Often with chronic pain, as your stress levels go up, so does the level of your pain. Think of a time when you were experiencing very low levels of pain and, for some reason, your stress levels went up. What happened to your level of pain? Most likely it also increased.

Periodically throughout this book, monitor both your level of stress and your level of pain. When asked to describe your pain or stress levels, use the stress scale above and the pain scale that follows, using the 10-point rating system. You will also want to be aware of whether your pain is more physiological (biological) or psychological/emotional. Please write down a personalized short descriptor for each of the ten levels of pain to individualize the pain scale that follows for you. For example, what words would describe your level-7 pain?

Looking at Two Pain Scales

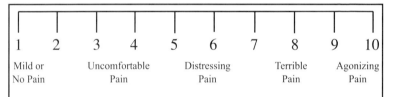

The second way to look at describing your pain level is by using a brief ten-point scale with short descriptors like the following one. As you review this ten-point scale, think how you would describe each of the ten levels in your own words. The important thing is for you to learn how to communicate your levels of pain accurately to your healthcare provider.

Level 1 = My pain is barely noticeable.

Level 2 = My pain is noticeable with no distress.

Level 3 = My pain is becoming disturbing but I have no distress.

Level 4 = My pain is causing me some distress but I have no coping problems.

Level 5 = My pain is causing me distress and I have some coping problems.

Level 6 = My pain is causing me distress and I have significant coping problems.

Level 7 = My pain is starting to interfere with my ability to function.

> Level 8 = My pain is causing moderate interference with my ability to function.
> Level 9 = My pain is causing severe interference with my ability to function.
> Level 10 = I'm unable to function at all because of my pain.
>
> Using the above scales, answer the following:
> 1. On my best days I would rate my pain at level ____ and my stress would be at level ____.
> 2. On an average day I would rate my pain at level ____ and my stress would be at level ____.
> 3. On my worst days I would rate my pain at level ____ and my stress would be at level ____.
>
> Many people find there is a definite correlation between their stress and their level of pain. That is why a good stress management plan is crucial for someone living with chronic pain. It is even more important if you are also in recovery from an addictive disorder, because stress turns on or exacerbates something called *Protracted* or *Post Acute Withdrawal*.
>
> As you are looking at the exercise—*Looking at Two Pain Scales*—think back to how you completed your *Identifying and Rating the Severity of Your Pain Symptoms* exercise. After looking at this pain level information, would you rate your symptoms the same way? Many people find they overrated the levels of their pain. However, some people find they actually underrated their symptoms the first time.

You are asked to use these charts to rate your pain and stress on your best days, on an average day, and on your worst pain day. The goal of this exercise is to help you see that pain and stress are connected, and good stress management can often reduce the intensity of your pain.

> *Please take a few minutes to complete this exercise in your* APM Workbook.

> Primary Goal:
> To show you the connection
> between stress and pain

Some of you may have difficulty accurately rating and communicating the type and levels of your pain. Some of you will benefit from using the pain scale in the exercise above, but others may need more help. One way is to develop a verbal description of each of the 1–10 levels of pain starting at level 1. Jean was able to do this quite easily, but Dean needed more help so he was given the *APM Expanded Pain Scale* shown in the following table.

The APM® Expanded Pain Scale

0	=	The absence of any pain signals
1–3	=	When I have pain at this level, my pain is a nuisance but I can almost always function normally without any extra effort. At these levels I might describe my pain as mildly troubling but no big deal. Most of the time I might not even notice that I'm in pain.
4–6	=	When I experience this level of pain, at times I can function normally with extra effort and at other times I struggle. At this level I might describe my pain as frustrating or even aggravating. When my pain gets to level six, it starts to feel like a very big deal, and I'm always conscious of being in pain.
7–10	=	When I reach this level of pain, most of the time I can't function normally even with medication and extra effort. At this level I'm truly "suffering" and might describe my pain as awful, horrible, or unbearable. When my pain gets to the 9–10 levels, I sometimes panic and mistakenly believe that it will never get better.

Both Jean and Dean were able to quickly see the connection between their stress and pain levels, and they used these scales throughout the remainder of their treatment. In many instances they both were able to report using stress identification and management to reduce their pain symptoms.

Once you are able to describe your pain symptoms and understand the biopsychosocial effects, the next task is to explore your use of pain medication. Prescription medication and other drugs (including alcohol) change how your brain and nervous system work. They either slow down, speed up, block out, change, or "blow up" (amplify) the messages and feelings sent out by your brain. These drug effects make you feel different for a little while, but they don't actually change anything in the real world. They usually mask the chronic pain and change how you think, feel, and act. But they don't make your life any better—often they make life worse.

In the next chapter you will see how Jean and Dean completed *Exercise Two* from the *APM Workbook*. It describes the biopsychosocial effects of medication and how the APM approach teaches you to make appropriate decisions regarding the use of medication.

- **Call to Action for the Fifth Chapter**

It is time to summarize what you have learned so far now that you have come to the end of the fifth chapter. Please answer the questions below.

1. What is the most important thing you have learned about yourself and your ability to help yourself as a result of completing Chapter Five?

2. What are you willing to commit to do differently as a result of what you have learned by completing this chapter?

3. What obstacles might get in the way of making these changes and what can you do to overcome these roadblocks?

Take time to pause and reflect, then
go to the next page to review Chapter Six.

Chapter Six
Effects of Prescription and/or Other Drugs

Pain Relief versus Euphoria

Some people with chronic pain who use addictive medication for pain management never experience negative consequences. So why do other people develop an addictive disorder? The answer to this question often depends upon various factors, such as genetics, coexisting disorders, and environmental dynamics. Educate yourself and expand your understanding of addiction. In Chapter Two you learned about the addictive disorder process that occurs and were introduced to the following table.

1.	Euphoria	6.	Inability to Abstain
2.	Craving	7.	Addiction-Centered Lifestyle
3.	Tolerance	8.	Addictive Lifestyle Losses
4.	Loss of Control	9.	Continued Use Despite Problems
5.	Withdrawal	10.	Substance-Induced Organic Mental Disorders

As you saw earlier, Dean was finally able to break through his denial and admit he often used his pain medication for its *euphoric effects* as well as for escape and emotional relief. This using for effect is a common realization for many chronic pain patients. I believe it is important to explore this further; I will be referring to information from the *Biopsychosocial Model of Alcoholism and Drug Addiction* (Gorski, 1999) to help make this concept more understandable.

Understanding Euphoria

So why do some people make a transition when they go from using their pain medication for pain relief to using it either for emotional coping or perhaps for its euphoric effects? This question can be answered, in part, by understanding the relationship of brain reward mechanisms and the behavior of using psychoactive medication, or alcohol and other drugs.

The brain reward mechanism demonstrates that the tendency toward *drug seeking behavior* is strongly linked to progressive alterations in the function of the brain and, in late stages, to the development of structural damage to the brain and other organ systems.

NIAAA (National Institute on Alcohol Abuse and Alcoholism) research clearly shows there are biomedical processes that occur within the brain that reinforce the regular and heavy use of psychoactive chemicals.

These *biomedical brain reinforcement processes* are different from the classic withdrawal syndrome. The following table shows a summary of this research first reported in the *Alcohol Alert* from NIAAA for July of 1996. It continues to be relevant today.

The Biomedical Brain Reinforcement Process

- People will tend to repeat an action that brings pleasure or reward. The pleasure or reward provided by that action is called *positive reinforcement* or *euphoria*.
- Certain behaviors, especially those associated with survival needs, are linked to biochemical processes within the brain that cause powerful *biological reinforcement* for these behaviors.
- This biological reinforcement is related to the release of specific brain chemicals when the behavior is performed. These brain chemicals produce a sense of pleasure or reward.
- Alcohol and other drugs of abuse (AODs), including pain medication, produce chemicals that are surrogates of the naturally occurring brain chemicals that produce biological reinforcement.
- As a result, the use of psychoactive chemicals causes a rewarding mental state (defined as euphoria) that positively reinforces the initial use of the drugs. (Euphoria is a state that is separate and distinct from the symptoms of intoxication.)
- As a result, individuals who receive positive reinforcement from drug use, because of the production of these brain chemicals, are more likely to engage in drug-seeking behavior and to use drugs regularly and heavily.
- The biochemical reinforcement that results from alcohol and other drug use is more powerful and persistently reinforcing than the biomedical reinforcement provided by other survival-related actions.
- As a result, people who experience this are more likely to feel that the use of alcohol and other drugs is more important than engaging

in other vital survival linked behaviors. They will tend to use drugs instead of actively meeting other vital needs.
- This perception that alcohol and other drug use is more important than meeting other survival needs results in *drug-seeking behavior*.
- After *drug seeking behavior* has been established, the brain undergoes certain *adaptive changes* to continue functioning despite the presence of the chemicals. This adaptation is called tolerance.
- Once this tolerance is established, further abnormalities occur in the brain when the drug is removed. In other words, the brain loses it capacity to function normally when drugs are not present.
- This low-grade abstinence-based brain dysfunction is distinct and different from the traditional acute withdrawal syndromes.
- This low-grade abstinence-based brain dysfunction is marked by feelings of discomfort, cravings, and difficulty finding gratification from other behaviors.
- This creates a desire to avoid the unpleasant sensations that occur in abstinence. This desire to avoid painful stimuli is called *negative reinforcement*.
- People who experience biological reinforcement (both positive and negative) are more likely to use drugs regularly and heavily.
- People who use drugs regularly and heavily are more likely to develop
    —physical dependence syndromes marked by tolerance and classic withdrawal symptoms and
    —biomedical complications resulting from alcohol and drug use.
- There is evidence that people who are genetically susceptible and exposed prenatally to addiction may have pathological brain reward mechanisms.
- When not using the drug of choice, this pathological brain reward mechanism is marked by a below average release of packets of brain reward chemicals.
    —When the drug of choice is used, the brain releases abnormally large amounts of brain reward chemicals.
    —When not using, the person experiences a sense of anhedonia (a decreased ability to experience pleasure) marked by a low-grade, agitated depression.
    —This feeling creates a craving for something, anything that will relive the feeling.
- When the person finds the drug of choice that releases large amounts of brain reward chemicals, they experience a powerful sense of

pleasure or euphoria. The experience feels so good that the patient begins seeking to repeat that experience.

> This biomedical condition leads to psychological and social reinforcement.

Psychological Reinforcement

Your mind is capable of formulating thoughts that produce strong, positive biological reinforcement. These thoughts often take the form of positive judgments about your behavior that results in self-talk, such as "Doing this is good for me!"

Positive judgments about your behavior can be reinforcing of and by themselves, because they are capable of activating the release of biologically reinforcing brain chemicals. When this occurs, the positive judgment is said to *trigger* the state of reinforcement.

> Psychological Reinforcement = Gratification

When the biologically reinforcing brain chemicals are automatically released in response to a behavior, you feel pleasure and are more likely to judge the behavior as positive, which stimulates the release of more reinforcing brain chemicals. When this occurs, the judgment you make is said to *enhance* the state of reinforcement.

Social Reinforcement

Social reinforcement develops when you judge the behavior of others or the response of the environment to be positive. These positive judgments about how people and the environment respond to you can trigger or enhance biological reinforcement.

> Social Reinforcement = Reward

Chronic pain patients who have addictive disorders or are in recovery should use the APM Medication Management Components, so special precautions must be taken. It must be determined whether or not the medication is being used appropriately.

That is why the following *Pain Medication Recovery and Relapse Indicators* chart was developed. Using this checklist, combined with *Exercise Two* from the *Addiction-Free Pain Management® Workbook,* gives you and your healthcare providers a better chance of avoiding potential problems.

Pain Medication Recovery and Relapse Indicators

Recovery Indicators	Relapse Indicators
1. I am using medication as prescribed and am in accordance with my *Medication Management Treatment Plan.*	1. I am not using medication as prescribed, nor am I in accordance with my *Medication Management Treatment Plan.*
2. I am using pain medication only for its analgesic pain relief.	2. I am using pain medication for its euphoric effects and/or for its emotional management properties.
3. I am not experiencing obsession for or intrusive thoughts about the medication.	3. I am experiencing obsession for and/or intrusive thoughts about the medication.
4. I am not experiencing compulsion to use the medication inappropriately.	4. I am experiencing compulsion to use the medication.
5. I am not experiencing a craving to use the medication inappropriately.	5. I am experiencing a craving to use the medication.
6. I am not experiencing a loss of control from using the medication.	6. I am experiencing a loss of control from using the medication.
7. I am not experiencing intoxication from using the medication.	7. I am experiencing intoxication from using the medication.
8. I am not experiencing negative consequences from using the medication.	8. I am experiencing negative consequences from using the medication.
9. I am not experiencing any secondary related problems due to using the medication.	9. I am experiencing secondary related problems due to using the medication.
10. I am not experiencing a pain rebound effect from using the medication.	10. I am experiencing a pain rebound effect from using the medication.

Expectations versus Reality

Exercise Two: Effects of Prescription and/or Other Drugs

In *Exercise Two, Part 1: What You Wanted versus What You Got*, you are asked to list the type(s), amount(s), and frequency of the medication(s) you currently use (or have used) to manage your pain. Alcohol needs to be included because many people with chronic pain often use alcohol to help manage their pain—or escape from it!

Your next step is to explore what you wanted the drugs to do, the effects the drugs actually produced that made you believe you were getting what you wanted, and finally, what you learned from completing the exercise. Please see the following table to review this exercise.

Prescription medication and other drugs (including alcohol) change how the brain and nervous system work. They slow down, speed up, block out, change, or "blow up" the messages and feelings that your brain sends out. These drug effects make you feel different for a little while, but they don't actually change anything in the real world. They mask your chronic pain and change how you think, feel, and act. But usually they don't make your life any better—in fact, they make life much worse.

In the following exercises you will be asked to list the type, amount, and frequency of the medication you are currently using (or have used during the past year) to manage your pain. Alcohol needs to be included because many people with chronic pain often use alcohol to help manage their pain. Some people also use some of the illicit drugs, e.g., marijuana, methamphetamine. If you use those chemicals, please list them as well. You will then explore what you wanted the drugs to do, the effects the drugs produced that made you believe you were getting what you wanted, and what you learned as a result of completing this exercise.

Part 1-A: What You Used and How Well It Worked

In this section list each drug you used for pain management (including alcohol or other nonprescribed drugs), how much you used, how often you used it, how long the effects lasted, and how much relief you received. Please rate the amount of relief on a 1-to-10 scale, with 1 being very minimal and 10 being total relief.

Part 1-B: What You Wanted Your Medication to Do

Please answer each of the following questions as fully and honestly as you can.

1. What are the three most important things you wanted your pain medication to do for you?
2. Could you do these things for yourself without using pain medication?
   ❐ Yes   ❐ No   ❐ Unsure   Please explain:
3. What are the three most important things you wanted the pain medication to help you cope with or escape from?
4. Can you cope with or escape from these things without using pain medication?
   ❐ Yes   ❐ No   ❐ Unsure   Please explain:
5. Looking back on it now, do you think that the pain medication did for you what you wanted it to do?
   ❐ Yes   ❐ No   ❐ Unsure   Please explain:

Part 1-C: What You Learned

6. List below the three most important things you have learned as a result of completing this exercise.
7. What are you willing to do differently as a result of what you learned?

Please take a few minutes to complete this exercise in your APM Workbook.

At this point it would be extremely beneficial to share this information with your counselor or therapist as well as your primary physician. If that doctor is not certified in addiction medicine, someone with that training should be consulted.

Remember—Teamwork Is a Must!

The second part of *Exercise Two* explores some of the most common side effects and problems experienced from using pain medication. In some instances prescription medication and other drugs (including alcohol) may seem to work for pain management.

However, they often have serious physical side effects and/or lead to psychological and social problems.

Exercise Two, Part 2: Medication Side Effects and Problems

Some of the most common problematic effects are listed below. You are asked to indicate how each applies to you, rating the degree of impact on you by writing in the appropriate level (on a scale of 1 to 10, with 1 being not a problem to 10 being extremely problematic). After reviewing the effects listed below, I will describe how Jean and Dean completed this exercise.

Effects of Substances Exercise

Level

1. Increased tolerance (needing more of the drug)
2. Nausea and/or vomiting
3. Feeling sleepy, fatigued, or drowsy
4. Becoming short-tempered (easily angered)
5. Impaired liver functions
6. Abdominal pain or cramping
7. Feeling down or depressed
8. Thoughts of suicide
9. Decreased sexuality or libido
10. Increased anxiety
11. Increased family or relationship problems
12. Euphoria—feeling high (intoxicated)
13. Becoming confused or disoriented
14. Blurred and/or double vision
15. Stomach pain and/or ulcers
16. Being dependent/addicted
17. Urine retention
18. Diarrhea
19. Decreased job performance
20. Difficulty having fun or experiencing pleasure

Jean's Answers to the Effects of Substances Exercise

	Effects of Substances	Level
1.	Increased tolerance (needing more of the drug)	9
2.	Nausea and/or vomiting	2
3.	Feeling sleepy, fatigued, or drowsy	4
4.	Becoming short-tempered (easily angered)	8
5.	Impaired liver functions	2
6.	Abdominal pain or cramping	4
7.	Feeling down or depressed	8
8.	Thoughts of suicide	3
9.	Decreased sexuality or libido	9
10.	Increased anxiety	10
11.	Increased family or relationship problems	8
12.	Euphoria—feeling high (intoxicated)	8
13.	Becoming confused or disoriented	8
14.	Blurred and/or double vision	1
15.	Stomach pain and/or ulcers	4
16.	Being dependent/addicted	10
17.	Urine retention	1
18.	Diarrhea	1
19.	Decreased job performance	8
20.	Difficulty having fun or experiencing pleasure	9

On her first attempt to complete this exercise, Jean greatly underrated many of the symptoms. As she processed the results during the session, she began to see how much she minimized the negative consequences and only focused on the benefits of using her medication.

Jean's second attempt was much more honest and showed an increase in most of her category levels. This exercise also opened up a discussion about other ways her use of pain medication was negatively impacting her life, as well as being problematic for her family and friends.

Now let's look at how Dean completed this exercise.

Dean's Answers to the Effects of Substances Exercise

Effects of Substances	Level
1. Increased tolerance (needing more of the drug)	8
2. Nausea and/or vomiting	2
3. Feeling sleepy, fatigued, or drowsy	3
4. Becoming short-tempered (easily angered)	9
5. Impaired liver functions	2
6. Abdominal pain or cramping	2
7. Feeling down or depressed	10
8. Thoughts of suicide	4
9. Decreased sexuality or libido	10
10. Increased anxiety	10
11. Increased family or relationship problems	10
12. Euphoria—feeling high (intoxicated)	8
13. Becoming confused or disoriented	9
14. Blurred and/or double vision	1
15. Stomach pain and/or ulcers	3
16. Being dependent/addicted	10
17. Urine retention	2
18. Diarrhea	2
19. Decreased job performance	10
20. Difficulty having fun or experiencing pleasure	10

Dean was very honest with his evaluation and reported that seeing all these negative side effects in one place was painful for him. He also noted that this realization never stopped him from using before, but now he wanted to learn how to use this information to increase his positive self-talk. Dean also noted that he experienced one other significant side effect from all the opiate medication—severe constipation—which impacts many people taking this type of medication. Again it was the *processing* of the exercise with someone else that had the most impact—not filling out the forms.

> *Please take a few minutes to complete this exercise in your* **APM Workbook**.

Medication and/or withdrawal from medication can lead to clinical symptoms of depression, a common side effect for someone coping with chronic pain. This is another area where teamwork is essential. If you are depressed, you need to seek help from someone who specializes in identifying and treating depression.

Examining grief and loss issues is a major part of the healing process for most people with chronic pain. Identifying and grieving the loss of your healthy self, and/or prior level of functioning, is essential to recovery. In later chapters you will see how Jean and Dean addressed these issues.

> It is very important to uncover the your beliefs about pain, as well as the benefits and disadvantages of taking the pain medication.

The next step in the assessment process is determining your beliefs about pain medication, your earliest experiences around pain and medication, and your perceived benefits and disadvantages of using your pain medication.

Exercise Three: Decision Making about Pain Medication

Exercise Three in the *Addiction-Free Pain Management® Workbook* is a series of four decision-making exercises, which are designed to assist you in looking at potential chemical dependency/abuse problems. *Part 1* explores your personal beliefs about pain and medication.

Exercise Three, Part 1:
Your Personal Beliefs about Pain and Medication

Often your decision to use pain medication has been made because a doctor prescribed it, usually after only a very brief consultation with you. Many doctors have minimal training in addictive disorders and may not be aware of the risks for some of their patients. On the other hand, some people mislead their doctors (intentionally or unintentionally) by not giving them an accurate picture of their past history (or family history) of alcohol or other drug problems. Other factors in medication decision making center on your response to, and beliefs about, pain.

> **Prerequisites of APM® Recovery**
> - Honest self-evaluation
> - Accurate self-monitoring
> - Healthy self-changing behaviors

The overall purpose of this exercise is for you to explore how you make decisions, so you can begin to make accurate, honest, and healthy choices about your pain management and use of pain medication.

You are asked to think back to the very first time you took any medication (including alcohol) for pain relief and write about it like a story with a beginning, middle, and end. Make sure to include: your age at the time, what you were doing, who you were with, what happened, what thoughts you had about your pain, how you were affected (or what feelings were produced) by the pain, who suggested the pain medication, what it was, and how much you used.

You are then asked what you wanted the medication to do for you and what you wanted the medication to help you cope with or escape from.

> **Ask Yourself**
> 1. **What did you want the pain medication to do for you?**
> 2. **Did you get what you wanted?**

See the following table for the questions asked in this exercise.

> **Part 1: Your Personal Beliefs about Pain and Medication**
>
> 1. Think back to the very first time you took any medication (including alcohol) for pain relief and write about it like a story with a beginning, middle, and end. Make sure to include your age at the time, what you were doing, who you were with, what happened, what you were thinking about your pain, how you were affected (or feelings produced) by the pain, who suggested the pain medication, what it was, and how much you used.
> 2. What did you want the medication to do for you?
> 3. What did you want the medication to help you cope with or escape from?
> 4. What happened when you were growing up in your family when someone was in pain? What were the messages you received about pain management?
> 5. What's the most important thing you learned from completing this part of the exercise and what can you do differently for your pain management as a result?

Both Jean and Dean experienced several useful insights after completing this exercise. Jean was able to see how her father frequently pushed pills at her when she complained about even mild symptoms. As a consequence, Jean learned from a very young age that pain was to be medicated, not tolerated.

Dean learned that pain must be hidden, not expressed. He remembers being shamed and humiliated by his father when he cried after spraining his ankle at age five. This set up his pattern of self-medicating and then hiding that he was doing so from others.

> *Please take a few minutes to complete this exercise in your* APM Workbook.

Exercise Three, Part 2: Pain Medication Problem Checklist

The next step is to determine the risk or level of a potential addictive disorder (substance abuse, addiction, or dependency). This is facilitated by *Exercise Three, Part 2: The Pain Medication Problem Checklist.*

Denial is one of the major symptoms of an addictive disorder, but in the case of someone addicted to prescribed pain medication for a *legitimate* pain condition the denial system is even more difficult to overcome. The *Pain Medication Problem Checklist* is designed to help you work around that resistance and denial—but is only possible if you are willing to answer the questions honestly.

This instrument originally included fifty "yes or no" questions using the addictive disorder criteria covered earlier, as well as the DSM-IV diagnostic criteria for substance abuse and substance dependency. However, they are rewritten in a less clinical manner and have only thirty items, making it much more user-friendly. Please review the following directions and questions from this exercise.

The Pain Medication Problem Checklist

Instructions

Sometimes when people start to use pain medication (including alcohol) and other drugs they may begin to experience problems. Please answer each question below as honestly as you can. The more questions you answer yes to, the more likely it is you may be having problems with your pain medication.

You may notice some of the questions may make you uncomfortable. As a matter of fact, you may notice you have an urge to rationalize or minimize (or even lie about) your answers. If this happens, it means you probably have an urge to defend yourself against acknowledging you have problems related to your use of pain medication and/or other drugs. This is definitely a sign something is wrong. You should talk to your counselor, therapist, and/or other healthcare providers about the questions that cause an urge to minimize, rationalize, or deny that you may have a problem with how you are using your pain medication.

Pain Medication Problem Checklist

1. Do you sometimes take medication in a larger dose than is prescribed by your doctor?
2. Do you sometimes take the medication more frequently than prescribed by your doctor?
3. Do you ever mix other medication (including alcohol or over-the-counter medication) with your prescribed medication without your doctor's knowledge or approval?
4. When you're using pain medication (including alcohol) and other drugs, do you ever put yourself in situations that raise your risk of getting hurt, having problems, or hurting others? (This includes things like driving while using prescriptions, alcohol, or other drugs; taking care of small children; getting into arguments; skipping work; committing crimes; etc.)
5. Have you noticed that you need to take more medication than you used to in order to get the pain relief you desire?
6. When you use the same amount of medication all the time, do you experience a reduction in your pain relief and are you tempted to increase the dose?
7. Have you ever felt sick or anxious (or experienced other withdrawal symptoms) when you suddenly stopped using your medication?
8. Have you ever used your medication or other drugs (including alcohol) to avoid withdrawal symptoms?
9. Have you ever hidden from (or not told) one doctor what you have been given by another doctor (or about use of over-the-counter medication)?
10. Have you ever had a persistent desire or made unsuccessful efforts to cut down or control your medication?
11. Have you ever used your medication (including alcohol) or other drugs to try to escape from or cope with a problem or situation you didn't know any other way to deal with?
12. Has anyone else (a spouse, parent, sibling, boss, or friend) told you they thought you might have a problem with your prescription drug use?
13. Have you continued to use your medication despite having physical or psychological problems caused by the medication

(e.g., impaired liver functions, loss of memory, irritability, or depression)?
14. Have you experienced legal problems due to substance-related issues (such as forging prescriptions or driving while taking your mood-altering medication)?
15. Have you used pain medication without really needing it for physical pain?
16. Have you used pain medication (including alcohol) to cope with uncomfortable feelings or to manage stress?
17. Have you thought your prescription drug use was becoming problematic?
18. Have you seen a counselor or other professional for help with your prescription drug (or alcohol and/or other drug) use?
19. Have you let other people down whom you cared about because you were using pain medication (including alcohol) or other drugs and were in withdrawal?
20. Have your family members or friends been concerned about the type, amount, or frequency of the pain medication you take (including alcohol)?
21. Have you continued using pain medication (including alcohol) or drugs even though you knew they were causing problems or making existing problems worse?
22. Has a doctor or counselor ever told you that he or she thought you had a serious problem with pain medication (including alcohol) or other drugs?
23. Have you experienced depression or even thoughts of suicide while taking pain medication?
24. Have you attended self-help meetings to deal with pain medication use or problems that occurred, at least in part, because you were taking the medication?
25. Do you ever use your medications to feel high (euphoria)?
26. If you were told you had to stop your pain medication because of a medical problem, would it be difficult for you to stop?
27. Have you ever lied to or mislead a doctor to receive more (or stronger) pain medication?

28. Do you feel deprived or even angry when you can't get your pain medication as quickly as you would like (or get enough of your pain medication)?
29. Do you find yourself making excuses to use more medication than was prescribed by your doctor?
30. Did you feel uncomfortable or have the urge to rationalize/minimize (or even lie) when answering any of the above questions?

Please take a few minutes to complete this exercise in your APM Workbook.

Exercise Three, Part 3:
Interpreting the Pain Medication Problem Checklist

The interpretation of the checklist follows in *Part 3*. It includes asking you to score the number of yes answers in two segments and then to check your level or risk of addiction. Please see the exercise in the following table.

1. Count how many times you answered yes to any of the questions numbered 1 through 15. How many yes answers did you check? _____
2. Count how many times you answered yes to any of the questions numbered 16 through 30. How many yes answers did you check? _____
3. From your yes answers above, check the box below that most accurately describes your level or risk of addiction based on your answers to the *Pain Medication Problem Checklist*.

☐ **Low Risk for Addiction:** If you answered no to all of the above questions, you are probably at a low risk for addiction.

☐ **High Risk for Addiction:** If you answered yes to three or more of the questions numbered 1 through 15 and answered no to all the remaining questions, you may be at a high risk of becoming addicted.

☐ **Early-Stage Addiction:** If you answered yes to three or more of the questions numbered 1 through 15 and answered yes to between two and four of the questions numbered 16 through 30, you may be in the early stages of addiction.

- ☐ **Middle-Stage Addiction:** If you answered yes to three or more of the questions numbered 1 through 15 and answered yes to between four and seven of the questions numbered 16 through 30, you could be in the middle stages of addiction.
- ☐ **Late-Stage Addiction:** If you answered yes to three or more of the questions numbered 1 through 15 and answered yes to seven or more of the questions numbered 16 through 30, you are probably in the late stages of addiction.

4. If you believe that pain medication (including alcohol) and other drugs can do things for you that you can't do without them, you are probably psychologically and/or socially dependent on those substances.
5. If you believe that pain medication (including alcohol) and other drugs can help you cope with or escape from things you can't handle without them, you are probably psychologically or socially dependent on pain medication (including alcohol) or other drugs to cope with pain and to solve problems.
6. Do you believe that the results of the *Pain Medication Problem Checklist* accurately describe your current level or risk of addiction to pain medication (including alcohol and other drugs)?

    ☐ Yes ☐ No ☐ Unsure   Please explain:

The discussion that follows this exercise is much more important than the exercise itself, so you should share this with your counselor or therapist and/or other trusted team members. This process helps you see clearly some of the problems you may have as a direct result of problematic medication use.

Jean and Dean saw themselves as addicted before completing this exercise, and the results of their checklists validated their impressions. Even though Jean and Dean were not in denial about being addicted, they were shocked at the seriousness of it; they were both surprised about how excessive their inappropriate medication use really was.

> *Please take a few minutes to complete this exercise in your* **APM Workbook.**

Exercise Three, Part 4:
Making a Decision to Do Something Different

This final part of *Exercise Three* asks you to explore both the benefits and disadvantages of using pain medication by completing the following form. The final question asks you whether you think the benefits you expected from your medication were worth the pain and problems that you experienced. See the table below.

1. **Benefits**: List the main things that were better for you because you used pain medication (including alcohol and other drugs)?	2. **Disadvantages**: List the main things that were worse for you, or problems that you had because you used pain medication (including alcohol and other drugs).

Biopsychosocial History

The final part of a complete self-assessment includes a biopsychosocial history including medication use/abuse, pain, and trauma. Your significant others and/or family members should be consulted when you're gathering this information, because you might have forgotten or blocked out crucial information. Family-of-origin issues and other traumatic situations have a significant impact on treatment planning and treatment outcome; it is essential that your counselor or therapist have the whole picture.

Pain literature clearly indicates that chronic pain conditions can restimulate posttraumatic stress disorders (PTSD). This was certainly the case for Jean and to a slightly lesser degree for Dean as well. As you will see in later chapters, this information can make a big difference in treatment approaches.

> Assessments need to be ongoing throughout the APM® treatment process.

Take note that the identification and self-assessment process needs to continue throughout the entire treatment process. The APM System is designed to facilitate this ongoing assessment. The more you learn about yourself, the more effective your recovery and pain management process becomes.

> *Please take a few minutes to complete this exercise in your* APM Workbook.

Exercise Four: Moving into the Solution

Another useful tool to help you avoid relapse early in treatment is *Exercise Four: Moving into the Solution* in the *Addiction-Free Pain Management® Workbook.* This exercise includes: a presenting problems report form, a relapse intervention plan, a medication management agreement, a craving management plan, and a nonpharmacological pain flare-up plan.

Part 1-A of this exercise asks you to identify your current problems and list how the problems are connected to any inappropriate use of pain medication or other self-defeating behaviors. It requests a commitment to stop your self-sabotage. You are also asked to identify a situation in the near future that could cause you to start using pain medication inappropriately.

Part 1-B gives you a chart to summarize the information. The intervention plan outlines the roles for you, your therapist, and at least three significant others. This exercise follows.

Jean and Dean had some difficulty in choosing appropriate significant others. It was also difficult for them to come up with effective intervention requests, since they were so used to isolating and depending only on themselves. Fortunately, after several attempts, they found supportive people who were willing and able to be an effective part of their relapse prevention network.

The other important parts of *Exercise Four* in the *Addiction-Free Pain Management® Workbook* are shown in the tables that follow.

Exercise Four, Part 1-A: Presenting Problems

1. **Presenting problems:** What are the presenting problems that caused you to seek help at this time? (Why did you seek help now? Why not yesterday or next week? What would have happened if you didn't seek help now? What problems or negative consequences can this workbook help you avoid?)

2. **Relationship to inappropriate use of pain medication:** How is each presenting problem related to your inappropriate use of pain medication and/or to an ineffective pain management program?

   How is this problem related to your inappropriate use of pain medication (including alcohol) or other mood-altering substances? Did the chemicals cause you to have this problem? (i.e., Would you have this problem if you never inappropriately used pain medication, including alcohol or other drugs?) Did inappropriate use of pain medication (including alcohol) or other drugs make this problem worse than it would have been if you hadn't been using it?

3. **Consequences of not stopping:** What additional problems could you experience if you keep inappropriately using pain medication (including alcohol) or other drugs despite these problems? (What are the benefits? What are the disadvantages? What is the best thing that could happen? What is the worst? What is the most likely thing that will probably happen?)

4. **Asking for a commitment to stop (The Abstinence Commitment):** Are you willing to make a commitment not to inappropriately use pain medication (including alcohol) or other drugs for <name the specific period of time: _____>? (This should be done with the assistance of your doctor and counselor.) Please explain your answer.

5. **Immediate high-risk situations:** Are you facing any situations in the near future that could cause you to inappropriately use pain medication (including alcohol) or other drugs despite your commitment not to? Please explain your answer.

6. **The APM® commitment:** Are you willing to make an agreement to complete the APM process to learn how to identify and manage those high-risk situations without inappropriately using pain medication (including alcohol) or other drugs?

   ❐ Yes ❐ No ❐ Unsure Please explain:

Exercise Four, Part 1-B: Presenting Problems Report Form

My Presenting Problems	Relationship to Inappropriate Pain Medication (Including Alcohol) or Other Mood-Altering Drug Use	Consequences If I Keep Using

Exercise Four, Part 2: The APM Medication Management Agreement

I, _____, do hereby agree to ABSTAIN from using any *inappropriate* medication (including alcohol) or other drugs and to continue an effective pain management program while I am completing this *APM Workbook*. Inappropriate medications are those that have not been authorized by my treatment team and include prescription medications (including quantity and frequency of use), over-the-counter medications, as well as alcohol and other mood-altering substances.

Should I return to using any inappropriate pain medication (including alcohol) or other drugs and/or deviating from my pain management program, I will immediately seek help from an appropriate treatment team member. I will also be open to having my treatment plan reevaluated and modified if determined necessary by my treatment team. This intervention may require transfer to a treatment facility for detoxification and/or stabilization before continuing with the *APM Workbook*.

I also agree to submit to random drug screens at the discretion of my treatment team. Unwillingness to submit to a breath, blood, or urine test will be interpreted as a clear indicator I have been using inappropriate mood-altering chemicals, including alcohol, and I need immediate intervention.

I will consult with my treatment team regarding any medications prescribed to me by any physician, and I will not use **anything** that is not approved by my treatment team including over-the-counter medications.

Signature _____ Date _____

Signature of Witness _____ Date _____

Exercise Four, Part 3:
Your Relapse Prevention Insurance Policy

Relapse Intervention Plan: One of the goals of completing this workbook is to prepare you to quickly stop the inappropriate use of pain medication (including alcohol) and other drugs, or ineffective pain management, should it occur. This exercise is called Developing a Relapse Intervention Plan.

Factors that stop relapse quickly: Your response to relapse will be determined in large part by the following three factors: (1) what you were told will happen if you start inappropriately using pain medication (including alcohol) or other drugs or start mismanaging your pain management program; (2) what you can do to stop using pain medication (including alcohol) or other drugs and/or get back to using an effective pain management program is relapse occurs; and (3) the approach of the treatment professionals who deal with you after the relapse has occurred.

Guidelines that stop relapse quickly should it occur: It's a mistaken belief that "if you take one dose of a drug, you will lose control and not be able to stop until you hit bottom." There are two reasons not to believe this: First, it's not true. Many chemically dependent people have short-term and low-consequence relapses and get back into recovery before serious damage occurs. Second, this approach programs you for a long-term catastrophic relapse episode. If you do start to inappropriately use pain medication (including alcohol) or other drugs, the misleading voice may pop into your head saying, "If you take one dose of a drug, you will lose control and not be able to stop until you hit bottom." You may then say to yourself, "Great, now I can keep medicating until I hit bottom." This does not mean it's perfectly fine to take single drug doses whenever the mood strikes or as long as your life doesn't fall apart. You still have to be vigilant. "Single dosing" is a high-risk situation. Fortunately, if you do start to inappropriately use pain medication (including alcohol) or other drugs, you will hit moments of sanity where you can choose to stop the relapse and get help. At these moments it is important to act immediately. If you wait, the urge to use again will come back and the opportunity will be lost. If you do start to use alcohol and drugs and hit a moment of sanity where you want to stop, the four most effective things for you to do are:

- Read your prepared relapse intervention plan, which should always be readily accessible. (You also should have given copies to significant others.)
- Immediately stop using and get out of the situation that supports inappropriate use of pain medication (including alcohol) and other drugs.
- Immediately call for help and get into a sobriety supportive situation.
- Call a counselor or sponsor, go to a treatment program or a support-group meeting.

The Relapse Intervention Plan: In its simplest form, developing a relapse intervention plan consists of processing the following three questions by developing a specific written plan in response to each question.

1. What is the counselor supposed to do if you relapse, stop coming to sessions, or fail to honor your treatment or abstinence contract?
2. What are you going to do to get back in recovery if you start inappropriately using pain medication (including alcohol) or other drugs so that you can stop using before you hit bottom?
3. Who are three significant others who have an investment in your recovery and what is each of them supposed to do if relaspe occurs? Make sure you have their day and night phone numbers accessible and they have a copy of this plan.

A. Name of Significant Other #1 _____
   Phone: _____
   What are they supposed to do? _____

B. Name of Significant Other #2 _____
   Phone: _____
   What are they supposed to do? _____

C. Name of Significant Other #3 _____
   Phone: _____
   What are they supposed to do? _____

Exercise Four, Part 4: Pain Management Craving Intervention Planning
Developing Your Personalized Craving Management Plan

When you have made a decision to take action and follow a healthy living plan and manage your pain in a recovery-prone manner, there is a strong possibility you may experience intense urges or cravings to once again use inappropriate medication (including alcohol and other drugs) to cope with stress or for pain relief and comfort. This doesn't mean you are weak or don't have a commitment to follow your *Medication Management Agreement* and recovery plan. It is normal for people who quit using medication inappropriately to have thoughts and even strong cravings to fall back into old ways.

You can avoid relapsing into old behaviors by creating an effective craving management plan. Below are ten examples of steps you can take to avoid giving into your cravings.

Directions: As you read each of the interventions below, rate **your** ability to implement each one on a scale of 1 to 10, with **1** meaning "I would probably not be able to do that" and **10** meaning "I could definitely do that."

Recognize and Accept: Recognize the craving and accept it as a normal part of your recovery. Remind yourself: "Just because I'm having a craving, doesn't mean there is something wrong with me. It is normal to have cravings." ____

Decide Not to Act on the Craving: Tell yourself the following: "No matter what happens, I'm not going to act on this craving. Instead I'll call someone." And/or "Cravings go away whether I use or not. I have proven this before and I can do what it takes to shut this down."
____

Change the Physical Setting: Change your physical and/or social location—**GET OUT OF THERE!** Sometimes something as simple as changing chairs makes a big difference. Don't be around negative people who pressure you to give in to your cravings. Be around positive recovery-prone people. ____

Meditation and Relaxation: Learn simple relaxation and/or meditation techniques (your healthcare provider can help you with this). Sometimes just taking a few deep breaths can also make a big difference. Some people report great benefit from meditation and/or relaxation cassettes. Check it out! Remember, contempt prior to investigation equals ignorance. _____

Negative Consequences: Remind yourself of the negative things that will probably happen if you give in to your craving and start to use again. Have this prepared before you start experiencing cravings. Remember all the pain and problems you have experienced and the pain your significant others had as a result of your giving in to your cravings before. _____

Benefits of Not Using: Remind yourself of all the good things that can happen if you do not give in to your cravings and adhere to your *Medication Management Agreement*. List some of the things that you can now accomplish because you are clean and sober that would have been difficult, if not impossible, to do while using. _____

Exercise: Have a regular, daily pattern of exercise and other pain management protocols developed, and practice them consistently. When you have a craving, you can begin using one of these activities to help you better manage your cravings. _____

Eat Healthy: Eating three balanced meals per day with nutritious snacks in between will be very helpful. Avoid eating as a "substitution" for using, but do fuel your body in a healthy way. Avoid sugar, caffeine, and nicotine as much as possible, especially when having cravings. _____

Mastery Imagery: Close your eyes and imagine yourself being successful and powerful by not giving in to your cravings. Imagine all the positive benefits you will experience and how good you will feel about yourself for not giving in to the cravings. _____

Do Anything Else That Works: You know yourself better than anyone else does, so use that knowledge to develop an action plan. You can be successful in handling urges and cravings. Allow yourself to succeed and improve the quality of your life. _____

My Personal Plan: Try to imagine yourself in a situation where you would begin to experience strong urges or cravings to use pain medication inappropriately, including alcohol and other drugs. Then using the above interventions as a starting point, list your step-by-step action plan in the space below. Your plan should be at least four steps—but in this case more is definitely better.

As you complete your craving management exercise, learn about the connections between addictive or other self-defeating thinking patterns and the uncomfortable emotions that lead to cravings. Understanding this connection can save you much pain and trouble in the future. The following chart can help achieve that understanding. This chart lists eight pairs of emotional continuums, and each pair has an intensity rating (the scale is 1–10, with 10 being very strong emotion). The higher the intensity the more likely you are to have addictive thinking that will lead to cravings. So before going on to the final exercise in this segment, please take time to review and think about this information.

Feelings and Cravings

Feeling + Addictive Thinking = Craving

❐	Strong	or	❐	Weak	*Intensity* = ___
❐	Angry	or	❐	Caring	*Intensity* = ___
❐	Happy	or	❐	Sad	*Intensity* = ___
❐	Safe	or	❐	Threatened	*Intensity* = ___
❐	Fulfilled	or	❐	Frustrated	*Intensity* = ___
❐	Proud	or	❐	Ashamed	*Intensity* = ___
❐	Connected	or	❐	Lonely	*Intensity* = ___
❐	Peaceful	or	❐	Agitated	*Intensity* = ___

Exercise Four, Part 5: Pain Flare-Up Planning

Developing Your Personalized Pain Flare-Up Plan

When you live with chronic pain, there will be times when your pain flares up. Sometimes you can determine why, and other times it comes as a complete surprise and you don't really know why. No matter why your pain flares up, you need to find safe, effective ways to cope with the amplified symptoms. This requires having a good plan in place. *Those who fail to plan, plan to fail!*

Below are several nonpharmacological (nonmedication) ways that other people have developed to manage their pain flare-ups. The important thing to remember is you **can** intervene in a way that helps you regain effective pain management. Sometimes the intervention may need to be pain medication, but changing your medication protocols should only be done with your healthcare provider's knowledge and permission. This worksheet can support you to adhere to your *Medication Management Agreement*.

1. **Breathing and Relaxation:** When you are in a pain flare-up, your body's automatic reaction often includes a reflexive tensing response. This can lead to being unable to relax the focus of the pain, which results in increased muscle tension in these areas. It is important to consciously practice relaxing the affected muscles. This will enable you to modulate your pain levels and bring the pain under control without increasing your medication. Using deep, slow breathing can help you soften and relax your overly tense muscles.

2. **Increasing Activity/Fitness:** When you experience pain flare-ups, you may become sedentary and avoid many types of activities. The two primary reasons for this are the pain itself and your own predictions (*anticipatory pain*) regarding the negative impact of the activity. Therefore, it is crucial to return to more nomal levels of activities, then slowly increase your stamina for physical activities to extinguish conditioned avoidance patterns.

3. **Diffusing/Reducing Emotional Overreactivity:** When you are experiencing intense uncomfortable emotions—especially about being in pain—your pain levels can actually intensify. Your emotions become like an amplifier circuit that increases the "volume" of your pain. It is necessary to practice specific methods of reducing this automatic process that occurs in the face of stressful triggers. As you do this, you will realize that you may not be able to eliminate those problematic emotional triggers. But you **can** learn different methods of reacting and managing your feelings.

4. **External Focusing/Distraction:** The more you focus on your pain, the more you actually intensify your experience of the pain. When you learn to shift and manipulate the focus of your attention in a positive way, your experience of the pain will be minimized. This can be accomplished by changing how you think and feel about your pain. You can then direct your attention to pleasant activities or tasks that take the focus off of your pain.

> 5. **Using Anything That Works:** When your pain flares up, there are many interventions that you can try. In addition to those listed above, you can use breathing, muscle relaxation, visual imagery, music, cold/heat, stretching, massage therapy, stress management, acupuncture, acupressure, TENS Unit, journaling, hydrotherapy, etc.
>
> **My Personal Plan**
>
> Try to imagine yourself in a situation where you are experiencing a pain flare-up and you want to intervene in a positive and proactive manner. Using the above interventions as a starting point, please list your step-by-step action plan. Your plan should have at least four interventions—again, the more the better.

This five-part exercise was a major turning point for both Jean and Dean. The most important thing they learned was that they could take action in order to manage their cravings, and they could develop a safe pain flare-up plan. Jean shared her completed exercise with her women's church group and asked for their support in implementing it.

Dean shared his answers to these exercises with a close friend in his Twelve-Step program and gave key people permission to remind him of his commitment and plan. Dean wanted to let his wife see his work, as well, because that was a simple way he could start emotionally connecting with her. I reminded Dean that his wife was also one of his three relapse intervention team members, so she needed to know his plan in order to fully support him in a positive way.

> Use Denial Management Counseling to manage any resistance and denial.

As you go through the exercises above, I hope you will be motivated and encouraged to continue to move forward in your ongoing recovery and effective pain management process. You will learn more about denial management in the following chapter.

Jean and Dean made commitments to stop abusing their pain medications in the past, but this time they were encouraged to put it in writing. They shared later that having this signed contract helped them to stop sabotaging themselves on several occasions.

> Connecting Cause and Effect

For Jean it was important to understand that seeing herself as a poor parent was directly connected to her inappropriate use of pain medication. Once she realized what the problem was, she was more than willing to make a commitment to stop using her old coping behaviors.

Other early treatment approaches—the Nonpharmacological Treatment Processes that include nonpsychoactive pain medication, physical therapy, hydrotherapy, nonchemical pain management, and chemical dependency education—should be implemented when needed to facilitate detoxification and stabilization. These, plus other treatment approaches, are covered in the next chapter and are sometimes necessary to implement early in your recovery/healing process.

- **Call to Action for the Sixth Chapter**

It is time to summarize what you have learned so far now that you have come to the end of the sixth chapter. Please answer the questions below.

1. What is the most important thing you have learned about yourself and your ability to help yourself as a result of completing Chapter Six?

2. What are you willing to commit to do differently as a result of what you have learned by completing this chapter?

3. What obstacles might get in the way of making these changes and what can you do to overcome these roadblocks?

> **Take time to pause and reflect, then go to the next page to review Chapter Seven.**

Chapter Seven
Utilizing Nonpharmacological/ Holistic Treatment Processes

> Active versus Passive Approaches

This chapter covers what some people call *nonpharmacological* treatment approaches or what others might refer to as *holistic* interventions. The term "nonpharmacological" simply means non-medication or nonmedical procedures. "Holistic health" is a term used by alternative medicine advocates to describe medical care that views physical, mental, and spiritual aspects of life as closely interconnected and balanced.

Holistic health is not new; it has been around for thousands of years, but it is relatively new to the United States healthcare system. It refers to the theory that whole entities, such as human beings, have an existence and a reality greater than the sum of their parts. Advocates of the holistic health philosophy typically seek or use a wide variety of alternative practices. The most common practices include acupuncture, chiropractice, naturopathy, yoga, aromatherapy, homeopathy, massage, and Tai Chi. In addition to some other early recovery approaches, you will see a brief description of several nonpharmacological interventions later in this chapter.

I mentioned earlier that the APM System is based upon the concept that people living with chronic pain require an active, multidimensional approach to obtain favorable treatment outcomes. This three-part approach includes: (1) a medication management plan, (2) a cognitive-behavioral treatment plan, and (3) a nonpharmacological pain management plan.

As was covered earlier, some addiction treatment programs and pain clinics have a tendency to put you in a passive role, which has proven to be counterproductive. In addition to assigning you to a passive role, some chronic pain programs fall short, as they lack a multidimensional approach.

There are many other pain management experts, though, that believe as I do that people living with chronic pain require an active, multidimensional approach to treatment. For example, the treatment plan might include exercises, chiropractic treatment, cognitive-behavioral strategies, and massage therapy, in addition to medication approaches. This combination is becoming known as *multidisciplinary integrated pain management*.

For some of you reading this book, the first step will be to move into a structured recovery process. Some of you may not recognize the need for this type of in-depth recovery approach. This is where the CENAPS® Model of Denial Management Counseling (DMC) could be helpful.

Denial Management Counseling

Denial Management Counseling (DMC) is a treatment modality designed to assist people with alcohol and drug-related problems or other self-defeating behaviors, who are also experiencing high levels of denial and treatment resistance. Many of you reading this book may need, and would benefit from, this type of approach.

The DMC process focuses upon developing appropriate treatment plans, targeted interviewing, and using a sequence of proven action steps to gain an initial commitment to treatment. The main goal of DMC is to help motivate people to look at accepting the need to seek additional help and follow through with specific action plans. Identifying and managing denial and resistance is often the missing link in many programs that treat addiction or chronic pain.

Goals of DMC

- Interrupt your patterns of denial
- Increase your recognition of any potential addiction-related or other self-defeating life problems
- Identify your real problems and negative consequences from these self-defeating patterns
- Motivate you to accept a referral to the next level of treatment

---

The *Addiction-Free Pain Management® Workbook* incorporates a portion of the DMC process by using a medication management contract and decision-making exercises that were explained earlier. However, the new *Denial Management Counseling for Effective Pain Management Workbook,* by Stephen F. Grinstead, Terence T.

Gorski, and Jennifer C. Messier, is an excellent resource for those of you who may need more comprehensive denial management work.

> Understanding and managing denial is crucial for effective pain management.

Along with DMC, other treatment modalities need to be added at the same time to address the synergistic effects of the addictive disorder and the chronic pain disorder (i.e., the *Addiction Pain Syndrome*®). The following table lists and briefly describes the twelve pain denial patterns from the *Denial Management Counseling for Effective Pain Management* workbook, used with full permission.

The Pain Denial Pattern Checklist

1. **Avoidance:** "I'll do anything not to talk about my pain management problems."
2. **Total Denial:** "No, not me! I don't have a problem with my pain!"
3. **Minimizing:** "My pain management problems aren't that big of a deal!"
4. **Rationalizing:** "If I can find good enough reasons for my problems with pain management, I won't have to deal with them."
5. **Blaming:** "If I can prove that my problems with pain management aren't my fault, I won't have to deal with them!"
6. **Comparing:** "Showing that others are worse off then me proves that I don't have serious problems with my pain management!"
7. **Compliance:** "I'll pretend to give you what you want so you'll leave me alone!"
8. **Manipulating:** "I'll play the game to convince others to do all the work for my pain management."
9. **Having a Flight into Health:** "Feeling better means that I'm cured and I can coast!"
10. **Fear of Change:** "If I don't focus on having a problem with my pain, I won't know who I am or how else to relate!"

> 11. **Diagnosing Myself as Beyond Help:** "Since nothing I do has ever worked for my pain management, I don't have to try anymore—I don't want to be let down yet again!"
> 12. **I Have the Right to Be This Way, AKA It's My Body:** "I have the right to whatever I want to do or don't want to do with my body and for my pain management, and no one has the right to tell me differently!"

More about Nonpharmacological Treatment Approaches

Some of the following pain management interventions will be familiar as they were briefly covered in an earlier chapter. In the following pages you will have an opportunity to obtain a more in-depth overview of some of the most utilized nonpharmacological pain management interventions; there are many more approaches than can be covered here. In fact, the only limitation for incorporating new nonpharmacological interventions is your imagination and that of your healthcare providers.

Avoidance by Distraction

Throughout this book you have seen the word *denial* used many times. It is important to note that the psychological defense mechanism called denial can be problematic, but at times it may also be helpful. When denial is automatic and unconscious, it can lead to life-damaging consequences and prevent people from taking needed action. However, some denial patterns can also be used strategically to help overcome problems.

One of these helpful patterns is a type of avoidance denial called Avoidance by Distraction. This denial pattern can be used in a very positive way to help someone with their pain management. For example, I treated one patient who learned to use this distraction tactic to focus on being present with her grandchildren instead of being overly caught up in her suffering. She discovered that when she was truly present with one of her grandchildren, she did not notice her pain as much. "Those who have something better to do, don't suffer as much" (W. Fordyce, Ph.D).

Unfortunately, some people take distraction to the extreme and cause even more damage to their bodies, as well as significantly increasing their pain levels. The goal here is to help people learn to focus their attention on something more interesting and positive than suffering. If you teach people to utilize this particular intervention, teach them proper activity pacing as well. Some people need to learn to slow down or take it easy, while others need to increase their activity levels and push themselves a little more.

Massage Therapy and Physical Therapy

One early pain management approach to consider is massage therapy. Remember, massage therapy will provide some immediate pain relief and reduced muscle tension, but it will be short-lived if not followed with other measures. This is understandable since there are many precursors or triggers for muscle tension that often resurface soon after the massage session. Therefore, other interventions must be implemented that are specific to the individual patient and used in the proper sequence.

Some of the methods that are successful in resolving other precursors to pain are: relaxation and meditation techniques, a customized exercise discipline, the use of biofeedback, and implementing proper nutrition, which is covered in a later chapter.

Using Physical Therapy with Hydrotherapy

Many healthcare providers promote the combination of physical therapy and hydrotherapy to help you strengthen and recondition your body, thus becoming an active participant in your healing.

Many pain management specialists agree that a program with hydrotherapy and water-based exercise can be an extremely helpful, active modality for people with chronic pain. Because water buoys the body, the stress and strain is removed while in the water. Exercising in the water for short periods of time has benefits equal to several times that of land-based exercise; it also comes without some of the negative side effects. Hydrotherapy and swimming were essential components of Dean's pain management program, especially because land-based exercise tended to be problematic for him.

TENS Units

TENS is an acronym for Transcutaneous Electrical Nerve Stimulation. With the development of modern medicine, doctors and scientists have perfected the use of electric pulses to treat and eliminate pain. TENS units use electro frequency at about 80 to 90 megahertz. According to doctors and medical professionals the TENS device is the most highly effective treatment for pain relief. Unlike prescription or over-the-counter drugs, TENS units are side-effect free when used as directed by a qualified healthcare professional.

A TENS unit transmits small square electrical pulses to the electrodes, which transmit this electrical pulse to the underlying nerves. The fundamental components of a TENS unit are the electrodes, a highly advanced computer chip, and an electrical battery source. A small amount of electricity is transmitted through the computer component then to the electrodes, which transmits the electrical waveform to the underlying nerves. The user can personalize the pulse frequency, which is the strength of the electrical current given to the electrode.

TENS units are prescribed for both acute pain and chronic pain conditions such as arthritis, joint pain, and fibromyalgia. For some people with chronic pain, a TENS unit provides pain relief that can last for several hours. For others, a TENS unit may help reduce the amount of pain medications needed. Some people hook the unit onto a belt turning it on and off as needed. The cost of a TENS unit can range from about $100 to several hundred dollars. These units can be purchased or rented. A prescription is usually necessary for insurance reimbursement of a TENS unit.

Biofeedback

Biofeedback has proved to be another effective, active method you can learn to apply to further participate in your own treatment. Biofeedback is a treatment technique where you are trained to improve your health by using signals from your own body. Physical therapists use biofeedback to help stroke victims regain movement in paralyzed muscles. Psychologists use biofeedback to help tense and anxious people learn to relax. Specialists in many different fields use biofeedback to help their patients cope with their chronic pain.

Devine (1988) discusses the condition of *dysponesis*, also called faulty bracing, where people tense up their muscles to pain thereby intensifying the pain experience. Dysponesis is defined by Doreland's Medical Dictionary as follows: "*A reversible physio-*

pathologic state consisting of unnoticed, misdirected neurophysiologic reactions to various agents (environmental events, bodily sensations, emotions, and thoughts) and the repercussions of these reactions throughout the organism." One of the most direct methods for coping with dysponesis involves the use of biofeedback. This procedure teaches you to let go of stress and tension.

According to many biofeedback practitioners, an effective biofeedback training program should be progressive and include several steps. The program starts with an accurate diagnosis of the problem followed by implementation of the proper treatment modality and time for you to practice in situations that simulate instances where the symptoms most often arise. Learning to use meditation and relaxation techniques to reduce stress would also be a helpful complement to the biofeedback process.

Hypnosis and Self-Hypnosis

Hypnosis has long been understood to produce varied effects in subjects. Although the public at large tends to associate hypnosis with stage performances and bad sitcom episodes, the medical community has approached the topic differently. Originally viewed as a magical cure-all, hypnosis has undergone tremendous amounts of scientific testing in modern times. When used in an appropriate manner, hypnosis has proved to be an effective tool in the management of pain and pain perception.

Watkins and Watkins (1990) stated that the most common psychological explanation for how hypnosis works is based upon a dissociation model. This model has been seen in patients with a multiple personality disorder. Dissociation eliminates pain by placing it in a sort of psychological storage area, away from your primary consciousness. This model of dissociation is commonly referred to as the "hidden observer" model of cognition.

Wall and Jones (1991) believe that stress reduction practice, as well as other nonpharmacological approaches, combined with biofeedback, has proved to be an excellent way to reduce pain symptoms. Wall and Jones also discuss hypnosis and meditation as effective "belief and attitude" therapy approaches that are successful in treating chronic pain. Dean was open to hypnotherapy, especially when he learned to use self-hypnosis to enhance his pain management.

> Self-hypnosis has proved
> effective for chronic pain management.

Self-hypnosis has proved to be an effective tool for other people and their pain management programs, aside from Dean's experience. A major benefit is that it releases you from a passive recipient role and supports you to become an active participant in your own healing. Self-hypnosis is a procedure where you are taught a simple technique to bring yourself to the alpha state—the place each of us goes every night just before we drift off to sleep. The difference, though, is that you do not sleep. You experience, instead, a heightened state of awareness where the "chatter" in your conscious mind is quieted and your subconscious mind is allowed to do what it does best—take care of your body. This opposite capacity of your body's reaction to stress has been called the alpha state, meditation, the sleep state, and the *relaxation response*. It is a conscious application of your body's innate ability to heal itself simply by relaxing.

The Emotional Link

Most addiction treatment professionals realize the importance of teaching their patients how to deal appropriately with emotional issues to reduce their stress and anxiety. The Gorski-CENAPS® Model is based in part on the belief that avoiding or covering up painful emotions will often lead a recovering person to relapse.

Unfortunately, many pain clinics do not focus on the emotional component. In their review of thirty-two multimodal pain treatment programs, Corey, Linssen, and Spinhoven (1992) found many interventions and treatment approaches being used; however, none of those programs used emotional modalities. Fortunately, over the past decade, this is changing at some of the truly multidisciplinary integrated pain management programs.

Corey and Solomon (1989) devote an entire chapter of their book to chronic pain and emotions. They explore the different treatment strategies needed to deal with emotions such as anger, depression, and anxiety. Some of the methods include cognitive-behavioral therapy exercises, as well as meditation and relaxation techniques.

Roy (1992) is another advocate of the link between chronic pain and emotions. Roy also believes in many cases, especially when there is clear and unambiguous evidence of suppressed or repressed emotional issues, that dynamic psychotherapy is an effective treatment modality.

> Using the Twelve Steps to Manage Pain

Martha Cleveland (1999), in her book *Chronic Illness and the Twelve Steps: A Practical Approach to Spiritual Resilience*, maintains that dealing with the emotional component of chronic pain is an extremely effective treatment approach. Cleveland adapts and incorporates the Twelve Steps of Alcoholics Anonymous, showing people with chronic pain issues how to improve the quality of their lives and effectively deal with their emotions. Jean and Dean used Cleveland's book as part of their healing process.

Meditation

Dealing with emotions and promoting faster healing can be facilitated through the use of meditation. Meditation involves using any number of awareness techniques to quiet the mind and relax the body. Concentration practices and mindfulness meditation are perhaps the best known. Research shows meditation can help relieve many arthritis symptoms, such as physical pain, anxiety, stress, and depression, as well as ease the fatigue and insomnia associated with fibromyalgia. It affects many body processes connected with well-being and relaxation. Recent studies suggest meditation may balance the immune system to help your body resist disease and even heal.

> Meditation has proved to be effective for chronic pain treatment.

Khalsa and Stauth (2002) discuss in their book, *Meditation as Medicine,* the process of using an adapted version of *Kundalini Yoga* and meditation to help the body heal itself. By committing to a daily structure of breathing and meditation, patients were able to reduce their pain and suffering.

Kundalini Yoga is a system of meditative techniques and movements within the yogic tradition that focuses on psycho-spiritual growth and the body's potential for maturation. The practice of Kundalini Yoga consists of a number of bodily postures, expressive movements and utterances, characterological meditations, breathing patterns, and degrees of concentration. Recently, there has been a growing interest within the medical community to study the physiological effects of meditation, and some of these studies have applied the discipline of Kundalini Yoga to their clinical settings.

Coffey-Lewis (1982) describes how the practice of meditation leads to true and lasting healing. Coffey-Lewis discusses how meditation takes on many different definitions for different individuals. For some, meditation is used for stress reduction; for others, it is a scientific way of interconnecting parts of the brain. Still, others find it helpful in healing the splits in personality and integrating wholeness.

Martha Cleveland also promotes the use of meditation for improving the quality of life and for self-healing. Meditation is also a part of the Twelve-Step process—the Eleventh Step. Reilly (1993) analyzes Step Eleven, showing people with chronic pain how to apply it towards their healing process and how to effectively use meditation. Jean and Dean spent a portion of many of their therapy sessions practicing breathing and meditation processes until they learned to automatically incorporate it into their daily schedules.

Evoking the Relaxation Response

There are many techniques and exercises for bringing about deep relaxation or the relaxation response. These include such things as breathing techniques, progressive muscle relaxation, visualizing a peaceful image, meditation, imagery, among others. In general, breathing exercises seem to be the easiest way to learn to elicit the relaxation response and is probably the most appropriate initial technique that you can use. The exercises are straightforward and require a minimal amount of body movement. This makes them easy to apply to most chronic pain conditions, even those where restriction of movement or position may be part of the functional problem.

Dr. Margaret Caudill (2001) devotes two chapters in her book, *Managing Pain before It Manages You,* to the importance of evoking this relaxation response as an integral component of pain management. However, you need to distinguish the difference between the *relaxation response* versus simply *relaxing*. When learning relaxation training as part of chronic pain management, some people often ask if they can simply do something they enjoy such as listening to music or sitting out in the backyard. Although these types of activities are certainly relaxing, they do not elicit this relaxation response.

The type of relaxation that works well in chronic pain management is a form of deep relaxation. Deep relaxation, or the relaxation response, refers to a specific physiological state that is the exact opposite of the way the body reacts when it is under stress. The relaxation response was first described by Dr. Herbert Benson and his colleagues at Harvard Medical School in the early 1970s. It involves a number of physical changes, including a decrease in
- heart rate,
- respiration rate,
- blood pressure,
- skeletal muscle tension,
- metabolism rate and oxygen consumption, and
- analytical thinking.

It also increases the alpha wave activity of the brain.

This type of deep relaxation or relaxation response can only be achieved with regular practice of a relaxation technique. Once you learn to elicit the relaxation response, you will notice feeling more relaxed even when not directly practicing the relaxation technique. The deep relaxation response also directly impacts the physical stressors associated with chronic pain and include

- pain reduction,
- control of medication side-effects such as nausea,
- enhanced immune response that may keep the patient healthier, and
- improved respiratory function.

Dealing with Grief/Loss Issues

One of the most difficult and crucial emotional issues that needs resolution is grief surrounding loss of health and/or prior level of functioning. Many people with chronic pain have lost careers, relationships, homes, and friends; other quality of life areas have been severely impacted as well.

Psychotherapists who facilitate the grieving process with their patients should be part of the APM team. A review of the works of Elizabeth Kubler-Ross on the grieving process would be helpful in this regard.

Grief work was an important part of healing for Jean and Dean, but especially so for Dean. One of the reasons Dean used medication was to help him function at a higher level of physical activity. Unfortunately, when he was under the influence of the pain medication, Dean overextended himself and, in some cases, exacerbated his old injury. Other times he incurred new injuries that increased the severity of his pain.

In addition, Dean had serious shame issues regarding what it meant to be a *real man*, especially in the area of sexuality. In fact, this sexuality/shame issue was a major precursor to a previous divorce, as well as his propensity to have affairs. These issues were also threatening his current marriage. For Dean, working through this grief/loss and shame was crucial to his avoiding future relapse episodes.

Acupuncture

Acupuncture is one of the oldest, most commonly used medical procedures in the world. Originating in China more than 2,000 years ago, acupuncture became better known in the United States in 1971 when *New York Times* reporter James Reston wrote about how doctors in China used needles to ease his pain after surgery.

The term "acupuncture" describes a family of procedures involving stimulation of anatomical points on the body by a variety of techniques. American practices of acupuncture incorporate medical traditions from China, Japan, Korea, and other countries. The acupuncture technique most studied scientifically involves penetrating the skin with thin, solid, metallic needles manipulated by the hands or by electrical stimulation.

Corey and Solomon (1989) discuss both the positive aspects of acupuncture and the fact that some people experience no benefit or limited benefit from it. Another drawback of this procedure is that frequent acupuncture treatments encourage a patient's passive role in treatment, which is counterproductive to effective ongoing pain management.

Jean experienced minimal benefit from acupuncture and discontinued it after a few sessions. Dean experienced only limited relief at first, but acupuncture eventually became a key intervention to help him reduce his major pain flare-ups. Many people with chronic pain experience significant benefits from acupuncture. An NCCAM (National Center for Complementary and Alternative Medicine, 2004) funded study recently showed that acupuncture provides significant pain relief, improves function for people with osteoarthritis of the knee, and serves as an effective complement to standard care.

Further research indicates there are additional areas where acupuncture interventions are useful. For example, promising results have emerged showing efficacy of acupuncture in adult postoperative and chemotherapy nausea and vomiting and in postoperative dental pain. There are other situations such as addiction, stroke rehabilitation, headache, menstrual cramps, tennis elbow, fibromyalgia, myofascial pain, osteoarthritis, low-back pain, carpal tunnel syndrome, and asthma where acupuncture may be useful as an adjunct treatment or as part of a comprehensive management program or even an acceptable treatment alternative.

Cold Laser Therapy

The term "cold laser" refers to the use of low intensity or low levels of laser light. Proponents claim that cold laser therapy can reduce pain and inflammation. The U.S. Food and Drug Administration (FDA) considers these laser devices investigational (experimental) and allows them to be used in studies based on evidence that they provide temporary pain relief.

Cold laser treatment is thought to help some types of pain, inflammation, and wound healing. These lasers are used directly on or over the affected area. Well-controlled scientific studies are underway using reliable low-level laser devices for pain, wounds, injuries, and other conditions. Certain types of cold laser treatments may eventually become part of conventional medical care.

Cold lasers are also used in acupuncture, where laser beams stimulate the body's acupoints rather than needles (see *Acupuncture* mentioned previously). This treatment regimen appeals to those who want acupuncture but fear pain or the idea of needles.

Chiropractic Treatment

Many people with chronic pain receive long-term pain reduction when undergoing chiropractic treatment. Chiropractic adjustments restore proper motion and function to damaged joints, thereby reducing irritation to associated muscles and nerves.

Most chiropractors are trained in nutrition and often include dietary changes and nutrient supplementation in their treatment plans. This process helps to build up your immune system while at the same time raising your pain threshold. Later in this chapter you will learn about the importance of using supplements as part of your healing process.

> Chiropractic care works very well for many chronic pain conditions.

There are a number of published studies supporting the effectiveness of chiropractic care for several types of chronic pain. For example, a study by Milne (1989) reported that out of 150 patients suffering migraine headaches, 98 percent experienced immediate relief of migraine through adjustments of the neck and through traction. Since many people are prescribed potentially addictive medication for migraine relief, chiropractic treatment could be a much safer and, often, a more effective alternative.

The largest comparative study of its time on treatment of back pain (Meade, 1995) concluded that chiropractic care was the superior treatment for chronic low-back pain. Some case studies on whiplash treatment (Osterbauer, 1992) suggest that chiropractic care is effective for relieving the chronic pain often experienced after these injuries.

Activator Methods® Chiropractic Technique

One of the newer, scientifically based chiropractic procedures is the *Activator Methods® Chiropractic Technique* (AMCT). The AMCT is described by Fuhr (1995) as a process of analysis and instrumentation designed to monitor and affect the neuromusculoskeletal system. The implement used is the *Activator Adjusting Instrument* (AAI), which is a patented, hand-held adjusting device, designed to generate reproducible and controlled results. However, as Fuhr points out, this process requires chiropractors to become certified via examinations to ensure a level of proficiency needed for effective and safe outcomes. So far, less than 20 percent of chiropractors have become certified.

Yoga for Pain Management

Living with chronic pain can be a cause of constant discomfort attacking your reserves of strength, energy, and feelings of well-being. Yoga is an ancient system developed in India that addresses the physical, mental, and spiritual aspects of the individual. There are many different forms of yoga practice, each of which emphasizes different skills and goals. Using Yoga techniques for pain management can help you minimize medication usage and help you lead a happier and fuller life.

Breathing • Relaxation • Meditation

Three of the best techniques for pain management are Yoga breathing, relaxation, and meditation (you saw examples of the latter two earlier). These three aspects of Yoga can distract the mind from pain, reduce the body's tension in reaction to pain, and provide an opportunity to *move through* the pain instead of resisting it.

The act of controlling the breath in Yoga reduces pain. Your body has a natural phenomenon built in to the nervous system that keeps tension in the muscles *on stand by* when the lungs are full or *pressurized.* Your muscles will relax upon exhalation, deflating the lungs. So lengthening the time of exhalation can help produce relaxation and reduce tension in your body.

Yoga works on the body to reduce or eliminate pain by helping your brain's pain center regulate the controlling mechanism located in the spinal cord. Yoga also assists your brain with secretion of natural painkillers through the body. The potential benefits of Yoga in pain management have recently begun to be documented. Studies have shown its positive effect on stress through a decrease in serum cortisol levels and an increase in alpha and theta brain waves. It may also be of benefit by increasing self-awareness, relaxation on physical and emotional levels, respiration, and self-understanding.

Movement Therapies for Improved Pain Management

Tai Chi and Qigong

Tai Chi and Qigong are gentle movement practices used for centuries in China for health, religious practice, and self-defense. As a form of exercise and relaxation, they have been used to improve balance and stability, reduce pain and stress, improve cardiovascular health, and promote mental and emotional calm and balance. Attitudes toward the basis of Tai Chi and Qigong vary markedly. Most Western medical practitioners, many practitioners of traditional Chinese medicine as well as the Chinese government, view Tai Chi and Qigong as a set of breathing and movement exercises that benefit health through stress reduction and exercise. Others see Tai Chi and Qigong in more metaphysical terms, claiming that breathing and movement exercises can influence the fundamental forces of the universe.

In the area of pain management, scientific studies have shown their benefit in reducing stress, as evidenced by alpha and theta brain wave increases, increases in B endorphin levels, and decreases in ACTH (Adrenocorticotropic hormone) levels. Effectiveness has also been shown for complex regional pain syndrome, fibromyalgia, and chronic low back pain when combined with education and relaxation training. Studies continue to clarify the mechanisms of action, benefits, and applications of these movement practices for health maintenance and disease management.

Developmental Model of Recovery Transition and Stabilization Tasks

Once you are engaged in treatment and have been withdrawn from problem medication, if needed, you are in what the Gorski-CENAPS® Developmental Model of Recovery refers to as the Transitional and Stabilization Stages of Recovery, covered earlier. According to this model there are four important tasks that need to be accomplished during these stages:
- Recovering physically from the withdrawal effects of chemicals
- Discontinuing a preoccupation with chemicals
- Learning to solve problems without using chemicals
- Developing hope and motivation for recovery

In a like manner, Stephanie Brown's (1989) Transitional Stage includes four tasks:

- Surrendering (hitting bottom)
- Forming of a new identity as an alcoholic and/or addict
- Discovering healthy behaviors to replace the addiction
- Learning relapse prevention strategies and abstinence skills

To give you the best hope of rapidly accomplishing these transitional tasks, you need to quickly integrate into the treatment milieu. At this point the DMC process, which was covered earlier, can be effectively implemented.

> APM® patients fit in better by attaining trust and safety.

Building trust and safety is crucial to help you fit in and bond. Many of you have learned to distrust others as a result of your dysfunctional family systems. By the time you enter treatment you may have become isolated or may be exhibiting paranoid and/or agoraphobic symptoms.

The DMC process will assist you in working through any denial or other defenses you may be using, while supporting you to trust others. This will enable you to admit and begin to accept your substance use disorder. You can then identify with others in the treatment program or support groups and transition into a stable recovery. Much of this work can be accomplished by participating in group therapy followed by individual sessions on an as-needed basis.

From Victim to Empowerment

Since one component of the preoccupation with medication usually stems from an appropriate need for pain reduction, nonpharmacological pain treatment modalities must be developed and put into place. The main goal during this phase of treatment is to empower yourself by transitioning away from your role as a passive participant in dealing with your pain. You need to believe that a proactive approach, including the above modalities and other cognitive-behavioral strategies, can be successfully implemented. Others have done it—so can you.

There are many other alternative, nontraditional pain management modalities a trained treatment team can prescribe and implement as indicated by the specific needs of each person. Some of these *Nonpharmacological Treatment Processes* were covered previously. All of the chosen strategies can become an integral part of your relapse prevention plan, which is covered later.

> APM® uses an individualized nonpharmacological team approach.

A traditional *cookie-cutter* approach has never delivered positive treatment outcomes with the *typical* addiction patient. Therefore, with the significantly more complicated problems that occur with chronic pain conditions (*Addiction Pain Syndrome*®), the approaches used must be individualized and wide-ranging. To that end, teamwork among all healthcare providers is essential. You must become the captain of your team and encourage all of your providers to communicate with you and each other, so everyone can work together as a team.

> Nutrition and Exercise

Nutrition and Healing

Until recently there has been a lack of information and a great deal of misinformation regarding the role of proper nutrition for effective pain management. The purpose of this section is to introduce you to some of the methods used as a part of the APM treatment approach.

Recent research studies by the National Fibromyalgia Association (NFA) have confirmed that diet and nutrition play a significant role in the management of pain. The NFA (2006) reports that success relies upon utilizing a multidisciplinary and multidimensional approach, incorporating lifestyle and dietary changes to achieve optimum health and well-being.

The NFA also states that nutritional therapy practitioners are successfully using diet to treat and prevent illness and restore the body to a natural healthy equilibrium. Some healthcare practitioners believe that deficiencies of minerals and vitamins could be responsible for much disease and weakness in the body. Examples of conditions resulting from deficiencies include fatigue, lethargy, and susceptibility to colds and viruses.

The role of proper diet and exercise as a part of addictive disorder recovery has been recognized for a long time. There is a significant amount of information about this in the recovery literature, such as the books *Passages through Recovery* (Gorski, 1989) and *Staying Sober* (Gorski & Miller, 1986).

There is also substantial pain management literature emphasizing the importance of nutrition and exercise in the healing process and effective pain management. In fact, Dr. Margaret Caudill (2001) devotes an entire chapter of her book, *Managing Your Pain Before It Manages You*, to nutrition in an effective pain management program.

> Nutrition impacts healing.

Later on, we will discuss and suggest some effective diet and exercise treatment plans and review the plans developed by Jean and Dean. Since in-depth coverage of nutrition and exercise is beyond the scope of this book, you will be introduced to several resources for additional research and information in the Appendix. You may also consider obtaining referrals to appropriate nutritionists in your area. Be sure to have consent releases signed to facilitate teamwork, treatment planning, and effective follow-up.

Nutrition and Pain
Foods That Help or Hinder

Murray and Pizzorno (1991) state that diet has little effect on a person's experience of pain, but it probably influences pain perception by the way it is associated with inflammation.

When metabolized, some fats and fatty acids may have a tendency to intensify the inflammation response, so their intake should be closely monitored. In addition, certain foods act as triggers for certain pain conditions, such as migraine headaches.

Some of the problem substances that are linked to increases in pain are caffeine, alcohol, monosodium glutamate (MSG), and aspartame (NutraSweet®). On the other hand, some foods have been credited with pain reduction—e.g., cherries and soy. (*Anthocyanins*, which give tart cherries their deep red color, have anti-inflammatory properties similar to those in aspirin. Soy can help relieve some osteoarthritis pain.) Caudill (2001) reports that foods linked to a decrease in pain include vegetarian diets as well as diets high in complex carbohydrates and low in protein.

Using a Food Diary

The use of a food diary can be beneficial in discovering which foods may be a part of the problem or part of the solution. For optimal success this should be done under the supervision of your doctor or nutritionist.

Ford (1994) reports that consumption of bioflavonoids, as found in fresh cherries—as well as eating other foods such as vegetables, legumes, whole grains, and some types of nuts—may supplement some of the vitamins that may be deficient in people with chronic pain. However, caution must be used when taking vitamin and mineral supplements, especially with the tendency of chronic pain patients to use megadoses—the mistaken belief being that if a little is good, a lot is better. Two conditions that seem to respond well to dietary changes are rheumatoid arthritis and gout.

The Naturopathy Controversy

Proper nutrition plays a role in the art of *naturopathy* (nature cure). Naturopathy is not universally accepted by the traditional medical society but has proved to be effective for many people.

Traditional naturopaths do not diagnose or treat disease, but instead focus on health and education. They teach their clients how to create an internal and external environment that is conducive to good health, enabling the clients to make their own choices. Naturopathy is based on the belief that the body is self-healing. The body will repair itself and recover from illness spontaneously if it is in a healthy environment. Naturopaths have many remedies and recommendations for creating a healthy environment so the body can spontaneously heal itself. The philosophy of naturopathic healing is based in part on the following:

- Discover and eliminate the primary cause of pain.
- Use the most natural, nontoxic, and least invasive therapy possible.
- Treat the whole person.
- Teach the person to develop a healthy diet.
- Support the body's own healing abilities.

Recent studies provide significant information and scientific data to ensure the safety and effectiveness of some naturopathic remedies. Although, as Murray and Pizzorno (1991) point out, some therapies using colonic irrigation may be dangerous and lead to unwanted side effects, such as infections. Dr. Stephen Barrett (2006) suggests that a closer look at naturopathy's philosophy will show it is simplistic and some of its practices are riddled with quackery.

Importance of Weight Management

Weight management is a key reason for good nutrition as many chronic pain conditions become worse the more weight a person gains. Catalano and Hardin (1996) discuss how gaining weight can lead to a rise in back pain and increase the pressure on degenerative joints; whereas, being underweight can lead to an impaired immune system and frequent illnesses. This is one of the reasons APM incorporates nutrition and exercise into every treatment plan.

> The human body functions most effectively at its optimal weight.

While Dean was near his optimal weight, Jean needed some additional interventions to reduce her weight by about forty pounds. Jean's extra weight made it difficult for her to want to exercise, due to her fear of being judged by those watching her. In addition to a proper food plan, a prescription to join a hydrotherapy class that catered to overweight patients was the turning point for Jean. As she began to lose weight, her pain started to decrease and her self-esteem and motivation to take better care of herself increased.

Herbal and Homeopathic Remedies

Some chronic pain practitioners use the pain relieving effects of herbs as an adjunct to a healthy nutritional plan. Murray (1995) states that according to the World Health Organization about 80 percent of the world uses herbal remedies. For example, the science of herbs is at the core of Chinese medicine. Also, a significant percentage of pharmaceutical products in the United States contain ingredients from plants. Fortunately, there has been an increase in research on herbal remedies, several have proved to be beneficial with negligible side effects.

On the other hand, some herbs have been found to have serious—and in some cases lethal—side effects. The vast majority of homeopathic medicines are also derived from plants, but before a remedy can be recognized as an official homeopathic medicine, it must be tested scientifically on healthy humans under a double-blind procedure to determine safety and effectiveness.

> Homeopathy—
> Science or Pseudoscience?

Homeopathy holds to the premise that treating the sick with extremely diluted agents in undiluted doses, produces similar symptoms in healthy individuals. Its adherents and practitioners assert that the therapeutic potency of a remedy can be increased by serial dilution of the drug, combined with what homeopaths call *succusion* or vigorous shaking.

Not altogether unlike conventional medicine, homeopathy regards diseases as *morbid derangements of the organism*. Homeopathy views a sick person as having a dynamic disturbance in a hypothetical *vital force*. This disturbance, homeopaths claim, underlies standard medical diagnoses of named diseases. However, many critics describe homeopathy as a pseudoscience and quackery. Homeopaths' claim that extreme dilution makes drugs more powerful is inconsistent with the laws of chemistry and physics.

Exercise and Healing

Most healthcare providers will readily agree that regular exercise is good for you and, when combined with a healthy diet, will help people gain or lose weight and generally improve their quality of life. Unfortunately, many people with a chronic pain condition mistakenly believe they can no longer get the full benefits of exercise. Egoscue (1998) is very adamant that flexibility and mobility are the keys to successful pain management. You must exercise, but it may be different than how you did it before. Pete Egoscue is responsible for establishing over twenty-five clinics worldwide, with corporate headquarters in San Diego, California. The Egoscue Method® is one of the world leaders in nonmedical pain relief.

Type, Frequency, and Style

Exercise can and should be part of all pain management plans. To develop an effective and safe program the type and frequency of exercise should be developed by someone with experience and clinical skills. Action, rest, and immobilization periods (or up-time and down-time) should also be an integral foundation of the plan.

Other considerations include the style of exercise, the progression of intensity, the frequency or quantity, and the prevention of additional injury. As mentioned earlier, hydrotherapy and water exercises can be very beneficial for people with chronic pain issues.

Most treatment providers working with pain management believe mobilization through exercise is an essential component of a successful treatment plan. Exercise helps increase range of motion, which is essential for increasing mobility and healing.

Again, the development of an exercise program should be done under the direction of a well-trained specialist. For some this will be their doctor, chiropractor, physical therapist, and/or personal trainer. Whichever specialist is chosen should become a part of your APM treatment team. Effective communication should be ongoing due to any exercise challenges that may occur for you.

> Using an exercise specialist is important.

Using an appropriate and trained exercise specialist is essential due to the different types of pain issues involved, as well as the different types of exercise modalities available to choose from.

> Three Types of Exercise
> Isotonic—Isometric—Isokinetic

There are basically three types of exercise and each achieves different results. The first type—isotonic—is active muscle contraction, moving a joint partially or thoroughly through its range of motion. Some examples of isotonic exercise include flexing and extending various limbs, with or without using resistance.

The second type is also an active exercise—isometric—where the joint remains still during the muscle contraction.

The third type—isokinetic—is where resistance is applied to force muscles to exert maximum force throughout the range of motion. Isokinetic exercise requires specialized equipment.

Dr. Margaret Caudill (2001) emphasizes the need for aerobic exercise at least three times a week to improve health and weight management. Many people with pain are afraid that their pain will increase if they become too active. However, the risks of not exercising far outweigh the fear of what "might" happen as a result of developing an exercise regime. Dr. Caudill states that if people are careful and progress slowly, they are not likely to worsen their condition.

Some of the forms of exercise recommended by Dr. Caudill include the following:
- Water exercise
- Stationary bike riding
- Treadmill use
- Walking
- Yoga or Tai Chi
- Indoor cross-country ski equipment use

When removing the pain is not possible, using exercise can increase your level of functioning and improve your quality of life, allowing you to more effectively manage your pain. As mentioned earlier, Egoscue (1998) believes that flexibility and mobility are the best pathways towards reducing debilitating chronic pain. Another benefit of exercise is the increased ability of your body to produce additional endorphins. As we discussed earlier, these neurotransmitters help the body manage pain.

Catalano and Hardin (1996) note the fact that people who gradually incorporate exercise into their pain management treatment plan return to a higher level of functioning and maintain more effective pain management. They also recommend a program of exercise that includes proper posture and stretching. Catalano and Hardin also show a secondary gain for exercise—reducing isolation tendencies.

Using Exercise to Socialize

As mentioned in an earlier chapter, isolation tendencies are common for people with chronic pain. Such was the case for Jean and Dean. Jean used her hydrotherapy and water exercise classes as a place to socialize and share with people in a similar situation. Dean socialized much less than Jean, but he was able to form a few close relationships with people who frequented the health club he joined.

Exercise and Stress Reduction

Reducing and managing stress is an additional reason for exercise. As discussed earlier, Jean and Dean noticed a high correlation between stress and the intensity of their pain symptoms. Each of these patients used their exercise program as an integral part of their stress management strategy.

Dean noticed that if his stress levels were above a level seven and he could go swim a few laps, he discovered that his level would go down to a four or five and he would be able to manage it more effectively. He also noticed that the distress he experienced as a result of his pain symptoms decreased at the same time.

In addition to effective stress management, Jean used exercise to reduce her weight and increase her energy level. She noticed that after she gained weight, her pain symptoms increased. When she began a proper diet and exercise program, she reduced her weight and her pain symptoms decreased.

Exercise and Depression

As mentioned earlier, depression is very common for people who live with a chronic pain condition. Managing depression is another reason for a person with chronic pain to exercise. Many therapists who work with people with various depressive mood disorders note that a regular exercise program is often a component of the treatment plan, but suggest that additional measures are often needed. These could include nutritional changes and even antidepressants in some appropriate cases.

Diet and Exercise for Healthy Recovery

In addition to being an important part of an effective pain management program, a proper nutrition and exercise plan are essential components of a chemical dependency recovery plan. When people use any psychoactive chemicals for a prolonged period of time, biochemical changes occur. Some of those changes were discussed earlier.

When people stop using drugs—whether it be prescription medication, alcohol, or other drugs—they often experience withdrawal symptoms. Fortunately, those symptoms are fairly short lived, from between three days to five or six weeks.

Unfortunately, what follows is a period of protracted or post acute withdrawal (PAW). PAW can last between eighteen months to three years. The symptoms of PAW will be discussed in the next chapter. Effective management for PAW includes a healthy nutritious diet and regular exercise as discussed earlier. Also, risk of relapse decreases significantly when people have an effective pain management and recovery program in place. This is covered in the following chapter.

> Nutrition and exercise are essential components of a relapse prevention plan.

An ongoing practice of healthy nutrition and exercise can be a challenge to accomplish, but isn't impossible. Over a long period of time your motivation may diminish, being replaced with boredom, forgetfulness, and distractions. However, your tendencies towards self-sabotage will significantly decrease by having an effective relapse prevention plan in place that includes nutrition and exercise, along with other components covered in the following chapter.

In an earlier chapter I talked about the *Addiction Pain Syndrome*®. A synergistic effect is produced when pain and addiction symptoms coexist, so it is essential to use a multidimensional treatment plan. That chapter emphasized the importance of combining the *Nonpharmacological Treatment Processes* with *Medication Management Components*. The next chapter emphasizes the use of a relapse prevention plan that treats the synergistic effects of the *Addiction Pain Syndrome*. This process is called *Reciprocal Relapse Prevention*. You will also learn how Jean and Dean completed APM *Core Clinical Exercises Five* and *Six*.

- **Call to Action for the Seventh Chapter**

It is time to summarize what you have learned so far now that you have come to the end of the seventh chapter. Please answer the questions below.

1. What is the most important thing you have learned about yourself and your ability to help yourself as a result of completing Chapter Seven?

2. What are you willing to commit to do differently as a result of what you have learned by completing this chapter?

3. What obstacles might get in the way of making these changes and what can you do to overcome these roadblocks?

Take time to pause and reflect, then
go to the next page to review Chapter Eight.

Chapter Eight
Reciprocal Relapse Prevention

The CENAPS® Model of Relapse Prevention

This stage of treatment is crucial because chronic pain is such a serious problem for many recovering people, often leading them to relapse. Over the past decade, relapse prevention planning has become a key ingredient in addiction treatment programs around the world. Many of these programs use the CENAPS® Model of relapse prevention, an innovative and dynamic process developed by Terence T. Gorski.

This method includes how to identify high-risk situations for relapse, analyze and manage high-risk situations, develop a relapse prevention network, and construct an early intervention plan to be implemented if you begin to experience serious signs of relapse.

Unfortunately, a literature review did not reveal any medical model pain clinics incorporating intensive relapse prevention plans into their treatment programs. However, some innovative pain programs that use a biopsychosocial approach do include some relapse prevention planning.

> Relapse prevention planning is a critical component of the APM® treatment plan!

This chapter will illustrate the relapse prevention protocols that I used with Jean and Dean. I will also review *Exercises Five* through *Eight* from the *Addiction-Free Pain Management® Workbook,* and you will see how Jean and Dean completed that portion of their relapse prevention and recovery planning work.

Redefining Relapse

Progressive Nature of Relapse: Stability to Dysfunction

Relapse education must start with a new definition of relapse:

> Relapse is a progressive series of events that takes an individual from stable recovery to a state of becoming dysfunctional in their recovery.

The relapse process is marked by predictable and identifiable warning signs that begin long before inappropriate pain medication, including alcohol and other drug use, or collapse occurs. This makes intervention possible for some of you before inappropriate medication use begins (including alcohol or other drugs). The appropriate response to a relapse is to stop the relapse quickly by using a preplanned intervention: being open to placement in the appropriate level of care and getting stabilized, honestly assessing the factors that contributed to your relapse, revising your recovery plan, and working your new personal recovery plan as quickly as possible.

When you begin the slide toward relapse, you undergo many changes; the first occurs in your thinking. Recovery-prone positive thinking is replaced by relapse-prone negative thinking and euphoric recall. Euphoric recall is remembering how good taking the pain medication used to be and self-talk about how awful it is not to be able to use your medication the way that you want to now.

This negative thinking leads to an experience of uncomfortable and/or painful emotions. These feelings produce self-defeating urges, which are often followed by self-destructive behaviors. Inappropriate use of pain medication may not be an option in the early stages of relapse, but the negative behaviors often lead you to experience more problems. Many of these problems also impact other people—often hurting those that you love the most.

Relapse and Post Acute Withdrawal

One of the biggest relapse triggers in early recovery is your inability to recognize and/or cope with the serious symptoms of protracted or post acute withdrawal (PAW). PAW is a series of biological and psychological symptoms that everyone in chemical recovery goes through. The brain chemistry is adapting and healing from the long-term toxic effects of the medication, including alcohol/drug use. Remember, in Chapter Two this toxic effect was called *Substance-Induced Organic Mental Disorders*.

> **There are six major symptoms of PAW:**
> - Cognitive (thinking) disturbances
> - Emotional management impairment
> - Sleep disturbances
> - Short-term and long-term memory problems
> - Physical coordination problems
> - An increased sensitivity to stress

When you are also experiencing chronic pain, post acute withdrawal symptoms are often amplified by the accompanying stress of that condition.

Relapse Prevention Planning

Relapse prevention starts with assessment and treatment planning followed by a high-risk situation identification process. High-Risk situations for people with chronic pain are events that create an urge to use inappropriate pain medication or other drugs (including alcohol) after making a commitment to work an effective pain management program and use only approved medication exactly as prescribed. They also include situations that make you want to stop using an effective pain management program despite promises to yourself to lead a healthy lifestyle.

Identifying and Managing Core Issues

Besides *core psychological issues* and *core addiction issues*, you also contend with *core pain issues*. Core pain issues are problems caused by a chronic pain condition and your response to that condition. An example of a core pain issue is the cyclical increase (flare-up) of pain due to the stresses of everyday living.

Core addictive issues are problems caused by the addiction itself that would not exist if the addiction had not developed. The issues create emotional pain and dysfunction in recovery and require a recovery plan. Denial is a prime example of a core addictive issue, and, in the case of people living with chronic pain, is often much stronger. For example, some of you might say, "I can't be an addict because I have a real pain condition and a doctor gave me the meds." Jean and Dean identified this type of denial as one of their mistaken beliefs.

Core psychological issues are repeating problems caused by unresolved issues from childhood or unresolved adult trauma. They create a deeply entrenched system of irrational beliefs that coexist with the core addictive issues. Some common examples are posttraumatic stress disorder (PTSD), depression, and personality disorders. In fact, a chronic pain condition will often retrigger PTSD. This is an area where a trained psychotherapist can have the greatest effectiveness.

Relapse Justifications

Relapse justifications are patterns of irrational thinking that create an immediate justification for inappropriate medication use. There are five common/basic justifications:
- Euphoric recall ("It worked in the past so it must be OK now.")
- Awfulizing sobriety ("Sobriety is and always will be a terrible struggle.")
- Magical thinking ("This time I know using chemicals will fix me.")
- Low tolerance for frustration ("I can't stand feeling so bad about...")
- Minimization ("This time I will only use a little," or "I'll use just this once.")

One of the most common relapse justifications for many people with chronic pain is: "I have a legitimate reason to be in pain; therefore, it's OK to do anything I can to stop my pain." It is critical to learn how to identify and talk back to your relapse justifications and find recovery-prone ways to manage your warning signs or high-risk situations.

Exercise Seven (Analyzing and Managing High-Risk Situations) in the *Addiction-Free Pain Management® Workbook* is an ideal tool for learning how to challenge old ways of coping as well as developing recovery-prone action plans. This exercise will be described later in the chapter.

Developing a Relapse Prevention Network

For effective warning sign or high-risk situation management, a relapse prevention network must be developed. An effective relapse prevention network consists of you, your therapist, appropriate family members and/or significant others, healthcare professionals, and appropriate Twelve-Step support people (including an appropriate sponsor).

You work together with this network to develop a relapse intervention plan. This is one more way you can take an active role in your recovery process. You share your high-risk situations and warning signs with your network and let each member know what to do if any active warning signs and/or symptoms of inappropriate medication use arise. Identifying early critical warning signs and sharing that knowledge with your relapse prevention network greatly increases your chances of stopping a relapse process before the actual chemical use begins.

> High-risk situations are any experiences that activate urges to self-medicate despite your best intentions not to relapse.

As discussed earlier, relapse prevention counseling starts with assessment and treatment planning followed by a high-risk situation identification process. A high-risk situation is any experience that can activate the urge to use inappropriate pain medication (including alcohol or other drugs) despite a commitment not to. It is a situation that makes you want to stop using your effective pain management program despite promises to yourself or others.

The following section explains *Exercise Five* in the *Addiction-Free Pain Management® Workbook*—the High-Risk Situation exercise.

Exercise Five: Identifying and Personalizing Your High-Risk Situations

Defining the concept of a high-risk situation can be complicated. Some situations activate self-defeating urges for some people and not others. The same situation can activate your self-defeating urges at certain times but not others.

Exercise Five is broken down into three separate parts. *Part 1* is designed to help you identify a high-risk situation you will be facing in the near future and then to personalize it. You start doing this by completing the following exercise from the *Addiction-Free Pain Management® Workbook*.

Exercise Five, Part 1: Identifying an Immediate Pain and Medication High-Risk Situation

Defining High-Risk Situations

A high-risk situation is something that happens that creates an urge to use inappropriate pain medication or other drugs (including alcohol) after making a commitment not to. It can also be a situation that creates an urge to stop using your effective pain management program despite your promises to yourself. You don't get into high-rish situations by accident. But sometimes you mistakenly believe you are drawn to these situations. Once you are in the situation, you don't know what to do. You convince yourself it's really not your fault you are in this situation. You didn't plan it. It just happened and there's nothing you can do about it. Defining the concept of a high-risk situation can be tricky. The same type of situation can be a problem at one time, but not another.

1. **Identify an immediate high-risk situation:** Please think ahead over the next several weeks, and identify a situation that could tempt you to deviate from your Medication Management Agreement despite your commitment not to use inappropriately. Or identify a situation that would cause you to stop working an effective pain management plan. Write a short sentence that describes that situation.

2. **How does this situation increase your risk of using pain medication?** Write one or two sentences that describe how this situation might change your thinking or behavior and lead you to violate your Medication Management Agreement or sabotage your effective pain management.

3. **Write a personal title:** In the space below write a word or short phrase that accurately describes your high-risk situation. This

word or phrase should be in your words and have emotional impact on you. Personal Title: _____

4. **Write a personal description:** Write a complete sentence that describes the high-risk situation. Do not use any of the words that you used in your Personal Title and follow this format: *I know I'm in a high-risk situation when <I do something> that causes <pain> and I think about or have an urge to use inappropriate pain medication (including alcohol or other drugs) to manage the pain or to solve my problems.* Example: I know I'm in a high-risk situation when <I stop swimming daily> and that causes <my lower back to start hurting> so I start fantasizing about taking my old pills to make my pain go away.

5. **Risk of using inappropriate pain medication:** How high a risk are you for using inappropriate pain medication or other self-defeating behaviors to manage this situation?
(Patients are asked to pick a rating between 0 and 10.)

6. **Why do you rate your risk at that level?** Please explain your answer.

Jean's High-Risk Situation

Jean identified a situation where she was going to have to meet with her oldest daughter's schoolteacher for parent-teacher night. She recognized that this situation increased her stress levels and intensified her pain. She reported feeling a strong sense of shame because the teacher knew about her medication problems; the school environment also triggered flashbacks from her own traumatic school history.

The title she chose was *"I Can't Do This."* She completed the sentence this way: "I know I'm in a high-risk situation when I get upset and ashamed, then my stress level goes up, which causes my pain to increase and I want to take a pill." She believed she had a 50 to 60 percent chance of using her medication inappropriately at this point, because she couldn't see any other options.

> Dean's High-Risk Situation

Dean chose a situation where it was likely he would have to confront his fear of talking about the affair he had. His wife asked him to start couples therapy with the expectation he would be emotionally open and truthful with her during their sessions.

The title he chose was *"Pure Panic."* He reported he was especially afraid, because if she found out about his past affairs, she would divorce him and he would be all alone. He completed the sentence this way: "I know I'm in a high-risk situation when I tell myself I need to take something to boost my courage and take the edge off my fear." He believed that he rated at a 60 to 70 percent chance of using, so he was very anxious.

> *Please take a few minutes to complete this exercise in your* APM Workbook.

Part 2 of *Exercise Five* in the *Addiction-Free Pain Management® Workbook* asks you to read the high-risk situation list that was developed specifically for the APM population. The following list contains nineteen common high-risk situations. You may relate to some of these.

Exercise Five, Part 2: Reading the APM High-Risk Situation List

Instructions:

As you read each of the high-risk situations (HRS) below, rate each high-risk situation on a scale of 0 to 10, with 0 meaning this has not, does not, and probably will not apply to me and 10 meaning that it has been, is, or could be a serious problem for me. Realize that you may have an urge to minimize or rationalize these situations, or some people may even start feeling very upset by what they read. If this happens to you, note it so you can share this reaction with someone you trust.

1. ☐ **We only want to stop because we have problems:** We experience a serious problem or crisis related to our pain medication (including alcohol) or other drug use. We feel an inner conflict. One part of us wants to keep taking the medication despite the problem. Another part of us says no and holds us back, because going back to using inappropriately would cause even more serious problems. We convince ourselves that it would be a good idea to stop taking the medication until the situation calms down, but we feel deprived. Since we don't believe we can continue coping with life without our pain medication, we leave the door open to change our mind later when things have calmed down.

2. ☐ **We don't see the connection:** We are blind to the relationship between our use of pain medication (including alcohol) or other drugs and the problems that we're having. We convince ourselves that we need to use pain medication despite the problems. Nobody has the right to make us stop. We tell ourselves that the real problem isn't our pain medication—it's the pain we have. Sure we've got some serious problems. That's why we're taking the medication—to help us cope with those problems. Besides, a doctor prescribed it for us, so it must be all right.

3. ☐ **We deny we have a problem with medication:** We tell ourselves we're in control of our pain medication use; it doesn't control us. We can stop forever if only the pain would stop for good. We're not taking the medication now and that proves we're in control. Nobody is going to convince us that we're weak-willed or some kind of a drug addict.

4. ☐ **We push away those who threaten our continued pain medication use:** We prove we're not an addict or drug abuser by telling ourselves that we have friends and people who care about us and they don't see a problem with our using the medication the way we are. There are other people who don't like us using the medication the way we are. It's these people, who aren't really our friends, who want us to stop and even suffer with our pain. If they were really our friends, they wouldn't be causing us problems by sticking their noses in where they don't belong. They would realize that we deserve

to have the medication. If they'd just leave us alone, then everything would be just fine.

5. ❐ **We only remember the good times:** We start remembering how good it was to use our pain medication in the past. We make our memories bigger than life by exaggerating the relief we got while minimizing or blocking out the emotional pain and the negative side effects we experienced. We start to convince ourselves that we always felt good and never experienced any pain or problems when we were taking our pain medication the way we wanted.

6. ❐ **We "awfulize" being without pain medication:** We start thinking about how hard it is to stay away from pain medication. We convince ourselves it is awful, terrible, and unbearable to have to live without using our pain medication the way we want. Sober living is nothing but pain, problems, and hassles. Without pain medication we can never have a pain-free, good quality of life.

7. ❐ **We use magical thinking:** We believe that pain medication can magically fix us. We mistakenly believe that pain medication would always make us feel good and solve all of our problems. We convince ourselves that this time we won't abuse it or lose control. We'll use it responsibly. Besides, it will just be this one time. We'll only use for a short period of time until the pain settles down. Then we'll just stop again.

8. ❐ **We get into problem situations:** We start putting ourselves into situations that create unnecessary stress, pain, and problems. Sometimes we make our pain worse when we have a legitimate pain flare-up by doing things that make it worse instead of better. We shoot ourselves in the foot by not using effective pain management and experience the negative consequences. Then we reload the gun and shoot ourselves in the other foot.

9. ❐ **We overcommit:** Sometimes we take on more than we can handle and start missing deadlines and letting other people down. This causes our stress to increase leading to our pain getting worse. Instead of talking openly about our problems, we go underground, put things off, blame others, and

try to cover our tracks. If we get caught, we get defensive and try to rationalize or explain our way out of it.

10. ☐ **We get frustrated:** Sometimes we get frustrated because we want something that we can't have—a totally pain free life. When this happens, we feel deprived because we should be able to have it. We deserve it. We're entitled to it. Others don't have the right to keep us from getting it, even if we need to use inappropriate pain medication to obtain it.

11. ☐ **We want to fit in:** We feel left out. It seems like no one likes us or wants to be around us since our pain condition limits us so much. We want to fit in and feel like a normal person again, but somehow we just can't see ourselves doing that without resorting to using inappropriate pain medication.

12. ☐ **We seek out a pain medication supportive environment:** We start putting ourselves in situations where we're around people, places, and things that make us want to use inappropriate pain medication despite our commitment not to. We might get into situations where we're feeling good, but we want to feel even better or enjoy ourselves more. We don't know how to without using inappropriate pain medication.

13. ☐ **We want to change our energy:** We might get into situations that stress us out or make us feel tired or bored. These situations leave us feeling like we need something to either calm us down or to pick us up.

14. ☐ **We see people enjoying themselves:** We might be in a social situation. The people we're with are having a very good time and being very active. We suddenly notice that everyone else is doing things that we can't do without taking extra pain medication. We don't want to use pain medication, but everyone else is having so much fun and we feel pressured. We remember how good it could be and ask ourselves, "Why not?" Besides no one will know.

15. ☐ **We want better sex:** We might get into a sexual experience that couldn't happen without using pain medication. Or

a sexual experience might not be going as well as we would like because of our pain. We know that pain medication could improve our performance, increase our pleasure, get rid of our limitations, and help us to seduce or please our partner.

16. ❐ **We face a loss:** A family member or friend might die. We have to go to the funeral and attend the social functions that surround it. We see people using alcohol or other drugs to cope with their pain. We know that one relative has tranquilizers and will give them to anyone who wants them. We remember that our old pain medication could help us feel better too. We don't give in but then we go home, alone, to deal with the pain and loss. We want to feel better, but we just don't know what to do without using pain meds.

17. ❐ **We remember the "good old days":** We find ourselves daydreaming about how healthy and active we used to be, or sometimes we wake up from dreaming about participating in our old favorite physical activities. When we realize it is only a dream, we feel cheated and frustrated. We need to grieve the loss of our healthy self, but we don't know how and instead we become tempted to use inappropriate medication to escape.

18. ❐ **We feel trapped:** We might get into a situation where we feel isolated or cut off from others. We might get backed into a corner and start feeling trapped because we don't know what to do. It seems like there is no way to fit in or get connected. To avoid situations like this, we might start spending more time alone and when we're by ourselves, we might start to feel lonely. When our pain is bad, we don't reach out; we suffer all alone.

19. ❐ **We get sick or injured:** We might get sick, injured, or start having different physical pain or discomfort. A doctor might offer us a prescription for pain medication, muscle relaxants, or tranquilizers. What's wrong with that? He/She is a doctor and we're sick or in pain, which is different than our other condition. We deserve relief. We don't mention our past problems with pain medication.

> *Please take a few minutes to complete this exercise in your* APM Workbook.

The next exercise in the *Addiction-Free Pain Management® Workbook* asks you to use what you learned by reading the high-risk situation list to modify the high-risk situation you chose in *Part 1*. See the following exercise.

Exercise Five, Part 3: Indentifying and Finalizing Your APM High-Risk Situation

Discussion Questions

1. What is the high-risk situation that you will be facing in the immediate future that could cause you to use inappropriate pain medication (including alcohol) or other drugs despite your commitment not to?

2. What did you learn from reading the APM High-Risk Situation List that can help you better understand and clarify this high-risk situation?

3. What was your previous personal title for the high-risk situation? Do you need to modify your personal title after reading the high-risk situation list? Remember that the title should stir up a feeling or emotion. The title should not be any longer than two or three words. An example of a personal title for the sample description below is "Getting Complacent." What is the new personal title for your high-risk situation?

    Personal Title: _____

4. See if you need to revise your personal description for the high-risk situation you selected. The description should start with the words "I know that I'm in a high-risk situation when I...." You should use something you learned by reading the high-risk situation list to make the description even more concrete and specific. Remember to use the general format below:

    I know that I am in a high-risk situation when <*I do something or get involved in something*> that causes <*pain and problems*> and I want to use inappropriate pain medication (including alcohol) or other drugs to manage the pain and solve the problems.

> **Example:** I know that I am in a high-risk situation when <*I stop swimming daily*> and that causes <*my back to start hurting more*> so I want to take a pill to make my pain go away.

Jean's Magical Thinking

Jean identified with the high-risk situation: **We use magical thinking**. *We believe that pain medication can magically fix us. We mistakenly believe pain medication will always make us feel good and solve all our problems. We convince ourselves that this time we won't abuse it or lose control. We'll use it responsibly. Besides, it will just be this one time. We'll only use for a short period of time until the pain settles down. Then we'll just stop again.*

She realized she was using the added stress and shame as an excuse to use pain medication to help her deal with an uncomfortable situation—the way she used to do it. She changed her title to *"I'm Doing It Again."* She changed her programming sentence this way: "I know I'm in a high-risk situation when I start fantasizing about how well my medication used to help me escape my feelings, and I begin to self-destruct by convincing myself I have a right to use any way I want."

Dean's Feeling Trapped

Dean chose the high-risk situation pertaining to fear: **We feel trapped.** *We might get into a situation where we feel isolated or cut off from others. We might get backed into a corner and start feeling trapped because we don't know what to do. It seems like there is no way to fit in or get connected. To avoid situations like this, we might start spending more time alone, and when we're by ourselves, we might start to feel lonely. When our pain is bad, we don't reach out; we suffer all alone.*

Dean realized that past situations like this led him to isolate and escape. He decided to change his title from "Pure Panic" to "Run and Hide." He decided that his programming sentence was good the way it was: "I know I'm in a high-risk situation when I tell myself I need to take something to boost my courage and take the edge off my fear." Dean's extramarital affairs were very serious issues, but now was not the time to attempt resolution—so he used the process of "bookmarking." However, Dean did agree that he needed to immediately learn how to face the situation of being more emotionally present and open with his wife.

> Using the *Bookmarking* Technique

Bookmarking is a technique that allows you to identify and clarify secondary issues and problems as they emerge, explore the relationship of those issues to the current target problem, write it down, and agree to work on it later in recovery. See the bookmarking steps listed in the following table.

- Briefly explain your problem or issue to a supportive other.
- Make sure you are listened to, understood, and taken seriously.
- Write down the issue on a card of sheet of paper.
- Remember this issue is important.
- Ask yourself what would happen to your ability to resolve this issue if you start to use inappropriate medication again, including alcohol or other drugs.
- Remember the tasks that you are trying to complete, and commit to the return to the bookmarked process as soon as appropriate.

Working on an emotionally-charged situation too soon, such as Dean's history of extramarital affairs, could very well lead to a relapse. It was in Dean's best interest to avoid being "brutally honest" at this point in his recovery process.

Using *Exercise Six: High-Risk Situation Mapping* was an appropriate intervention to teach Dean how to deal with his immediate high-risk situation in a safe way, allowing him to focus on being open and present with his wife. Dean also talked with his sponsor about not rushing in with a *true confession* until his recovery was more stable. His sponsor reminded him that he was only on Step Three of his Twelve-Step Program and *Making Amends* was in Step Nine. He had some time before it would be necessary for him to deal with his extramarital affairs.

> *Please take a few minutes to complete this exercise in your* APM Workbook.

Exercise Six: High-Risk Situation Mapping

Exercise Six is divided into three parts. *Part 1* asks you to think of a specific time when you experienced your high-risk situation and coped with it in a way that caused you to use inappropriate pain medication or other drugs (including alcohol) and/or used ineffective pain management. You are asked to think about the experience as if it were a story with a beginning, middle, and end.

Part 2 asks you to think of a specific time when you experienced this high-risk situation and managed it using effective pain management and/or avoided using inappropriate pain medication or other drugs (including alcohol). Unfortunately, many of you may have no experience of coping with some high-risk situations without using medication inappropriately or indulging in other self-defeating behaviors. When this is the case, ask yourself, "What would it look like to manage such a situation effectively?"

In *Part 3* you are asked to think of the most important high-risk situation you will be experiencing in the near future. You are asked to imagine yourself using ineffective pain management or other self-defeating behaviors that would cause you to use inappropriate pain medication or other drugs (including alcohol). You are asked to imagine yourself doing the things you would have done in the past to convince yourself it is justifiable to use inappropriate pain medication or other drugs (including alcohol).

Jean and Dean were able to identify appropriate mapping situations that brought them more clarity about past using incidents. By answering the remaining questions in the mapping processes, they were able to identify three intervention points where they could have done something different to change the outcome. The remainder of the questions for the mapping processes follows.

Exercise Six—Parts 1, 2, and 3: Discussion Questions

2. What did you want to accomplish by managing this situation the way you did?

3. Did you get what you wanted by managing the situation this way?
   ❏ Yes ❏ No ❏ Unsure

Please explain: _____
_____
_____

4. On a scale of 1 to 10, what were your stress levels when you managed the situation this way? _____
5. On a scale of 1 to 10, what were your pain levels when you managed the situation this way? _____
6. Can you think of some things you could have done differently to manage the situation without having to use inappropriate pain medication (including alcohol) or other drugs or other self-defeating behaviors?
7. **Avoiding the situation:** What could you have done to responsibly avoid getting into this situation?
    If you avoid this situation, how will it change the outcome?
8. **Decision point #1:** What could you have done differently near the beginning of the situation to produce a better outcome? (How could you have thought differently? managed your feelings and emotions differently? responded to your self-destructive urges differently? acted or behaved differently? treated other people differently?)
    If you do these things, how will it change the situation?
9. **Decision point #2:** What could you have done differently near the middle of the situation to produce a better outcome? (How could you have thought differently? managed your feelings and emotions differently? responded to your self-destructive urges differently? acted or behaved differently? treated other people differently?)
    If you do these things, how will it change the outcome?
10. **Decision point #3:** What you have done differenly near the end of the situation to produce a better outcome? (How could you have thought differently? managed your feelings and emotions differently? responded to your self-destructive urges differently? acted or behaved differently? treated other people differently?)
    If you do these things, how will it change the outcome?
11. **Stop relapse quickly:** If you start using inappropriate pain medication (including alcohol) or other drugs, what can you do to stop?

> 12. **Most important thing learned:** What is the most important thing you've learned by completing this exercise?
>
>   **Note:** If you do relapse, it is important not to despair. You can choose to learn from that situation and discover that in the future you will be able to intervene before you use inappropriately or experience life-damaging consequences. The important thing is that you learn to intervene as soon as you are able. For some people the recovery process seems to move steadily forward, but for many others it goes forward, the person hits a stuck point, consolidates their resources, and then moves forward again. Whatever your recovery pattern is, you must not give up. Remember, recovery is a lifelong learning process.

> *Please take a few minutes to complete this exercise in your* APM Workbook.

Up to now most of this work has been to help you uncover and understand the problems associated with the *Addiction Pain Syndrome*®. In the next chapter you will see how Jean and Dean learned to further understand and manage their high-risk situations. This was accomplished through the use of the TFUAR Process.

- **Call to Action for the Eighth Chapter**

It is time to summarize what you have learned so far now that you have come to the end of the eighth chapter. Please answer the questions below.

1. What is the most important thing you've learned about yourself and your ability to help yourself as a result of completing Chapter Eight?

2. What are you willing to commit to do differently as a result of what you have learned by completing this chapter?

3. What obstacles might get in the way of making these changes and what can you do to overcome these roadblocks?

> **Take time to pause and reflect, then go to the next page to review Chapter Nine.**

Chapter Nine
The TFUAR Process and Recovery Planning

Exercise Seven: Analyzing and Managing High-Risk Situations

Exercise Seven in the *Addiction-Free Pain Management® Workbook* is focused on analyzing and managing high-risk situations using the *TFUAR Process*. As I mentioned earlier, TFUAR stands for thoughts, feelings, urges, actions, and reactions or relationships. The following chart shows the TFUAR Process.

TFUAR Process	
• Thoughts (T) Cause Feelings (F)	• Actions Cause Social Reactions (R)
• Thoughts Plus Feelings Cause Urges (U)	• Two Types of TFUAR Sequences:
• Urges Plus Decisions Cause Actions (A)	—Self-Defeating —Addictive

In this exercise you learn how to analyze your high-risk situation by identifying the thoughts, feelings, urges, actions, and reactions of others that are related to coping with the high-risk situation in a way that leads to relapse or self-defeating behaviors. Once you analyze your problematic or addictive TFUARs, you then have an opportunity to develop new recovery-prone ways to manage your TFUARs.

Some of you may have difficulty separating your TFUARs. You might not be able to distinguish thoughts from feelings. You may not believe that the way you think has any effect on your feelings. You may not be able to distinguish feelings from urges or recognize that each feeling carries with it a specific urge. You may not realize you can experience a feeling—sit still and breathe through it until it dissipates without acting upon it. You may not be able to recognize the space between an urge and an action.

Impulse control lives in that space between the urge and the action. You can learn to expand this in-between space so you will be

able to pause and notice the urge, but do nothing about it. From a peace-centered place of *reflection* you can begin to ask yourself the following questions:
- What do I have an urge to do?
- What has happened when I've done similar things in the past?
- What is likely to happen if I do that now?

Now you can make an appropriate decision. What do I choose to do this time? And finally affirming—I know I am responsible for my behavior and its consequences.

Some of you may not be able to distinguish action from social reaction. You may believe that people are reacting to you for no reason at all. You may not be able to link the responses of others to your own behaviors.

The following flowchart shows the progression from the high-risk situation trigger all the way to the social reaction. You will also see an item labeled *positive self-talk,* which is the starting point for moving out of the problem and into the solution. The chart shows some areas where you can interject this way of thinking in order to have a more positive outcome. As you can see, the last place positive self-talk can help change the outcome is at the decision point, but the best place is to already have a plan to implement when you hit a high-risk situation. Relapse prevention means learning a concept called *time-line competency*—learning from the past then taking that knowledge into the present in order to plan for the future. To overcome negative social reactions you need to learn to plug in positive self-talk when you get into a high-risk situation.

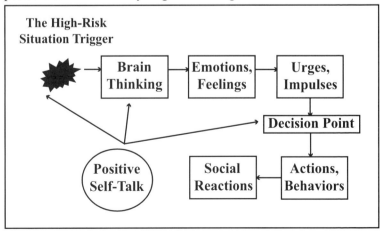

With the above information in mind, let's look at *Exercise Seven* in the *Addiction-Free Pain Management® Workbook*, which has six parts. *Part 1* asks you to list the high-risk situation you are working on and then analyze your TFUARs. This six-part exercise is reproduced in the following table.

Exercise Seven, Part 1: Looking at Your Personal Reactions to High-Risk Situations

High-risk situations, such as the ones you mapped out in the previous exercise, can activate deeply entrenched habits of thinking, feeling, acting, and relating to others that create an urge to abuse your pain medication or stop your effective pain management practices. To effectively manage these high-risk situations, you must learn to understand and control the way you react in these situations. Your chances of managing high-risk situations without using pain medication, including alcohol or other drugs, go up as you get better at recognizing and managing your thoughts, feelings, urges, actions, and social reactions that create the urge to deviate from your medication management agreement.

Let's define some words that will help you understand the process of learning how to manage your reactions to high-risk situations.

Personal reactions are automatic habitual things you do when situations occur. There are four things that automatically take place when these situations come up: you think about it, you have feelings or emotional reactions to it, you get an urge to do something about it, and you actually do something about it. So each automatic personal reaction can be broken down into its component parts, which are: (1) automatic thoughts, (2) automatic feelings, (3) automatic urges, and (4) automatic actions. To learn how to effectively manage high-risk situations, you must learn to change automatic reactions into conscious choices.

Personal responses are different from personal reactions. A personal reaction is automatic and unconscious. A response is something you consciously choose to do. A conscious response is a choice. In order to manage high-risk situations without using pain medication, including alcohol or other drugs, you must learn to make better choices about how to respond to situations. In other words, to change automatic responses into conscious choices, you must choose what you think, how you manage and express your feelings, how you manage your urges, and what you actually do in these situations.

Addictive thinking is an irrational way of thinking that convinces you that using inappropriate pain medication, including alcohol and other drugs, is an effective way to manage the pain and problems caused by irresponsible thinking and behavior.

Irresponsible thinking is an irrational way of thinking about something that causes unnecessary emotional pain and motivates you to do things that will make your problems worse.

Addictive behavior is a way of acting that puts you around people, places, and things that make you want to use inappropriate pain medication, including alcohol or other drugs.

Irresponsible behavior is a way of acting out or behaving that causes unnecessary pain and problems.

There are **emotional consequences** to thoughts and actions. All thoughts and behaviors have logical consequences. Sober, responsible, or rational thinking allows you to deal with life without experiencing unnecessary emotional pain or the urge to use inappropriate pain medication, including alcohol or other drugs, to manage unpleasant feelings. Sober and responsible behavior allows you to conduct your life and solve your problems without producing unnecessary complications for yourself or others and without having to center your life around the inappropriate use of pain medication, including alcohol or other drugs.

Instant gratification is the desire to feel better now even if it means you will hurt worse in the future. When you seek instant gratification, you want to do something, anything that will instantly make you feel better. **You want to feel better now without having to think better or act better first.** This results in a **quick-fix mentality.** When you seek instant gratification, you want to feel good all of the time. You tend to place "feeling good" above all other priorities. This is often based on the mistaken belief that "If I feel better, I will be better and my life will be better!" You are not interested in living according to a responsible set of principles that will make your life work well. You want what you want when you want it regardless of the consequences.

Deferred gratification is the ability to feel uncomfortable or to hurt now in order to gain a benefit or to feel better in the future. When you use deferred gratification, you **think and act better first in order to feel better later.** To learn how to develop deferred gratification you must get in the habit of **thinking things through before you act them out.** Deferred gratification is based on the belief that there are rules or principles that will make your life work well in the long run and will give you a firm sense of meaning, purpose, and satisfaction allowing you to get through the inevitable periods of pain, hard feelings, and frustration that are a normal part of life and living.

You can learn how to **challenge addictive and irresponsible thoughts.** You must learn how to identify and challenge your addictive and irresponsible thoughts if you want to make responsible choices that will allow you to build an effective and satisfying way of life. The following way of thinking can help you challenge the tendency to seek instant gratification. The healthy goal is to live a good life regardless of how it feels at the moment. Feelings change; effective principles don't. Sober and responsible people live a life based on principles, not feelings. Instant gratification provides what looks like an easy way out. The problem is that this easy way out becomes a trap. Once trapped in a conditioned pattern of instant gratification, you will feel cravings when you attempt to break the pattern. But once the pattern is broken, the urges disappear because the long-term beneficial consequences of responsible living kick in.

In the following exercise on *Managing Personal Reaction to High-Risk Situations*, you will learn how to analyze your high-risk situations by identifying the thoughts, feelings, urges, actions, and social reactions that make you want to deviate from your medication management agreement. Then you will learn how to manage them in a new and more effective way without using inappropriate pain medication, including alcohol or other drugs.

The first thing you need to do is to understand how thoughts, feelings, urges, actions, and social reactions relate to one another. Here are some basic principles that can help you understand how this works.

1. *Thoughts cause feelings.* Whenever you think about something, you automatically react by having a feeling or an emotion.
2. *Thoughts and feelings work together to cause urges.* Your way of thinking causes you to feel certain feelings. These feelings, in turn, reinforce the way you are thinking. These thoughts and feelings work together to create an urge to do something. An urge is a desire that may be rational or irrational. The irrational urge to use inappropriate pain medication, including alcohol

or other drugs, even though you know it will hurt you, is also called *craving*. It is irrational because you want to use even though you know it will not be good for you.
3. *Urges plus decisions cause actions.* A decision is a choice. A choice is a specific way of thinking that causes you to commit to one way of doing things while refusing to do anything else. The space between the urge and the action is filled with a decision. This decision may be an automatic and unconscious choice you have learned to make without having to think about it, or this decision can be based on a conscious choice that results from carefully reflecting on the situation and the options available for dealing with it.
4. *Actions cause reactions from other people.* Your actions affect other people and cause them to react to you. It is helpful to think about your behavior like invitations that you give to other people to treat you in certain ways. Some behaviors invite people to be nice to you and to treat you with respect. Other behaviors invite people to argue and fight with you or to put you down. In every social situation you share a part of the responsibility for what happens, because you are constantly inviting people to respond to you by the actions you take and how you react to what other people do.

Relapse usually involves one or more of the following problems:
1. *You can't tell the difference between thoughts and feelings.* You also tend to believe you can think anything that you want and it won't affect your feelings. Then when you start to feel bad, you can't understand why and convince yourself the only way to feel better is to use pain medication, including alcohol or other drugs.
2. *You can't tell the difference between feelings and urges.* You believe each feeling carries with it a specific urge. You don't realize you can experience a feeling, sit still and breathe into the feeling, and it will go away without being acted on.
3. *You can't tell the difference between urges and actions.* You don't realize there is a space between urge and action—the *decision point.*
4. *You can't control your impulses.* You believe you must do whatever you feel an urge to do. You have never understood that to learn impulse control you must learn how to pause, relax, reflect, and decide even when you feel a strong urge to act immediately. The following are four steps of the impulse control process:

- *Pause* and notice the urge without doing anything about it.
- *Relax* by taking a deep breath, slowly exhaling, and consciously imagining the stress draining from your body.
- *Reflect* on what you are experiencing by asking yourself, "What do I have an urge to do? What has happened when I have done similar things in the past? What is likely to happen if I do that now?"
- *Then decide* what you are going to do about the urge. Make a conscious choice instead of acting out in an automatic and unconscious way. When making the choice about what you are going to do, remind yourself that you will be responsible for both the action that you choose to take and its consequence.

Remember: Impulse control lives in the space between the urge and the action.

5. *You can't tell the difference between actions and social reactions.* You tend to believe that people respond to you for no reason at all. You don't link the responses of others to what you do when you are with others. In reality, what you do gives an invitation to other people to treat you in certain ways. Ask yourself, "How do I want to invite other people to treat me in this situation?"

With this in mind, the following exercise will help you identify and change the thoughts, feelings, urges, actions, and social reactions that can lead you back to using pain medication, including alcohol and other drugs.

Part 1 of this exercise is meant to be an educational component designed to help you understand what you are going to be doing and why it is so important. Like most of the patients I worked with, Dean and Jean were able to complete the following exercises much more effectively after reading and discussing this information. Please make sure you understand the exercise above before going on to the next section. If you get stuck, ask someone for help.

Exercise Seven, Part 2: Managing Thoughts That Cause You to Use Inappropriate Medication

In order to manage high-risk situations, you must learn to identify the thoughts that can create an urge to use inappropriate pain medication, including alcohol and other drugs, and/or indulge in other self-defeating behaviors. Think of a high-risk situation you want to learn how to manage more effectively.

1. Go back to the exercise, *Identifying and Personalizing Your High-Risk Situations*, and write the title and description of a high-risk situation that you will be facing in the near future in the spaces below:

Title of Your High-Risk Situation:
Description of the High-Risk Situation: *I know that I'm in a high-risk situation when I*_____.

2. Keeping the situation you described above in mind, read each of the thoughts listed below. Ask yourself if you tend to think *similar* thoughts when you are in this high-risk situation. If you do, put a check in the box in front of the thought. Check as many boxes as you need to.

- ☐ 1. I don't have a serious pain medication problem, so there is no good reason for me not to use pain medication to deal with this situation.
- ☐ 2. I have a right to use pain medication in this situation, and nobody has the right to tell me to stop.
- ☐ 3. If I use pain medication to deal with this situation, nobody will know about it. So what difference will it make?
- ☐ 4. If I use pain medication to deal with this situation, nothing bad will happen to me as a result.
- ☐ 5. If I don't use pain medication, I won't be able to effectively manage this situation.
- ☐ 6. If I don't use pain medication, I won't be able to handle the stress and pain that this situation will cause.
- ☐ 7. Pain medication can help me manage this situation more effectively.
- ☐ 8. I shouldn't have to do anything special to manage this situation. If I just go with the flow, everything will be OK.

3. What are the three thoughts you tend to have in this kind of high-risk situation that makes you want to use pain medication? You can use the thoughts above as a starting point, but it is important for you to write down these thoughts in your own words.

Part 2 asks you to think of the high-risk situation you want to learn how to manage effectively without using inappropriate pain medication and/or other drugs (including alcohol). First, read each of the addictive thoughts and ask yourself if you think similar thoughts when you are in the high-risk situation. If you do, check the box in front of the thought(s) you picked, put the thoughts in your own words, and then come up with a challenge for each one.

Jean's Addictive Thought Selections

In this exercise Jean picked numbers 2, 4, and 5. This exercise helped her to see previously unconscious thoughts that led to the inappropriate use of her pain medication. She specifically focused on number 2 because she realized this was connected to one of her major denial patterns named: *I have the right to be this way; AKA it's my body*. Jean also realized she needed help in dismantling her magical thinking in 4 and 5 regarding her minimization and rationalization about what would happen if she used. She was excited to learn more effective thinking management skills.

Jean put her three major self-defeating thoughts in her own words. "They don't know what it's like, so they should just get off my case." Other thoughts she had were: "It won't get out of control this time" and "I'll freak if I don't use." It took Jean a long time to come up with effective challenging interventions for those thoughts. Her top three were: (1) "People are concerned—I should listen"; (2) "I know better—It will get out of control"; and (3) "I have new tools now—I'll be OK." She realized this was just a starting point and looked forward to the remainder of the exercise.

Dean's Addictive Thought Selections

Dean chose numbers 2, 3, and 7, but he also stated that some of the others could apply to him as well. Dean was very surprised at how many of these thoughts he actually experienced when he was in high-risk situations. His special focus was number 3. This was related to his major isolation pattern as well as the way he avoided being totally honest with anyone—especially his wife.

Dean realized that the pattern of convincing himself that it was necessary to keep secrets was connected to one of his major denial patterns named *Rationalizing*. Like Jean, he saw that he used another favorite denial pattern, *I have the right to be this way; AKA it's my body,* to justify his continued use of self-defeating behaviors, including isolation and inappropriate medication use so he could avoid feeling uncomfortable emotions.

Dean put his three major self-defeating thoughts in his own words. "Screw them! I'm the one in pain here," "They'll never know," and "Using will get me through this." It took Dean a long time and much frustration before he was able to come up with effective challenging interventions for those thoughts. His top three were: (1) "They really want to help me—I'll let them"; (2) "Keeping secrets hurts me and those I love"; and (3) "I can do this without using." He saw that painful emotions, especially guilt and shame, were a problem area and looked forward to learning new feeling management skills.

> *Please take a few minutes to complete this exercise in your* APM Workbook.

Part 3 uses the same feeling checklist that was previously covered in an earlier chapter. This time Jean and Dean saw some differences.

The feelings Jean and Dean chose in *Exercise One, Part 3* were: *weak, angry, sad, lonely, threatened, and frustrated.* Jean rated *weak* at level 10 while Dean rated it at level 5. Jean rated *sad* at level 8 and Dean rated it at 4. Both rated *anger* and *frustration* at a level 10. Jean rated *ashamed* at level 10, while Dean did not rate either *proud* or *ashamed*. This time Dean was able to see that *ashamed* was near level 10, and his *sad* rating moved up to level 8. Both rated *lonely* at level 10 this time.

Jean and Dean were very happy to work on the "Feeling Management Skills" part of this exercise (shown in the following table) as they began to learn how they could better manage their uncomfortable feelings.

The instructions for this exercise require you to read each statement and rate how true it is for you on a scale of 0–10. (0 means the statement is not at all true. And 10 means the statement is totally true.) You are then asked to pick two or three of the tools you would like to focus on.

> Learning Feeling-Management Skills

Jean noted that before she started the APM treatment she would not have been able to have any items near level 10, but now she had three at level 10—items 1, 5, and 8.

Dean had a similar reaction to this exercise. In the past he tended to be a victim of his feelings and would often use pain medication to cope with his uncomfortable emotions. The three most important management skills for him were items 3, 12, and 14. Number 14, *seeking help to deal with feelings*, was a major step forward in Dean's recovery. Although this checklist worked well for Dean and Jean, many of you may need additional help to identify and/or articulate your uncomfortable emotions. Additional tools are the Feeling Faces Poster (*http://www.ctherapy.com/feelings_home.asp*) and the Feeling Faces Cards (*http://www.feelingfacescards.com/*). These products are commonly used in many treatment programs.

Exercise Seven, Part 3: Managing Feelings That Cause You to Use Inappropriate Medication

The following exercise will show you how to more effectively manage the feelings and emotions you will tend to experience in your immediate high-risk situation:

1. Before completing this part of the exercise, go back and read the title and description of the high-risk situation you are learning how to manage.

2. When you are in this high-risk situation, do you tend to feel…
   ☐ Strong?   or   ☐ Weak?
   How intense is the feeling? (0–10) _____
   Why do you rate it this way?

3. When you are in this high-risk situation, do you tend to feel…
   ☐ Caring?   or   ☐ Angry?
   How intense is the feeling? (0–10) _____
   Why do you rate it this way?

4. When you are in this high-risk situation, do you tend to feel…
   ☐ Happy?   or   ☐ Sad?
   How intense is the feeling? (0–10) _____
   Why do you rate it this way?

5. When you are in this high-risk situation, do you tend to feel…
   - ☐ Safe?   or   ☐ Threatened?
   How intense is the feeling? (0–10) _____
   Why do you rate it this way?
6. When you are in this high-risk situation, do you tend to feel…
   - ☐ Fulfilled?   or   ☐ Frustrated?
   How intense is the feeling? (0–10) _____
   Why do you rate it this way?
7. When you are in this high-risk situation, do you tend to feel…
   - ☐ Proud?   or   ☐ Ashamed?
   How intense is the feeling? (0–10) _____
   Why do you rate it this way?
8. When you are in this high-risk situation, do you tend to feel…
   - ☐ Connected?   or   ☐ Lonely?
   How intense is the feeling? (0–10) _____
   Why do you rate it this way?
9. When you are in this high-risk situation, do you tend to feel…
   - ☐ Peaceful?   or   ☐ Agitated?
   How intense is the feeling? (0–10) _____
   Why do you rate it this way?
10. What are the three strongest feelings you tend to have in this kind of high-risk situation that make you want to use inappropriate pain medication, including alcohol or other drugs?
11. Keeping these three feelings in mind, read each of the following statements about your ability to manage your feelings, and rate how true it is on a scale of 0–10. (0 means the statement is not at all true. 10 means the statement is totally true.) Place your answer on the line in front of each statement.
    ____ A. **Skill #1:** I am able to anticipate situations that are likely to provoke strong feelings and emotions.
    ____ B. **Skill #2:** I am able to recognize when I am starting to have a strong feeling or emotion.
    ____ C. **Skill #3:** I am able to stop myself from automatically reacting to the feeling without thinking it through.
    ____ D. **Skill #4:** I am able to call a time-out in emotionally charged situations before my feelings become unmanageable.
    ____ E. **Skill #5:** I am able to use an immediate relaxation technique to bring down the intensity of the feeling.

___ F. **Skill #6:** I am able to take a deep breath and notice what I'm feeling.

___ G. **Skill #7:** I am able to find words that describe what I'm feeling and use the feeling list when necessary.

___ H. **Skill #8:** I am able to rate the intensity of my feelings using a ten-point scale.

___ I. **Skill #9:** I am able to consciously acknowledge the feeling and its intensity by saying to myself, "Right now I'm feeling _____ and it's OK to be feeling this way."

___ J. **Skill #10:** I am able to identify what I'm thinking that's making me feel this way and ask myself, "How can I change my thinking in a way that will make me feel better?"

___ K. **Skill #11:** I am able to identify what I'm doing that's making me feel this way and ask myself, "How can I change what I'm doing in a way that will make me feel better?"

___ L. **Skill #12:** I am able to recognize and resist urges to create problems, hurt myself, or hurt other people in an attempt to make myself feel better.

___ M. **Skill #13:** I am able to recognize my resistance to doing things that would help me or my situation and force myself to do those things despite the resistance.

___ N. **Skill #14:** I am able to get outside of myself and recognize and respond to what other people are feeling.

- Please select two or three of these feeling management skills that you are willing to commit to getting better at and list them below.
- Who can you ask to help you with these skills? What could stop you from following through?
- What are any potential obstacles that could keep you from learning these new feeling management skills?
- What are some ways you can overcome any potential obstacles from learning these new feeling management skills?

Please take a few minutes to complete this exercise in your **APM Workbook.**

The fourth part of this exercise focuses on the self-defeating urges that come up in high-risk situations. The following exercise asks you to explore these urges and answer a few simple questions.

Exercise Seven, Part 4: Managing Urges That Cause You to Use Inappropriate Medication

High-risk situations often cause the urge to use pain medication, including alcohol and other drugs, or engage in other self-defeating behaviors. When this urge or craving is activated, you almost always experience an inner conflict between two parts of yourself. One part, your addictive self, wants you to use chemicals. Another part of you, the sober self, wants you to manage the situation without using chemicals. This exercise will help you explore these two parts of yourself.

1. Before completing this part of the exercise, go back and read the title and the description of the high-risk situation you are learning how to manage.
2. When you are in this high-risk situation, what self-defeating urges do you have?
3. Is there a part of you that wants to use pain medication, including alcohol and drugs? Tell about that part of you.
4. Is there another part of you that wants to manage the situation without using pain medication, including alcohol or drugs? Tell about that part of you.
5. If you wanted to manage this high-risk situation more effectively, what part of you do you need to listen to and why?

Please take a few minutes to complete this exercise in your **APM Workbook.**

Using the Inner Dialogue Process

At this point in the process I find it helpful to use a tool called the *Inner Dialogue Process*. This process can be used to help you identify and clarify the components of internal dissonance—when a part of you feels one way and another part feels the opposite. Most people have an inner conflict between

the irresponsible self—the part of you that mistakenly believes that the use of irresponsible coping behaviors is good for you, and

the responsible self—the part of you that recognizes the problems with irresponsible coping behaviors.

The inner dialogue technique asks you to identify the battle between these two sides of your personality and to learn how to engage in conscious dialogue and train the responsible self to win the arguments. The Inner Dialogue Process includes the following steps.

The Inner Dialogue Process

1. You need to pay careful attention to signs that you may be experiencing an inner conflict.
2. When you seem conflicted but don't want to say anything, pause and ask, "What's happening? There seems to be a conflict going on inside of me. Is there? What is it?"
3. If you are strongly asserting one position that supports continued inappropriate coping behavior, ask yourself, "How strongly do I believe that? Rate your belief on a scale of 1–10. (1 being not very strong and 10 being as strong as it can get.) If you say 10, ask yourself, "Am I sure? Is it possible that there's a small part inside of me that thinks that I might be wrong? Can I talk to that part of me for a moment?"
4. The goal is to identify both sides of the argument. Then you ask yourself, "Which side of this argument represents my *irresponsible self*? Why do I think so? Which part of this argument represents my *responsible self*? Why do I think so?"
5. Invite the two parts of yourself to engage in a conversation by asking, "What would my *irresponsible self* say about this?" Then ask, "What would my *responsible self* say about this?"
6. The final step would be to objectively look at both sides of the argument/self-talk and then ask yourself, "If I want to have an ongoing positive quality of life and avoid negative consequences, which side do I need to listen to and why do I believe that?"

This process worked very well for Jean and Dean. Jean discovered there was a *responsible* part of her that wanted to quit reacting to her self-defeating urges in ways that hurt her and those she loved. She rated the part that wanted to use medication inappropriately as being very strong—level 7–8 on a 0–10 scale. She was surprised to discover that she enjoyed talking back to her *irresponsible* self and realized she did have choices. Dean's process was very similar. Once *Part Four* was completed, they immediately moved to *Part Five*, which is listed in the following table.

Exercise Seven, Part 5:
Managing Actions That Cause You to Use Inappropriate Medication

1. Before completing this part of the exercise, go back and read the title and the description of the high-risk situation you are learning how to manage.

2. Keeping this high-risk situation in mind, read the following list of *self-defeating behaviors* that can be used to mismanage this high-risk situation. Check the behaviors you are most likely to use in this situation.

- ☐ 1. **Procrastinating:** I put off dealing with the high-risk situation by finding excuses or reasons for not doing it now.

- ☐ 2. **Distracting myself:** I get too busy with other things to pay attention to managing the situation.

- ☐ 3. **Saying "It's not important":** I convince myself that other things are more important than effectively managing this high-risk situation.

- ☐ 4. **Thinking I'm cured:** I convince myself that because I'm OK now and don't have a pain medication problem, there is no need to learn how to manage this high-risk situation more effectively.

- ☐ 5. **Playing dumb:** Even though a big part of me knows what I need to do to manage this situation more effectively, I let myself get confused and convince myself that I can't understand what I'm supposed to do.

- ☐ 6. **Getting overwhelmed:** I feel scared and start to panic. I use my fear as an excuse for not learning how to manage the high-risk situation more effectively.

> ☐ 7. **Playing helpless:** I pretend to be too weak and helpless to manage the situation more effectively.
> ☐ 8. **Wanting the quick fix:** I want a guarantee that I can quickly and easily learn to manage the high-risk situation more effectively or I won't even try.
> 3. What are the three self-defeating behaviors you tend to have in this kind of high-risk situation that make you want to use pain medication, including alcohol or other drugs? You can use the self-defeating behaviors above as a starting point, but it is important for you to write the descriptions in your own words.

Exercise Seven, Part 5 is about identifying addictive and/or self-defeating tactics you've used in the past. In this exercise you are asked to read the list of self-defeating behavioral tactics to learn how to identify and manage them so you can creatively implement interactions that will improve your pain management and recovery. You are asked to check the tactic(s) you have used in the past and then list three self-defeating behaviors you have used in past high-risk situations. In addition to identifying the three behaviors, you are asked to identify a more recovery-prone way of behaving in those types of high-risk situations.

This exercise is an effective tool for helping you uncover previously automatic and unconscious scripts you have played out over and over again in the past. The first step toward change is recognition that a problem exists. If you are familiar with Transactional Analysis (TA), you may find some of the above tactics very familiar. Some of the TA tools can be extremely effective in enhancing your recovery process, and many therapists are familiar with them.

> Jean and Dean learned to identify
> and overcome self-defeating behaviors.

When Jean and Dean saw on paper in front of them some of the tactics they had used, they began to realize just how damaging and self-defeating those behaviors were to their recovery process. Jean's most significant realization was noticing a pattern she played out when getting to number 7—"Playing helpless." She looked at several of her past significant relationships and saw how she mistakenly believed she could not handle her own situation. After asking inappropriate people for help, she could then justify using when they let her down.

Dean's biggest awareness was number 8—"Wanting the quick fix" or instant gratification. He was able to identify times in his past where he could have avoided using if he would have stuck to his pain management plan, but he stated, "I want it now." The process of analyzing and learning to manage high-risk situations is yet another tool to assist the APM patient in moving from experiencing themselves as a victim to discovering their own sense of empowerment.

> *Please take a few minutes to complete this exercise in your* APM Workbook.

Tying It All Together

Jean and Dean experienced some confusion while working on the following exercise but eventually moved through their stuck points. Once they realized they had already processed this exercise in the previous worksheets, they became excited. When they finished putting all their answers in the *Part 6* table, they had a much better picture of how to more effectively manage any future high-risk situations. To get the greatest benefit from these workbook exercises, you should work with a professional who has been trained in the CENAPS® Model.

> Treatment works best when patients become more proactive in their healing.

Exercise Seven, Part 6: Managing Your Personal Reactions to High-Risk Situations

This exercise will help you tie together everything you have learned by completing the previous TFUAR management exercises.

1. Before completing this part of the exercise, please go back and read the title and the description of the high-risk situation you are learning how to manage. Then review your answers to all of the questions in the previous exercises. Take time to reflect on what you are really saying in your answers. See if you can sense how the answer to each question is somehow connected to all of your other answers. Then complete the following questions:

2. When you're in this high-risk situation, what do you tend to think?

2-a. What is another way of thinking that will allow you to manage this high-risk situation without inappropriately using pain medication?

3. When you're in this high-risk situation, how do you tend to feel?

3-a. What is another way to manage those feelings that would let you manage this situation without inappropriately using pain medication?

4. When you're in this high-risk situation, what do you have a self-defeating urge to do?

4-a. What is another way of managing this urge that would allow you to manage the situation without inappropriately using pain medication?

5. When you're in this high-risk situation, what self-defeating actions do you usually do?

5-a. What are some other things that you could do that will allow you to manage this situation without inappropriately using pain medication?

6. When you're in this high-risk situation, how do other people usually react in ways that cause you distress?

6-a. How could you invite other people to react to you in a way that would help you manage this situation without inappropriately using pain medication?

> *Please take a few minutes to complete this exercise in your* APM Workbook.

Exercise Eight: Recovery Planning

Developing a Recovery Plan

The last clinical exercise in the *Addiction-Free Pain Management® Workbook* is focused on recovery planning. Having insight and understanding is only the starting point for successful relapse prevention. Developing an effective recovery plan and following it makes the difference between treatment success and failure for most people. At this point I often share a phrase I learned from Mr. Gorski: "Insight without action is the booby prize." Dean and Jean thought this was a great way to frame the importance of continuing to be proactive and take action.

> "Insight without action is the booby prize!"—T. Gorski

While the remainder of this chapter explains recovery planning, the next chapter describes measuring treatment effectiveness. *Exercise Eight* in the *Addiction-Free Pain Management® Workbook* assists you in developing and then testing your recovery plan.

Having a structured daily plan assists you in your recovery process and helps you practice more effective pain management. The recovery activities suggested in *Exercise Eight, Part 1* are a combination of clinical and Twelve-Step activities along with revisiting many of the nonpharmacological interventions. These recovery principles have been proven by outcome studies from hundreds of addiction treatment centers across the United States and by the successful recovery of millions of people working Twelve-Step recovery programs around the world.

> Effective pain management requires a recovery and pain management plan.

Along the same lines, people who are most effective with their pain management have learned to develop a recovery/management plan; however, this plan needs to be individualized to obtain maximum efficiency. Building a personalized recovery, pain management, and relapse prevention plan is essential for optimal treatment success.

Referring to the following *Addiction-Pain Syndrome®* diagram, which was first introduced in an earlier chapter, a relapse prevention plan must address all three zones concurrently: the *Addictive Disorder* Zone, the *Pain Disorder* Zone, and the *Addiction Pain Syndrome* Zone.

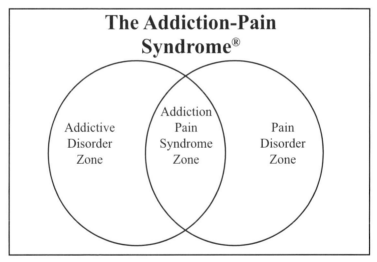

There are seven basic recovery activities described in the following table that will address these zones. They are essential habits of good, healthy living. Anyone who wants to live a responsible, healthy, and fulfilling life will get in the habit of regularly doing these things.

For people in recovery these activities are essential. For those who also have a chronic pain disorder (*Addiction Pain Syndrome®*), these steps become even more crucial. A regular schedule of these activities—designed to match your unique profiles of recovery needs, pain management requirements, and high-risk situation management—is necessary for your brain and body to heal from damage caused by an addictive disorder and your chronic pain condition.

You are instructed to read the following list of recovery activities and identify which ones you think will be helpful for your personal recovery and pain management program. You are asked to notice the obstacles you may face in doing them on a regular basis, and indicate your strategies to overcome those obstacles. You are then asked if you are willing to put the activities on your recovery plan.

The seven recovery activities are listed in the following table.

Exercise Eight, Part 1: Selecting Your Recovery Activities

Having a plan for each day will help your recovery and enable you to practice better pain management. People who successfully recover and effectively manage their pain tend to do certain things. These recovery principles are proven. In AA there is such a strong belief in them that many people with solid recovery will say, "If you want what we have, do what we did!" and "It works if you work it!" The same applies to pain management; those who are most effective with pain management have learned to develop a recovery/management plan. However, not everyone does exactly the same things. Once you understand yourself and the basic principles of recovery, pain management, and relapse prevention, you can build an effective personalized program for yourself.

When people first read the following list, they tend to get defensive. "I can't do all of those things!" they say to themselves. I invite you to think about your recovery as if you were hiking in the Grand Canyon and had to jump across a ravine that was about three feet wide and 100 feet deep. It's better to jump three feet too far than to risk jumping one inch too short. The same is true of recovery. It's better to plan to do a little bit more than you need to do than to risk not doing enough. In AA they say, "Half measures availed us nothing!"

The following basic recovery activities are actually habits of good, healthy living. Anyone who wants to live a responsible, healthy, and fulfilling life will get in the habit of regularly doing these things. For people in recovery, these activities are essential, and if you also have a chronic pain condition, these steps become even more crucial. A regular schedule of these activities, designed to match your unique profile of recovery needs, pain management requirements, and high-risk situations, is necessary for your brain and body to heal from the damage by medication use and your chronic pain condition.

Instructions

Read the following list of recovery activities and identify which activities you think will be helpful for your recovery and pain management program. Notice the obstacles you face in doing them on a regular basis, and indicate your strategies to overcome those obstacles.

1. **Professional counseling:** The success of your recovery and effective pain management will depend on regular attendance at education sessions, group therapy sessions, and/or individual therapy or counseling sessions. The scientific literature on treatment effectiveness clearly shows that the more you invest in professional counseling and/or therapy during the first two years of recovery, the more likely you are to stay in recovery. This process needs to include pain management treatment planning.

    A. Do I believe that I need to do this?
        ❒ Yes ❒ No ❒ Unsure   Please explain:
    B. The obstacles that might prevent me from doing this are:
    C. Possible ways of overcoming these obstacles are:
    D. Will I put this on my recovery plan?
        ❒ Yes ❒ No ❒ Unsure   Please explain:

2. **Self-help programs:** There are a number of self-help programs—such as Alcoholics Anonymous (AA), Pills Anonymous (PA), Chronic Pain Anonymous (CPA), Chronic Pain Support Groups, Narcotics Anonymous (NA), Rational Recovery, and Women for Sobriety—that can support you in your efforts to live a sober and responsible life. These programs all have several things in common: (1) they ask you to abstain from inappropriate mood-altering substances and to live a responsible life; (2) they encourage you to regularly attend meetings, so you can

meet and develop relationships with other people living sober and responsible lives; (3) they ask you to attend regularly with an established member of the group (usually called a sponsor) who will help you learn about the organization and get through the rough spots; and (4) they promote a program of recovery (often in the form of steps or structured exercises for you to work on outside of meetings) that focuses on techniques for changing your thinking, emotional management, urge management, and behavior.

Scientific research shows that the more committed and actively involved you are in self-help groups during the first two years of recovery, the greater your ability to avoid relapse. You should also consider joining a chronic pain support group, because research indicated personal empowerment is crucial for developing effective, long-term chronic pain management.

  A. Do I believe that I need to do this?
     ❒ Yes ❒ No ❒ Unsure   Please explain:
  B. The obstacles that might prevent me from this are:
  C. Possible ways of overcoming these obstacles are:
  D. Will I put this on my recovery plan?
     ❒ Yes ❒ No ❒ Unsure   Please explain:

3. **Proper diet:** What you eat can affect how you think, feel, and act. Many chemically dependent people find they feel better if they eat three well-balanced meals a day, use vitamin and amino-acid supplements, avoid eating sugar and foods made with white flour, and cut back on or stop smoking cigarettes and drinking beverages containing caffeine, such as coffee and colas. Recovering people who do not follow these simple principles of healthy diet and meal planning tend to feel anxious and depressed, have strong and violent mood swings, feel constantly angry and resentful, and periodically experience powerful cravings. They're more likely to relapse. Those who follow a proper diet tend to feel better and have lower relapse rates. Proper nutrition is also crucial for effective pain management.

  A. Do I believe that I need to do this?
     ❒ Yes ❒ No ❒ Unsure   Please explain:
  B. The obstacles that might prevent me from doing this are:
  C. Possible ways of overcoming these obstacles are:
  D. Will I put this on my recovery plan?

☐ Yes ☐ No ☐ Unsure   Please explain:

4. **Exercise program:** If your chronic pain condition permits, doing thirty minutes of aerobic exercise each day will help your brain recover and help you feel better about yourself. Fast walking, jogging, swimming, and aerobic classes are all beneficial. It's also helpful to do strength-building exercises (such as weight lifting) and flexibility exercises (such as stretching) in addition to the aerobic exercise. You need to work with your doctor or healthcare practitioner to determine the most effective (and safest) exercise program for you. Many pain management providers state that flexibility and mobility are essential for effective pain management.
   A. Do I believe that I need to do this?
      ☐ Yes ☐ No ☐ Unsure   Please explain:
   B. The obstacles that might prevent me from doing this are:
   C. Possible ways of overcoming these obstacles are:
   D. Will I put this on my recovery plan?
      ☐ Yes ☐ No ☐ Unsure   Please explain:

5. **Stress management program:** Stress is a major cause of relapse. In addition, as you read earlier in this book, an increase in stress often leads to an increase in pain. Recovering people who learn how to manage stress without using self-defeating behaviors tend to stay in recovery and learn how to more effectively manage their chronic pain symptoms. Those who do not learn to manage stress tend to relapse or suffer more with their pain. Stress management involves learning relaxation exercises and taking quiet time on a daily basis to relax. It also involves long hours of working and taking time for recreation and relaxation. Meditation can also be part of this program.
   A. Do I believe that I need to do this?
      ☐ Yes ☐ No ☐ Unsure   Please explain:
   B. The obstacles that might prevent me from doing this are:
   C. Possible ways of overcoming these obstacles are:
   D. Will I put this on my recovery plan?
      ☐ Yes ☐ No ☐ Unsure   Please explain:

6. **Spiritual development program:** Human beings have both a physical self (based on the health of our brains and bodies) and a nonphysical self (based on the health of our value systems and spiritual lives). Most recovering people find they need to

invest regular time in developing themselves spiritually (in other words, exercising the nonphysical aspects of who they are). Twelve-Step programs, like AA, provide an excellent program for spiritual recovery, as do many communities of faith and spiritual programs. At the heart of any spiritual program are three activities: (1) fellowship, where you spend time talking with other people who use similar methods; (2) private prayer and meditation, where you take time to be conscious of yourself in the presence of your Higher Power or to consciously reflect on your spiritual self; and (3) group worship, where you pray and meditate with other people who share a similar spiritual philosophy.

- A. Do I believe that I need to do this?
  - ❒ Yes ❒ No ❒ Unsure Please explain:
- B. The obstacles that might prevent me from doing this are:
- C. Possible ways of overcoming these obstacles are:
- D. Will I put this on my recovery plan?
  - ❒ Yes ❒ No ❒ Unsure Please explain:

7. **Morning and evening inventories:** People who avoid relapse and successfully obtain lifelong recovery learn how to break free of automatic and unconscious self-defeating responses. They learn to live consciously each day, being aware of what they're doing and taking responsibility for it and its consequences. To stay consciously aware, they take time each morning to plan their day (a morning planning inventory) and they take time each evening to review their progress and problems (an evening review inventory). They discuss what they learn about themselves with other people who are involved in their recovery program.

   For people with chronic pain, it is important to keep a pain journal that identifies stress and trigger patterns as well as associated thoughts, feelings, and behaviors. During times of increased pain, keeping a daily pain journal is essential, leading to more effective pain management. Incorporating the *Identifying and Rating the Severity of Your Pain Symptoms* worksheet from *Exercise One* in this book would be an important addition to your pain journaling.

   - A. Do I believe that I need to do this?
     - ❒ Yes ❒ No ❒ Unsure Please explain:

> B. The obstacles that might prevent me from doing this are:
> C. Possible ways of overcoming these obstacles are:
> D. Will I put this on my recovery plan?
>   ❐ Yes ❐ No ❐ Unsure   Please explain:

> *Please take a few minutes to complete this exercise in your* APM Workbook.

Exercise Eight, Part 2: Completing Your Schedule of Recovery Activities

After you identify the recovery activities you will use to avoid relapse, then develop a schedule of those activities. *Exercise Eight, Part 2* assists you by introducing a weekly planner (see the *APM Workbook*, page 84). A reproduction of this exercise is in the following table.

Instructions

On the next page is a weekly planner (see workbook, p. 84) that will allow you to create a schedule of weekly recovery and pain management activities. Think of a typical week and enter the pain management and recovery activities you plan to routinely schedule in the correct time slot for each day. *Recovery activities* and/or *pain management activities* are specific things that you do at scheduled times on certain days. If you can't enter the activity on a daily planner at a specific time, it's not a recovery and/or pain management activity. Most people find it helpful to have more than one scheduled activity for each day.

Remember, recovery activities fall into four quadrants:

- **Biological:** This quadrant includes activities that improve the health of your physical self. Some examples include abstinence from inappropriate medications, regularly scheduled balanced meals, scheduled exercise regimen, physical therapy appointments, daily hygiene, etc.
- **Psychological:** This quadrant includes activities that help you identify and change negative thinking patterns and

cope with uncomfortable emotions. Some examples include counseling/therapy appointments, reading recovery literature, anger management training, etc.

- **Social:** This quadrant includes activities that help you let go of enabling or addiction-prone relationships and encourages developing relationships with recovery-prone people who will support your recovery. Some examples include finding an appropriate sponsor who understands both the pain management and chemical recovery processes and saying goodbye to problem people, places, and things that could trigger relapse, etc.

- **Spiritual:** This quadrant includes activities that will help you develop or improve your relationship with your inner self or Higher Power. Some examples include prayer and meditation, visits to nature, attending religious or spiritual services, etc.

The examples above are only a starting place. You need to develop your own personalized recovery schedule. It needs to contain activities that will help you identify and manage problem high-risk situations without putting you at risk of using inappropriate pain medication, including alcohol or other drugs, or cutting back or eliminating effective pain management activities.

Please take a few minutes to complete this exercise in your APM Workbook.

Once you have developed your calendar, *Exercise Eight, Part 3* is designed to test your scheduled events. You are asked to complete the following exercise.

Exercise Eight, Part 3:
Testing Your Schedule of Recovery Activities

Instructions

1. Go back and review the primary high-risk situation that you want your recovery and pain management program to help you identify and manage. Read the personal title and description and the thought, feeling, urge, and action statements carefully. What is the personal title and description of this high-risk situation?

Title: _____

Description: *I know that I'm in a high-risk situation when I ...*

2. Review your Weekly Planner. What is the most important recovery and/or pain management activity that will help you manage your high-risk situation?

    A. How can you use your recovery and/or pain management activity to help you identify your high-risk situation should it occur? (Remember, most high-risk situations develop in an automatic and unconscious way. A trigger is activated and you start using the old ways of thinking and acting without being consciously aware of what you are doing. To prevent relapse it's helpful to regularly schedule recovery and/or pain management activities that will encourage you to talk about how you are thinking, feeling, and acting, and then receive feedback if you experience high-risk situations.)

    B. If you start to experience your high-risk situation again, how can you use this recovery activity to manage it? (Remember, managing a high-risk situation means changing how you think, feel, and act. How can this recovery activity help you stop thinking and doing things that make you feel like relapsing? How can it help you start thinking and doing things that make you want to get back into recovery?)

3. Review your Weekly Planner again. What is the second most important recovery activity that will help you manage your high-risk situation?

    A. How can you use this recovery activity to help you identify your high-risk situation?

B. If you start to experience your high-risk situation again, how can you use this recovery activity to manage it?
4. Review your Weekly Planner one last time. What is the third most important recovery activity that will help you manage your high-risk situation?
   A. How can you use this recovery activity to help you identify your high-risk situation should it occur?
   B. If you start to experience your high-risk situation again, how can you use this recovery activity to manage it?
5. What other recovery activities can you think of that could be more effective in helping you identify and manage future high-risk situations should they occur?

Please take a few minutes to complete this exercise in your APM Workbook.

The Importance of a Pain Medication Management Plan

Another useful tool for someone in recovery for pain and substance use is the twelve-item protocol for managing pain medication in recovery developed by myself and Sheila Thares that was covered in an earlier chapter. This information was introduced to Jean and Dean who eventually used it very effectively.

By the time Jean and Dean reached the end of the workbook exercises they were fairly stable. Dean did experience a brief and minor relapse episode related to a very emotional couples therapy session where he finally talked about his affairs. Fortunately, he used his relapse intervention plan immediately with his relapse prevention network to quickly restabilize.

Jean did not relapse, but her life became very stressful and she needed to backtrack into some basic self-care treatment planning. In addition, both Jean and Dean were encouraged to start working in the *Denial Management Counseling for Effective Pain Management Workbook* and then move on to the *Relapse Prevention Therapy Workbook* as soon as they were stable. Their progress in those processes will be covered in future publications.

An ounce of relapse prevention planning is worth a pound of treatment cure.

When thinking about relapse prevention for chronic pain and addiction, remember the old saying "An ounce of prevention is worth a pound of cure." You must learn to get and stay active with your recovery and not wait until after you are in relapse mode.

It is helpful to look at a relapse prevention plan like a car insurance policy. Many people are fortunate not to collect on that insurance, but it sure is nice to know that it will be available if they need it. A solid relapse prevention plan works the same way. You may never need to use the interventions you set up, but should you start that downward spiral, it is comforting for you to know a plan is in place that will support you to put the brakes on relapse.

> Relapse prevention is simple but not easy.

Like many other things in recovery, relapse prevention is simple—but not easy. And although relapse prevention is an inside job, that does not mean you have to do it alone. Help is out there for those who need it, want it, and reach out for it.

However, you have a much better chance of quality recovery when your healthcare providers use a combination of the APM *Core Clinical Exercises* combined with, as needed, *Medication Management Components* and appropriate *Nonpharmacological Treatment Processes*. It is the healthcare providers' responsibility to be aware of all potential resources in their communities, and you should hold them accountable.

In the next chapter, which is the final exercise in the *Addiction-Free Pain Management® Workbook,* you will learn Jean and Dean's self-evaluation outcomes. This exercise is also described in the final chapter of this book and is designed to help you complete a final evaluation to learn how much you have benefited from all your hard work. This is also a useful tool for your healthcare provider to help them determine the effectiveness of the treatment process.

- **Call to Action for the Ninth Chapter**

It is time to summarize what you have learned so far now that you have come to the end of the ninth chapter. Please answer the questions below.

1. What is the most important thing you have learned about yourself and your ability to help yourself as a result of completing Chapter Nine?

2. What are you willing to commit to do differently as a result of what you have learned by completing this chapter?

3. What obstacles might get in the way of making these changes and what can you do to overcome these roadblocks?

Take time to pause and reflect, then
go to the next page to review Chapter Ten.

Chapter Ten
Measuring Treatment Effectiveness

Determining the effectiveness of addiction treatment is relatively straightforward. If you remain abstinent from alcohol and other psychoactive drugs, the treatment is deemed successful. Determining the outcome of APM treatment is much more complex.

It is not enough for you to achieve abstinence from inappropriate medication. You must also experience an improvement in your pain management and quality of life. In addition, you must have a solid relapse prevention and pain management plan that you continue to evaluate and modify frequently.

Benchmarks for Effective Treatment

You should schedule follow-up reviews with your team to be completed at different intervals, using specific benchmarks that gauge successful treatment. The first benchmark occurs at the completion of the APM process, followed by reviews at three months, six months, nine months, and one year.

These benchmarks include assessing improvement in your quality of life. Improvements are determined by such factors as returning to work or other significant increases in the quality of your life. They are also determined by the absence, or significant reduction, of psychoactive drug use. Family members and significant others should be asked for their input.

To be considered a total treatment success the following criteria must be met: After one year you must not be taking any inappropriate medications (including alcohol or other drugs), report an increase in your quality of life, and report a decrease both in your inactivity due to pain and an overall pain level reduction. However, please remember that in some cases the most optimal outcome will be a reduction in the problematic medication, not total elimination.

> **Successful APM® Treatment Criteria**
> - Reduction or elimination of inappropriate medication
> - Decreased pain symptoms
> - Decreased inactivity due to pain
> - Increased quality of life

Utilizing the Pain Outcome Profile (POP) Instrument

A relatively new instrument, the *Pain Outcome Profile (POP)*, was developed by the American Academy of Pain Management and Drs. Michael Clark and Ron Gironda at the James A. Haley Veterans Hospital in Tampa, Florida.

The POP assesses three domains of your pain experience with twenty core clinical items: pain perception, perceived physical impairment due to pain and several aspects of emotional functioning. These domains are assessed using two pain intensity scales, three self-reports of functional impairment scales, and two scales that address self-reported emotional functioning (seven scales total).

Evaluating Your Pain and Addiction Management Skills

You also need to have an effective method to evaluate and rate your own progress for overall pain and addiction recovery. On page 88 in the *Addiction-Free Pain Management® Workbook* you will find such a tool. After completing the first eight clinical exercises in the workbook you will have a chance to complete a final evaluation. The following table gives you the process that you are asked to complete.

Completing Your Final Evaluation Exercise

Instructions

The ultimate test of whether you have benefited from completing the exercises in this workbook will be your ability to increase effective pain management and avoid relapse. It may be helpful, however, to review what you have accomplished. A careful evaluation may help you identify areas in your Relapse Prevention Plan that are incomplete. By going back and completing these areas, you may avoid unnecessary relapse and the resulting pain and problems.

Here is a checklist that can help you decide if you have accomplished the objectives of completing this workbook. Read each statement and ask yourself if you have fully completed that objective, partially completed it, or not completed it at all. Remember, this is a self-evaluation designed to help you determine if you have the skills needed to avoid relapse. Be honest with yourself. If you relapse because you haven't learned the skills to stay in recovery, you are the one who will pay the price.

1. **Understanding Your Pain:** I understand and can explain the common effects of my chronic pain, the main effects that I personally experienced, and can differentiate between my physical and psychological/emotional pain symptoms.

    Level of Completion:
    ❏ None (0)   ❏ Partial (5)   ❏ Full (10)   Score (0–10) ___

2. **The Effects of Prescription and/or Other Drugs (Including Alcohol):** I understand and can explain the benefits I obtained from using prescription or other drugs and what I wanted to get from using these chemicals. I can also understand and explain the problems I experienced as a result of using.

    Level of Completion:
    ❏ None (0)   ❏ Partial (5)   ❏ Full (10)   Score (0–10) ___

3. **Decision Making about Pain Medication:** I understand and can explain the reasons I started using pain medication, alcohol, or other drugs inappropriately. I understand and can explain the reasons why I stopped using pain medication, including alcohol and other drugs, as well as what I did to adhere to my medication agreement.

Level of Completion:
❐ None (0)   ❐ Partial (5)   ❐ Full (10)   Score (0–10) ___

4. **Moving into the Solution:** I can define what my medication management agreement and recovery plan includes. I have completed and signed a medication management agreement, committing to maintain adherence to the plan and practice effective pain management. I have developed a relapse prevention intervention plan. It describes my responsibilities, and those of my counselor and significant others (two or three), to stop relapse quickly should it occur.

   Level of Completion:
   ❐ None (0)   ❐ Partial (5)   ❐ Full (10)   Score (0–10) ___

5. **Identifying High-Risk Situations:** I am able to identify the immediate high-risk situations that can cause me to use inappropriate pain medication (including alcohol) or other drugs and/or stop using an effective pain management program despite my commitment not to by developing an *Initial High-Risk Situation List* and identifying my immediate high-risk situations.

   Level of Completion:
   ❐ None (0)   ❐ Partial (5)   ❐ Full (10)   Score (0–10) ___

6. **Personalizing High-Risk Situations:** I am able to concretely and specifically describe the immediate high-risk situations, having developed meaningful personal titles and personal descriptions.

   Level of Completion:
   ❐ None (0)   ❐ Partial (5)   ❐ Full (10)   Score (0–10) ___

7. **Mapping Past Mismanaged High-Risk Situations:** I am able to use *Situation Mapping* to objectively describe past high-risk situations that were managed in a way that led to using inappropriate pain medication (including alcohol) or other drugs and/or ineffective pain management.

   Level of Completion:
   ❐ None (0)   ❐ Partial (5)   ❐ Full (10)   Score (0–10) ___

8. **Analyzing Past Mismanaged High-Risk Situations:** I am able to use *High-Risk Situation Analysis* to identify the thoughts, feelings, urges, actions, and relationship patterns caused by the past mismanagement of the high-risk situation.

Level of Completion:
❐ None (0)   ❐ Partial (5)   ❐ Full (10)   Score (0–10) ___

9. **Managing High-Risk Thoughts and Feelings:** I am able to (1) identify the general way of thinking that is driving situation management; (2) show the relationship between these thoughts and the feelings driving this mismanagement; and (3) use positive self-talk techniques to challenge the thoughts and feelings driving situation mismanagement.

Level of Completion:
❐ None (0)   ❐ Partial (5)   ❐ Full (10)   Score (0–10) ___

10. **Developing a Recovery Plan:** I am able to develop a schedule of recovery activities that will support my ongoing identification and management of high-risk situations and help me to intervene early should I be tempted to violate my medication management agreement and/or use ineffective pain management.

Level of Completion:
❐ None (0)   ❐ Partial (5)   ❐ Full (10)   Score (0–10) ___

11. **Overall Skill Level:** I have developed an overall ability to identify and manage my high-risk situations that lead me from stability to violating my medication management agreement and/or ineffective pain management. I have developed a schedule of recovery activities that will support my ongoing high-risk situation identification and management.

Level of Completion:
❐ None (0)   ❐ Partial (5)   ❐ Full (10)   Score (0–10) ___

> *Please take a few minutes to complete this exercise in your* **APM Workbook.**

Although this exercise can be an effective benchmark for you to evaluate yourself, follow-up sessions are needed to determine the ongoing effectiveness of your recovery and pain management program.

A New Beginning

> Using the APM® System increases positive treatment outcomes.

The Road Map to APM Recovery

APM recovery utilizes detailed, accurate assessments followed by multidimensional treatment plans. These treatment plans include the *Core Clinical Exercises* and, when needed, the *Medication Management Components*. They also include the *Nonpharmacological Treatment Processes,* as well as the proven CENAPS® relapse prevention protocols. These methods are implemented to help ensure ongoing recovery.

> **An Integrated APM® Treatment Approach**
> - Core clinical exercises
> - Medication management components
> - Nonpharmacological treatment processes

More and more people are benefiting from the implementation of APM methodologies than from either traditional addiction treatment or pain management care at chronic pain clinics. By going through this process you will be able to resume healthy and productive lives and experience an overall improved quality of life.

This was the case for Jean; she stopped using all of her problematic pain medication and her family relationships improved. In addition, she built trust and safety in her women's group and continues to work an effective pain management program.

Dean, however, continues to struggle but has learned some valuable lessons from his recent relapse. He is much more hopeful now that he will eventually succeed in becoming a high functioning member of society. His prognosis has significantly improved as a result of the APM process. Based on other signs of progress, he should become totally stabilized and move into a healthy, ongoing recovery.

Spreading the Word—APM® Works

Having gone through the *Recovery Guide* and completed the exercises in the *Addiction-Free Pain Management® Workbook,* you are now a part of the APM recovery family. This is a new beginning. It is up to you to continue the work of further developing your personalized APM recovery and relapse prevention plan. You can do this by practicing what you have learned and sharing your progress to support other people in chronic pain.

- **The Final Call to Action for the APM® Recovery Guide**

It is time to summarize what you have learned now that you have come to the end of the final chapter. Please answer the final questions below.

1. What is the most important thing you have learned about yourself and your ability to help yourself as a result of completing this book?

2. What are you willing to commit to do differently as a result of what you have learned by completing this book?

3. What obstacles might get in the way of making these changes and what can you do to overcome these roadblocks?

**You haven't finished *Addiction-Free Pain Management® Recovery Guide* yet.
Go to the next page to review additional information in the Appendix.**

Appendix

Medical Marijuana Controversy Update
By Dr. Stephen F. Grinstead, LMFT, ACRPS, CADC-II

Since I first published this article in 2002 I find that the same old controversies about marijuana are still raging. One of these issues is the use of marijuana as a legitimate medication. Dr. Clifford Gevirtz (2007) points out that cannabis has a very long history in medicine with early records going back 5,000 years to China; it was then used to treat such conditions as malaria, constipation, and rheumatic pains. Nonetheless, today there are two primary polarized camps fueling this debate. One side preaches the evils of using this herb as medication and the other side extols the virtues of medical marijuana.

Over the past several decades I have listened to both sides of this issue and have seen the impact of this controversy on many of my patients. Unfortunately, until recently, there has been an important piece missing: reliable double-blind studies designed to test how effective marijuana really is as a legitimate medication. Unfortunately, there are very few of these studies and some of them have small numbers of participants. In addition, several of these research study outcomes are somewhat inconclusive. Gevirtz (2007) also points out that there have been no studies evaluating the analgesic effects of smoked cannabis (marijuana) or other smoked cannabinoids.

Robson (2001) published his analysis of nine randomized controlled trials with a total of 222 adult patients. These studies' subjects had either cancer pain, chronic nonmalignant pain, or were patients with postoperative pain. In these trials oral THC 5-10 mg, an oral synthetic THC (NIB) 4 mg, and intramuscular levonantradol (Marinol) 1.5-3 mg were used. These studies compared those interventions with oral codeine 60-120 mg and oral secobarbital (it has no analgesic properties but does have a sedative agent) 50mg. Although the therapeutic benefits proved to be small and variable in these studies, they had clinical relevance because of the minimal side effects.

Gevirtz's (2007) conclusions included noting a wide range of efficacy across various cannabis preparation but related poorly with efficacy compared with nonsteroidal anti-inflammatory drugs or other simple analgesics. He also noted that increasing the cannabinoid dose to increase analgesia resulted in more adverse side effects.

There are also legality issues to consider because of the way in which the Drug Enforcement Agency (DEA) rates or "schedules" drugs. For Schedule I substances, the criteria that need to be considered are whether the substance has a high potential for abuse, has no currently accepted medical use in treatment in the United States, and has a lack of accepted safety for use under medical supervision. While Schedule I drugs cannot be used medically, the law does allow supervised research.

For substances to be rated as Schedule II, the DEA considers its high potential for abuse, whether it has a currently accepted medical use in treatment in the United States or a currently accepted medical use with severe restrictions and whether abuse of the substances may lead to severe psychological or physical dependence. While legal for medical use, doctors need to go through additional legal steps when prescribing these drugs.

A substance is placed on Schedule III based on its potential for abuse relative to substances in other schedules, whether it has a currently accepted medical use in treatment in the United States, and its relative potential to produce physical or psychological dependence is less.

What has been available for several years as a legitimate medication is Marinol (dronabinol), a synthetic THC (delta-9-tetrahydrocannabinol, the active psychoactive chemical in marijuana). While marijuana is still listed as a Schedule I drug by the DEA and illegal for medical use, Marinol, the synthetic form of THC has finally been reduced from Schedule II to a Schedule III drug.

Marinol has been used in treating glaucoma, people undergoing chemotherapy, and people with AIDS. Again, sides are split on the effectiveness of this medication. One side says Marinol works great; therefore, there is no need to legalize the medical use of marijuana. The other side states that Marinol is not nearly as effective as smoked marijuana.

After working with many individuals who have used Marinol and also smoked marijuana, I see that both sides have good points. For example, after helping some of my patients work through denial issues surrounding marijuana abuse, they become honest and share that the Marinol did work as well for controlling nausea or increasing appetite, but they didn't get high. On the other hand, several patients who needed help for nausea caused by chemotherapy treatment were not able to ingest the Marinol tablets and found smoking marijuana to be a better option for them.

There are many risks associated with marijuana, especially smoked marijuana, which must be considered not only in terms of immediate adverse effects on the lung; e.g., bronchi and alveoli, but also long-term effects in people with chronic diseases and those with a poor immune status. The major problems I have with someone smoking marijuana as a medicine is the inability to regulate the dosage and, even more important, the delivery system. The level of THC varies so greatly in the marijuana that is currently available, that coming up with a therapeutic dose is extremely difficult. In addition, marijuana has other ingredients that may have problematic side effects. Then there is the dangerous delivery system—the issue of smoking it. The components of the smoke are hazardous, especially in the immuno-compromised patient. No other medication we have is administered that way because of the potential dangers.

Because of the lack of more positive research outcomes, there has been minimal exploration of a safer delivery system for the active ingredient of marijuana (THC). There have been suggestions that an aerosol delivery system for the THC or Marinol would eliminate the dosage and the unsafe smoking problems. Why is this not being given due consideration?

One of the reasons may be that there is not enough profit for drug companies, but I believe the main reason is the stigma that has historically surrounded marijuana. I think marijuana is a serious drug of abuse that leads to dependency (addiction), but this is also true of many legal prescription medications. For example Vicodin and OxyContin have both been increasingly abused in the past several years, and Valium and Xanax have been a serious abuse problem for at least the past decade.

Another problem with medical marijuana is that it is often prescribed for conditions that may not be medically indicated. In fact, several of my patients received medical marijuana prescriptions for stress management and chronic pain management. I am not aware of any legitimate research that indicates marijuana is a medically effective treatment for either of these conditions. That is why quality research needs to be undertaken to prove once and for all the legitimacy of using marijuana—or at least its active ingredient THC—to treat specific medical conditions.

Joy, Watson, and Benson (1999) published their book *Marijuana and Medicine: Assessing the Science Base*. One major finding of this book was that although marijuana smoke delivers THC and other cannabinoids to the body, it also delivers harmful substances, including most of those found in tobacco smoke. In addition, plants contain a variable mixture of biologically-active compounds and cannot be expected to provide a precisely defined drug effect. For those reasons, the book concludes that the future of cannabinoid drugs lies not in smoked marijuana, but in chemically-defined drugs that act on the cannabinoid systems that are a natural component of human physiology. Until such drugs can be developed and made available for medical use, the report recommends interim solutions. The development of these appropriate drugs depends upon thorough double-blind clinical trials.

I understand this is a very controversial issue. While I am not in favor of legalizing "street drugs," I do advocate utilizing a potentially effective medication after it has undergone the same level of testing as the other medications we currently use. Like Gevirtz (2007), I do not believe there is enough valid evidence to support the introduction of cannabinoids into widespread clinical practice for pain management. I believe that in addition to verifying the effectiveness, the delivery system and dosage problems need to be resolved before I would feel comfortable endorsing the use of medicinal marijuana for any of my patients.

Medical Marijuana Controversy Bibliography

Gevirtz, C. (2007). An emerging therapy: The future role of cannabinoids in pain management. *Topics in Pain Management*, *22*, #8, 1–5.

Holdcroft, A., Maze, M., & Dore, C. B. (2006). A multicenter dose-escalation study of the analgesic and adverse effects of an oral cannabis extract (Cannador) for post-operative pain management. *Journal of Anesthesiology, 104*, 1040–1046.

Joy, J., Watson, S. J., & Benson, J. A. (Eds.). (1999). *Marijuana and Medicine: Assessing the Science Base*. Washington; DC. National Academies Press.

Pertwee, R. G. (1999). Cannabis and cannabinoids: Pharmacology and rationale for clinical use. *Rorsch Komplementarmed, 6*, (suppl 3): 12–15.

Reynolds, J. R. (2005). Therapeutic uses and toxic effects of *Cannabis indica. Lancet*, 1890; i: 637–638.

Robson, P. (2001). Therapeutic aspects of cannabis and cannabinoids. *British Journal of Psychiatry*; #178: 107–115.

Recovery and Smoking Just Don't Mix
By Dr. Stephen F. Grinstead, LMFT, ACRPS, CADC-II

Throughout my professional addiction treatment career I have been an advocate for the cessation of all addictions when people decide to get into recovery; this includes cigarette smoking and chewing tobacco. Unfortunately, many of my addiction treatment colleagues do not agree—in fact, many of them still use nicotine addictively themselves. On the positive side more and more addiction programs are now addressing nicotine addiction as part of their treatment curriculum, and my hope is that this trend continues.

In an attempt to present some objective reasons why people in recovery from alcohol and other drugs should also be in recovery for their nicotine addiction—and that nicotine recovery is possible and preferable—I offer the following perspective. Part of my motivation is that I am tired of watching the people I care about, personally and professionally, slowly killing themselves with nicotine and not truly seeing what they are doing to their health. Many continue because they simply do not believe they have any other choice. My commitment is to do what I can do as an addiction professional, family member, and friend. I say there always is a choice if one is willing and proceeds with an open mind and an open heart.

In my research I found a 2005 report by Alcohol Alert from the National Institute on Alcohol Abuse and Alcoholism (NIAAA) that stated until recently alcoholism treatment professionals have generally not addressed the issue of smoking cessation, largely because of the belief that the added stress of quitting smoking would jeopardize an alcoholic's recovery. This report goes on to state that current research does not confirm this belief.

Following the lead of other healthcare facilities, many addictions treatment facilities are becoming smoke free, providing a *natural experiment* on the effectiveness of dual recovery programs. Initial evaluations suggest that no-smoking policies are feasible in this setting, but additional research is needed. In addition, this report noted that Canadian scientists have found evidence that the nicotine in cigarettes can induce a craving for alcohol.

The report concludes with a summary by NIAAA Director Enoch Gordis, M.D.; *Alcohol and Tobacco—A Commentary.*

Alcohol and tobacco are frequently used together, may share certain brain pathways underlying dependence, and because of their

> *numerous social and health-related consequences, are a continuing source of national public policy debate.*
>
> *Many alcoholism treatment professionals have not actively pursued smoking cessation among their patients based on the belief that the stress of quitting smoking while undergoing alcoholism treatment might cause relapse. As a physician who has seen the ravages caused by both alcoholism and smoking, I am pleased that we now have research evidence showing that both can be treated simultaneously without endangering alcoholism recovery. As basic science learns more about how alcohol and nicotine act singly and together within the brain, new treatments for alcohol and nicotine dependence will follow.*
>
> *Finally, society has attempted to minimize the consequences of using both alcohol and tobacco through public policy actions, including health warning labels, restrictions on advertising, and age restrictions on use…*

We have known for well over a decade that smoking while in recovery for addiction can be a relapse trigger. The research I quote here goes as far back as 1992. Alcoholics who smoke, generally, are less successful in achieving and maintaining sobriety than are nonsmoking alcoholics (Hughes; *Journal of the American Medical Association 275*:1097–1103, 1996). Furthermore, in alcoholics treated for both addictions, relapse to smoking is considered a risk factor for alcohol relapse (Johnson & Jennison; *International Journal of the Addictions 27*:749–792, 1992).

Many people who are chemically dependent have also developed either HIV or the Hepititus C Virus (HCV), usually directly from their addictive and/or self-destructive behaviors. When these people get into a recovery process, many continue to use nicotine—which has serious negative health implications for them. The information below is from an article by Jill Cadman in 2002. The study reported in Ms. Cadman's article (partial text below) appeared in the April 8, 2002, issue of the *Archives of Internal Medicine.*

> *About four million people in the U.S. have the hepatitis C virus (HCV). HCV can cause an infection of the liver that is usually spread through blood contact with an infected person. Many HIV-positive people are also infected with HCV. If not treated, hepatitis can cause cirrhosis (scarring) of the liver. This can lead to severe sickness or even death.*
>
> *A new study has found that people with HCV should avoid smoking cigarettes and drinking alcohol because both habits can further damage their livers. The study used levels of the liver enzyme ALT*

> to check for liver damage. (Higher ALT levels can be a warning sign of liver damage.)
>
> The researchers found that drinking alcohol and smoking more or less doubled the risk of having high ALT levels. People who smoked a pack or more of cigarettes each day and frequently drank alcohol had a risk of elevated ALT levels that was seven times higher than for those who did not drink or smoke.
>
> The researchers who conducted the study stated that people who have HCV "are strongly advised not to smoke and drink alcohol to reduce the possible risk for aggravating (their) liver dysfunction."
>
> A person with HIV and HCV can become very sick. The added strain that HCV puts on the immune system makes it even harder for the body to fight diseases and infections. If you have HIV and HCV, you need to get regular medical attention for both conditions and take care of your body by avoiding habits, such as smoking and drinking.

Other interesting information was published in *Counselor* magazine in 1996 in an article written by Terence T. Gorski. I've included a brief passage from that article below.

> Actively drinking alcoholics have a reduced life expectancy of approximately eleven years. Abstinent alcoholics who continue to smoke cigarettes don't do much better. Their life expectancy is reduced by nine years. The major causes of death in sober recovering alcoholics are cancer and heart disease related to smoking. Studies conducted by Janet K. Bobo in Seattle and Richard Sandor at the Betty Ford Center show that there is no higher incidence of relapse in people who quit smoking during their treatment for chemical dependency. The research also shows that recovering people who do not smoke have higher recovery rates from all drugs than those who do smoke. In other words, the relapse rates are significantly higher among recovering people who smoke than among recovering people who don't smoke.

The adverse health effects of nicotine have been widely addressed and nicotine may also contribute to an addiction relapse, but even this does not motivate people in recovery to stop. So why do people keep smoking or using chewing tobacco when they know it is dangerous to their health? There are a number of reasons why this is so, but what I believe needs to be addressed first and foremost is the automatic and unconscious defense mechanism called denial.

My personal opinion is that being totally clean and sober from all addictions will lead to a truly happy, joyous, and free life. My professional opinion is that addiction recovery and smoking just don't mix.

Brief Red Flags Checklist for Pain Medication Addiction
By Dr. Stephen F. Grinstead, LMFT, ACRPS, CADC-II

Many people in chronic pain are afraid to take their narcotic medication (opiates, etc.) because they have heard horror stories of people getting hooked on pain pills. This leads to a decision to under-medicate and to suffering as a result. If you happen to be in recovery for alcoholism or any other drug addiction, the problem is even worse. If you under-medicate, it could trigger a relapse. Of course, the other side of the coin is overmedication, which could lead to rapid tolerance building and finally reactivation of your addiction.

Telling the difference between appropriate and effective use of pain medication and the beginning of medication abuse can sometimes be difficult for you or your healthcare providers to determine. There are progressive stages of problematic use including medication dependency, medication abuse, pseudo-addiction, and finally addiction. The confusion and uncertainty of this progression is a challenge for both you and your treatment provider.

Below is the brief list of "red flags" or indicators that you are using your pain medication in a manner that could eventually lead to problems or even addiction. If you would like the full version, go to my Web site *http://www.addiction-free.com,* and register on the *Articles Page*. Both you and your treatment providers need to be familiar with these red flags and to seek professional help from a person trained in addiction who also has experience, understanding, or training in pain management.

Instructions: *Please review each of the items below and rate each on a 0 to 10 scale with 0 meaning this item is not and has never been a problem for me to 10 meaning this could be a serious problem for me.*

☐ 1. After adjusting to the medication, you still experience a sense of euphoria (feeling buzzed).

☐ 2. You start having urges or cravings for your medication between scheduled times.

☐ 3. You are unable to take your medication exactly as prescribed.

- [ ] 4. You are experiencing problems with your thinking, feelings, and/or behavior.
- [ ] 5. Your quality of life and/or relationships are being impacted by your use of medication.
- [ ] 6. You use medications in physically dangerous situations, e.g., driving a car, operating power tools, providing childcare, etc.
- [ ] 7. You find yourself not informing one healthcare provider what medication another provider is prescribing for you.
- [ ] 8. You have a history—or a family history—of alcoholism or other drug addiction.
- [ ] 9. You start using your medication to cope with psychological/emotional type pain or to cope with stressful or uncomfortable situations.
- [ ] 10. Family members or friends report concerns about your use of medication.
- [ ] 11. You start thinking you might be having a problem with your medication.
- [ ] 12. You find yourself needing early refills and may rationalize this by coming up with unusual excuses: I lost it, someone else took it, it fell in the water, etc.

Some of the items above may be difficult to determine, which is why sharing this with someone else is so essential. This collaboration should include you, your support network, other healthcare providers, or any other sources that could help you be more accurate in completing the above. If 2–3 of the red flag areas have scores above a 3–5, or more than 1 have scores in the 8–10 range, it's time to seek a referral to an appropriate addiction specialist to make a more accurate assessment of a potential medication abuse/addiction problem.

From Denial to Effective Pain Management
By Dr. Stephen F. Grinstead, LMFT, ACRPS, CADC-II

Learning to identify and manage denial is a necessary first step for people living with chronic pain who want to learn how to develop and implement an effective pain management plan. The *Denial Management Counseling for Effective Pain Management Workbook* is designed for people who have experienced significant problems related to living with chronic pain, but who honestly don't believe—or don't want to believe—that their decisions and behaviors are undermining what could be an effective pain management plan.

A major obstacle to recognizing these self-sabotaging behaviors and achieving effective pain treatment is the denial system—a psychological defense mechanism that protects us from devastating pain and problems and is automatic and unconscious. Remember that this system of defense was developed to protect us from being overwhelmed by what I call *Painful Reality*.

There are situations when denial can help us cope with painful reality; e.g., the death of a loved one, an unforeseen medical crisis, etc. Unfortunately, denial can also prevent us from looking at or dealing with a situation that is causing life-damaging consequences.

If we don't realize how serious our problem really is, it can be extremely difficult for us to find a solution. For example, many people have a mistaken belief that "I can't be addicted because I'm in pain and a doctor gave me the medication." This can be a type of denial if, in fact, they have been abusing or are addicted to their medication and experiencing life-damaging consequences. Denial can be even subtler than this. It can also lead people to behave in ways that are inconsistent with appropriate treatment recommendations.

There are four levels of denial. The first is a *lack of information*—in this case what ineffective pain management or medication abuse/addiction really is. This example demonstrates the first level—the mistaken belief that because a doctor prescribed the medication, there won't be an addiction problem. The solution here is education and up-to-date information about addiction. It is crucial for people living with chronic pain to learn as much as possible about effective pain management, pain disorders, and substance use disorders—i.e., prescription drug abuse or prescription drug addiction.

The second level of denial is *conscious defensiveness*. At this level we know that something is wrong, but we don't want to look at the problem and face the pain of knowing. The solution is to recognize there is an inner conflict occurring where one part of us knows there's a problem, but another part doesn't want to admit it. To resolve this conflict we must be willing to listen to the part that knows the truth and take action. The old saying "the truth will set you free" is certainly relevant in this case.

The third level is denial as an *unconscious defense mechanism*. We get to this level when we have stayed in the inner conflict, mentioned above, and the defensive voice keeps winning. Once this happens, denial becomes an automatic and unconscious defense mechanism. The solution is much more difficult. It usually takes an outside intervention, or what is called a *motivational crisis*, to break through this defense and allow us to know the truth, and then start addressing the problem. For some of my patients this motivational crisis was generated when their treating physicians became concerned about their mismanaged chronic pain or use/abuse of pain medication. For others it was family members intervening and urging them to seek help.

The fourth level is denial as *a delusional system*, which is the toughest level to address. This delusion is a mistaken belief that is firmly held to be true despite convincing evidence that it is not true. If someone was experiencing denial at this level, they probably wouldn't be open to reading this book. People at this level of denial usually need long-term psychotherapy to resolve their delusional system.

The *Denial Management Counseling for Effective Pain Management Workbook* can be very effective in overcoming the first three levels of denial. The workbook is divided into nine exercises. Each exercise explains basic information about denial or denial management and then asks clients to answer a series of questions that helps them apply that information to their current situation. In the table that follows is a brief summary of each exercise from the workbook.

Exercise #1: Understanding Denial as a Part of the Human Condition: This exercise explains that denial is a normal and natural part of the human condition. Denial is related to our need to search for the truth about what is happening to us despite our tendency to make mistakes. Whether we like to admit it or not, we all sometimes have fragile egos that can be easily hurt when we make mistakes. This creates the tendency for us to lie to ourselves when we do make mistakes, to avoid the pain. We are all capable of convincing ourselves that the lies we tell ourselves are in fact true. Once we start believing our own lies, we can become deceptive and start lying to others whether we mean to or not. As a result, we all need to develop personal and social systems for finding the truth while protecting ourselves from self-deception and the lies of others. Denial management is a personal system for finding the truth while protecting us from self-deception.

Exercise #2: Understanding the Principles of Denial Management: This exercise explains the basic information that is needed to understand and recognize denial so we can make a choice between continuing to lie to ourselves or facing and dealing with the truth. Denial is the natural tendency to avoid the pain that is caused by thinking and talking about serious problems. This pain is avoided by using a set of automatic and unconscious thoughts, feelings, and actions that keep us from thinking and talking about our problems. Denial is a normal psychological defense that has both benefits and disadvantages. The major benefit of using denial is that it allows us to avoid feeling the pain caused by serious or overwhelming problems. The major disadvantage is that it prevents us from seeing what is really going on and effectively managing our problems. Fortunately, there are two antidotes for denial: (1) accepting the truth about what is going wrong with our lives and (2) developing effective problem solving strategies to address our problems. The four primary feelings that drive denial are anger, fear, guilt, and shame. The good news is that denial can be recognized. We can face the truth about what is happening in our lives, and as a result, we can turn our lives around.

Exercise #3: Recognizing Your Personal Denial Patterns: This exercise describes twelve common denial patterns people tend to use to deny they have serious problems. You will be asked to review a denial pattern checklist that explains these denial patterns and to select and personalize the three denial patterns you tend to use most often or the ones that cause you the most problems.

Exercise #4: Managing Your Denial: This exercise shows you how to begin to challenge your inner saboteur (denial) by identifying and managing the thoughts, feelings, urges, actions, and social reactions that drive your personal denial process. This process allows your *responsible/wise self* to empower you in making positive changes in your life. You will be guided through a strategic step-by-step process and asked to be as thorough and honest with yourself as possible.

Exercise #5: Stopping Denial as You Think about Your Problems: This first application exercise will test your ability to recognize and manage your own denial as you think and talk about the problems that caused you to seek help. First you will be asked to describe the problems that generated your desire to seek help. Then you will be asked to look at the relationship of your problems to self-defeating behaviors—including possible prescription medication problems—and the potential consequences, both good and bad, of continuing to use these self-defeating patterns. You will then be asked to tie all of this information together in your mind, look at the big picture of what is happening at this moment in your life, and make a hard decision about what you want to do about your problems. At each step in this process, you will be asked to notice if you were able to recognize and stop your denial when it was turned on, by reviewing a mini denial pattern checklist and answering a few simple questions.

Exercise #6: Stopping Denial as You Think about Your Pain History: In this exercise you will be asked to review the important things that have happened to you in the course of your pain history and think about how self-defeating patterns were related to each of the key events. Again, at each step in this process, you will be asked to notice if you were able to recognize and stop your denial when it was turned on.

Exercise #7: Stopping Denial as You Think about Your Prescription Medication Use: In this final application exercise you will review thirty questions from the *Prescription Medication Problem Checklist* that indicate whether or not you could be experiencing medication abuse or even addiction. Then you will have a chance to determine which ones apply to you. You will then be able to see the potential level of problem you may be experiencing by completing the *Interpreting the Prescription Medication Problem Checklist* exercise. At each step in this process, you will be asked to notice if you were able to recognize and stop your denial when it was turned on.

Exercise #8: Stopping Denial as You Decide What to Do Next: In this exercise you will be asked to decide what you are going to do next. You can decide to stay in denial and pretend your problems don't exist, or you can decide to recognize your problems and enter an appropriate process to learn how to effectively manage your chronic pain problems and get your life back on track.

Exercise #9: Evaluating Your Denial Management Skills: In this exercise you will evaluate how well you learned the skills needed to recognize and manage your denial. If you have been honest with yourself and others while completing this workbook, you no longer have to be like the ostrich with your head in the sand. You can now enjoy safe and effective pain management.

Pain Management Reference List and Recommended Reading List

Barrett, S., et al. (2006). *Consumer health: A guide to intelligent decisions.* Columbus, OH: McGraw-Hill.

Boriskin, J. (2004). *PTSD and addiction: A practical guide for clinicians and counselors.* Center City, MN: Hazelden.

Carr, D., Loeser, J., & Morris, D. (2005). *Narrative, pain, and suffering.* Seattle, WA: IASP Press.

Catalano, E., & Hardin, K. (1996). *The chronic pain control workbook: A step-by-step guide for coping with and overcoming pain.* Oakland, CA: New Harbinger.

Caudill, M. (2001). *Managing pain before it manages you.* New York: Guilford Press.

Cleveland, M. (1999). *Chronic illness and the twelve steps: A practical approach to spiritual resilience.* Center City, MN: Hazelden.

Colvin, R. (2002). *Prescription drug addiction: The hidden epidemic.* Omaha, NE: Addicus Books.

Corey, D., & Solomon, S. (1989). *Pain: Free yourself for life.* New York: Penguin Books USA.

Davis, M., Eshelman, E. R., & McKay, M. (1995). *The relaxation & stress reduction workbook* (fourth edition). Oakland, CA: New Harbinger Publications, Inc.

Deardorff, W. (2004). *The psychological management of chronic pain.* Continuing Ed Courses.Net: *www.continu ingedcourses.net.*

Deardorff, W., & Reeves, J. (1997). *Preparing for surgery: A mind-body approach to enhance healing and recovery.* Oakland, CA: New Harbinger Publications, Inc.

Egoscue, P. (1998). *Pain free: A revolutionary method for stopping chronic pain.* New York, NY: Bantam.

Ford, N. (1994). *Painstoppers: The magic of all-natural pain relief.* West Nyack, NY: Parker.

Fuhr, A. (1995). Activator methods chiropractic technique: The science and art. *Today's Chiropractic*, July/August, 48–52.

Gorski, T. (2006). *Depression and relapse: A guide to recovery.* Independence, MO: Herald House/Independence Press.

Gorski, T., & Grinstead, S., (2006). *Denial management counseling workbook*, revised. Independence, MO: Herald House/Independence Press.

Gorski, T., & Grinstead, S. (2000). *Denial management counseling professional guide.* Independence, MO: Herald House/Independence Press.

Grant, M. (2005). Pain control with EMDR: An information processing approach. Submitted for publication.

Grinstead, S. (2007). *Managing pain and coexisting disorders: Using the addiction-free pain management® system.* Independence, MO: Herald House/Independence Press.

Grinstead, S. (2007). *APM® module one: Understanding and evaluating your chronic pain symptoms.* Independence, MO: Herald House/Independence Press.

Grinstead, S. (2007). *APM® module two: Examining your potential medication management problems.* Independence, MO: Herald House/Independence Press.

Grinstead, S. (2007). *APM® module three: Understanding and developing effective pain management.* Independence, MO: Herald House/Independence Press.

Grinstead, S., Gorski, T., & Messier, J. (2006). *Denial management counseling for effective pain management.* Independence, MO: Herald House/Independence Press.

Grinstead, S., & Gorski, T. (2006). *Addiction-free pain management®: Relapse prevention counseling workbook*, revised. Independence, MO: Herald House/Independence Press.

Grinstead, S. (2002). *Addiction-free pain management® recovery guide: Managing pain and medication in recovery.* Independence, MO: Herald House/Independence Press.

Grinstead, S., & Gorski, T. (1999). *Addiction-free pain management®: The professional guide.* Independence, MO: Herald House/Independence Press.

Khalsa, D., & Stauth, C. (2002). *Meditation as medicine: Activate the power of your natural healing force.* New York: Fireside.

Kennedy, J., & Crowley, T. (1990). Chronic pain and substance abuse: A pilot study of opioid maintenance. *Journal of Substance Abuse Treatment, 7*(4), 233–238.

Kingdon, R., Stanley, K., & Kizior, R. (1998). *Handbook for pain management.* Philadelphia, PA: W. B. Saunders.

McKay, M., & Harp, D. (2005). *Neural path therapy: How to change your brain's response to anger, fear, pain & desire.* Oakland, CA: New Harbinger.

Meade, T., et al. (1995). Randomized comparison of chiropractic and hospital outpatient management for low back pain: Results from extended follow-up. *British Medical Journal, 311,* 349–351.

Melzack, R., & Wall, P. (1965). Pain mechanisms: A new theory. *Science, 150,* 971–979.

Melzack, R., & Wall, P. (1982). *The challenge of pain.* New York: Basic Books.

Osterbauer, P., et al. (1992). Three-dimensional head kinetics and clinical outcome of patients with neck injury treated with manipulative therapy: A pilot study. *Journal of Manipulative Physiological Therapy, 15*(8), 501–511.

Pinsky, D., et al. (2004). *When painkillers become dangerous.* Center City, MN: Hazelden.

Reilly, R. (1993). *Living with pain: A new approach to the management of chronic pain.* Minneapolis: Deaconess.

Rogers, R., & McMillin, C. (1989). *The healing bond: Treating addictions in groups.* New York: W. W. Norton & Company.

Roy, R. (1992). *The social context of the chronic pain sufferer.* Toronto: University of Toronto Press.

Sarno, J. (1998). *The mind body prescription: Healing the body, healing the pain.* New York: Warner Books.

Sarno, J. (1991). *Healing back pain: The mind body connection.* New York: Warner Books.

Stacy, C., Kaplan, A., & Williams, G. (1992). *The fight against pain.* New York: Consumers Union.

Stanford, M. (1998). *Foundations in behavioral pharmacology: For social workers, psychologists, therapists, and counselors.* Santa Cruz, CA: Lightway Centre.

Stimmel, B. (1997). *Pain and its relief without addiction.* New York: Haworth Medical.

Stimmel, B. (1983). *Pain, analgesics, and addictions.* New York: Raven.

St. Marie, B., & Arnold, S. (Eds.). (2002). *When your pain flares up.* Minneapolis: Fairview Press.

Tennant, F., Shannon J., Nork, J., Sagherian, A., & Berman, M. (1991). Abnormal adrenal gland metabolism in opioid addicts: Implications for clinical treatment. *Journal of Psychoactive Drugs, 23* (2), 135–149.

Turk, D., Rudy, T., & Sorkin, B. (1993). Neglected topics in chronic pain treatment outcome studies: Determination of success. *Pain, 53* (1), 3–16.

Wall, P., & Jones, M. (1991). *Defeating pain: The war against the silent epidemic.* New York: Plenum.

Warfield, C. (1996). *Expert pain management.* Spring House, PA: Springhouse.

Watkins, J., & Watkins, H. (1990). Dissociation and displacement: Where goes the ouch? *American Journal of Clinical Hypnosis, 33*(1), 1–10.

Vertosick, F. (2000). *Why we hurt: The natural history of pain.* New York: Harcourt.

(2006). *Substance abuse in brief fact sheet. Pain management without psychological dependence. Summer 2006, 4,* Issue 1: U.S. Department of Health and Human Services.

Useful Internet Resources

Addiction-Free Pain Management®
http://www.addiction-free.com
   Addiction-Free Pain Management® describes the treatment system developed by Dr. Stephen F. Grinstead to help people suffering with chronic pain who also have coexisting addiction problems due to their prescription medication use.

American Academy of Pain Management
http://www.aapainmanage.org
   The American Academy of Pain Management is the largest multidisciplinary and physician-based pain society in the United States. The academy is a nonprofit multidisciplinary credentialing society providing credentialing to practitioners in the area of pain management.

American Society of Addiction Medicine
http://www.asam.org
   This national medical specialty society is dedicated to educating physicians and improving the treatment of individuals suffering from alcoholism and other addictions, including those with pain and addiction.

American Society of Pain Management Nursing
http://www.aspmn.org
   The American Society for Pain Management Nursing is an organization of professional nurses dedicated to promoting and providing optimal care of individuals with pain, including the management of its sequelae. This is accomplished through education, standards, advocacy, and research.

Body Mind Resources
http://www.bodymindresources.com
   This site was founded to help keep people out of pain. Liam is a massage therapist and a structural bodyworker with a mission to help and guide all those who are bold enough to begin the adventure of **putting their bodies back together and getting out of pain.**

Drug Free at Last
http://www.drugfreeatlast.com/index.html
Selecting a drug rehab for yourself or someone you care about is one of the most important decisions you will make. On this site you can find the right treatment for drug abuse. Their services are free to the public. This site also includes valuable information about many of the drugs of abuse.

Enhanced Healing through Relaxation Music
http://www.enhancedhealing.com
On this site you will find relaxation music, positive affirmations, and online counseling for reducing stress and anxiety and promoting health, wellness, and healing, as well as improving self-esteem.

Gorski-CENAPS® Corporation
http://www.cenaps.com
This is the home site of Terence T. Gorski and the CENAPS® training team. Visit here for information on training and consultation services for recovery and relapse prevention issues for addiction and related mental disorders, personality disorders, and lifestyle problems.

Grant Me the Serenity: Self Help and Recovery
http://www.Open-Mind.org/Links
This site is intended to help those in, or seeking, recovery from various addictions, obsessions, and compulsions—such as drugs, alcohol, sex, and food. It is also intended for family, friends, anxiety sufferers, and abuse survivors, to find information, support, and resources.

Holistic Health Solutions
http://www.holistichelp.net
On this site you will find sources for life management and support for people living with chronic illness, chronic pain, or disability. This site also offers education, consultation, pamphlets, articles, and e-books.

International Association for the Study of Pain
http://www.iasp-pain.org

Founded in 1973, IASP brings together scientists, clinicians, healthcare providers, and policy makers to stimulate and support the study of pain and to translate that knowledge into improved pain relief worldwide. Currently, IASP has more than 6,300 members from 108 countries and in 69 chapters.

Metropolitan Pain Management Consultants
http://www.pain-mpmc.com

MPMC specializes in injuries and disease of the back, such as work-related injuries, persistent back pain before and after surgery, degenerative disc disease, spinal arthritis, disease of the facet joints, injury to muscles or ligaments, or pinched nerves in the neck and back. We treat complex regional pain syndrome (RSD), peripheral neuropathy, and pain associated with vascular conditions.

The National Center for Complementary and Alternative Medicine (NCCAM)
http://nccam.nih.gov

NCCAM is dedicated to exploring complementary and alternative healing practices in the context of rigorous science; training complementary and alternative medicine (CAM) researchers; and disseminating authoritative information to the public and professionals.

National Fibromyalgia Association (NFA)
http://www.fmaware.org/index.html

The National Fibromyalgia Association (previously known as the National Fibromyalgia Awareness Campaign) is a [501(c) 3] nonprofit organization whose mission is to develop and execute programs dedicated to improving the quality of life for people with fibromyalgia.

NI-COR (Network International-Coalition for Online Resources)
http://www.ni-cor.com

This site offers articles and directories for: health and wellness, addictions and prevention, addiction recovery, medical terms, mental health issues, social issues, research, education, spirituality, and family.

Pemarro Treatment Program
http://www.pemarro.com/main.html
   Pemarro offers an integrated multidisciplinary team approach to successfully treat the complex issue of chronic pain and a coexisting addictive disorder. Pemarro's Chronic Pain Program incorporates the Addiction-Free Pain Management® System (APM) developed by Dr. Stephen Grinstead. Proper pain management utilizing pharmacological, nonpharmacological, and innovative holistic methods allows Pemarro to meet the unique needs of those suffering from chronic pain and substance use disorders.

Prolotherapy
http://www.prolotherapy.org
   This Web site offers a comprehensive description of the *prolotherapy* procedure as well as the many pain conditions that it effectively treats. The site also has a *prolotherapist* location-search-capability option as well as an interactive contact-us and ask-questions function.

Scripps McDonald Center
http://mcdonald-center.scripps.org
   The Scripps McDonald Center is a nationally recognized organization dedicated to treating alcohol and drug abuse. The center provides a healing environment. People needing help, and their families, receive the tools and support they need to rebuild their lives.

Sierra Tucson
http://www.sierratucson.com
   Sierra Tucson is in the process of becoming the first Addiction-Free Pain Management® Center of Excellence in their new chronic Pain Management program. For more than twenty-four years Sierra Tucson's compassionate care and clinical excellence have helped people rebuild their lives. Internationally respected as a leader in the treatment of coexisting disorders, Sierra Tucson offers programs for chemical dependency, mood disorders, eating disorders, sexual and trauma recovery, pain management, and complex assessment and diagnosis. Dually licensed as a Special Hospital and a Level-1 Psychiatric Acute Hospital, professional staff incorporates medical and psychiatric services with Twelve-Step philosophy; traditional, experiential, integrative therapies;

and a comprehensive family program. It is accredited by JCAHO and is a member of CRC Health Group. For information or a confidential consultation, please call 1-800-842-4487.

SouthCoast Recovery Center
http://www.southcoastrecovery.com
SouthCoast Recovery provides highly effective, yet affordable, state-licensed detox and treatment near the beach in southern California. We treat alcohol and drug addictions with our on-staff psychologist, family counselors, and addiction specialists with individualized care that treats the body, mind, and spirit. Call 1-866-847-4506 now for a free assessment and ask about our financing options.

Terence T. Gorski's Clinical Development
http://www.tgorski.com
Terry Gorski's Addiction and Clinical Development Web site is designed to keep decision makers, program managers, and clinicians up-to-the-minute on new developments regarding the Gorski-CENAPS® Model of Treatment.

Valley Forge Medical Center Addiction/Pain Program
http://www.vfmc.net/
In addition to addiction specific treatment, Valley Forge Medical Center (VFMC) offers chronic pain management (CPM) services developed specifically for those patients suffering from co-occurring issues of chronic pain and substance abuse and/or addiction. Many of the VFMC staff have been trained by Dr. Grinstead in the Addiction-Free Pain Management® System.

Notes

Notes